AF552777

OTHER LOTUS TITLES

Hindustan Times Leadership Summit	*The Peace Dividend: Progress for India and South Asia*
Hindustan Times Leadership Summit	*India and the World: a Blueprint for Partnership and Growth*
Hindustan Times Leadership Summit	*Building a Better Future*
Hindustan Times Leadership Summit	*India the Next Global Superpower*
Hindustan Times Leadership Summit	*Imagine the India that Can Be*
Hindustan Times Leadership Summit	*Ambitions for the New Century*
Hindustan Times Leadership Summit	*Vision 2020: Challenges for the Next Decade*
Ajit Bhattacharjea	*Sheikh Mohammad Abdullah: Tragic Hero of Kashmir*
Amarinder Singh	*The Last Sunset: The Rise and Fall of the Lahore Durbar*
Anil Dharker	*Icons: Men & Women Who Shaped Today's India*
Aitzaz Ahsan	*The Indus Saga: The Making of Pakistan*
Alam Srinivas & TR Vivek	*IPL: The Inside Story*
Amir Mir	*The True Face of Jehadis: Inside Pakistan's Terror Networks*
Ashok Mitra	*The Starkness of It*
Dr Humanyun Khan & G. Parthasarthy	*Diplomatic Divide*
Gyanendra Pandey & Yunus Samad	*Faultlines of Nationhood*
H.L.O. Garrett	*The Trial of Bahadur Shah Zafar*
M.J. Akbar	*India: The Siege Within*
M.J. Akbar	*Kashmir: Behind the Vale*
M.J. Akbar	*The Shade of Swords*
M.J. Akbar	*Byline*
M.J. Akbar	*Blood Brothers: A Family Saga*
Maj. Gen. Ian Cardozo	*Param Vir: Our Heroes in Battle*
Maj. Gen. Ian Cardozo	*The Sinking of INS Khukri: What Happened in 1971*
Madhu Trehan	*Tehelka as Metaphor*
Mushirul Hasan	*India Partitioned. 2 Vols*
Mushirul Hasan	*John Company to the Republic*
Mushirul Hasan	*Knowledge, Power and Politics*
Nayantara Sahgal (ed.)	*Before Freedom: Nehru's Letters to His Sister*
Nilima Lambah	*A Life Across Three Continents*
Robert Hutchison	*The Raja of Harsil: The Legend of Frederick 'Pahari' Wilson*
Sharmishta Gooptu and Boria Majumdar (eds)	*Revisiting 1857: Myth, Memory, History*
Shashi Joshi	*The Last Durbar*
Shashi Tharoor & Shaharyar M. Khan	*Shadows across the Playing Field*
Shrabani Basu	*Spy Princess: The Life of Noor Inayat Khan*
Shyam Bhatia	*Goodbye Shahzadi: A Political Biography*
Thomas Weber	*Gandhi, Gandhism and the Gandhians*
Thomas Weber	*Going Native: Gandhi's Relationship with Western Women*

FORTHCOMING TITLES

CNN-IBN	*Real Heroes: Ordinary People Extraordinary Service*
Jaiwant Paul	*The Greased Cartridge: The Heroes and Villians of 1857*

WINNING
IN TESTING TIMES

Edited by
Namita Bhandare

LOTUS COLLECTION
ROLI BOOKS

Lotus Collection

First published in 2011
The Lotus Collection
An imprint of
Roli Books Pvt Ltd
M-75, G.K. II Market
New Delhi 110 048
Phone: ++91 (011) 40682000
Fax: ++91 (011) 2921 7185
E-mail: info@rolibooks.com; Website: rolibooks.com

Also at
Bangalore, Chennai, Mumbai

Cover: Deven Das
Layout Design: Sanjeev Mathpal
Photo Credit: HT Media Ltd

ISBN: 978-81-7436-852-2

Typeset in Photina MT by Roli Books Pvt Ltd
printed at Sanat Printers, Haryana.

WINNING
IN TESTING TIMES

Hindustan Times
Leadership Summit

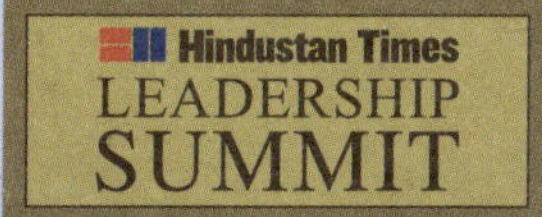

His Holiness The Dalai Lama

Shashi Ruia
Chairman, Essar Group

Nandan Nilekani
Chairman, Unique Identification Authority of India

Kapil Sibal
Hon. Minister for Human Resource Development, India

Prof. Dipak C. Jain
Dean Designate, INSEAD and Dean Emeritus, Kellogg School of Management

Chas Edelstein
CEO, Apollo Group, USA

Jairam Ramesh
Hon. Minister of State for Environment and Forests, India

Sunita Narain
Director, Centre for Science and Environment

Rishi Kapoor
Actor and Film Director

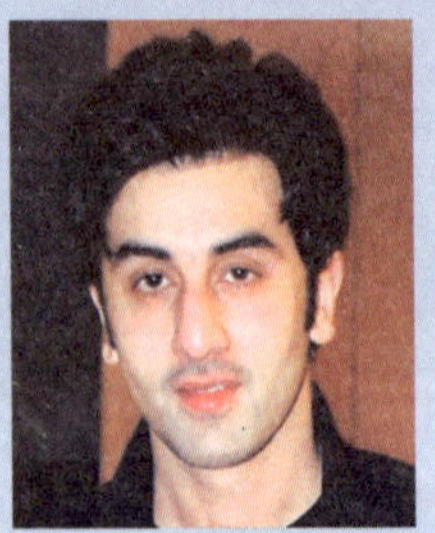

Ranbir Kapoor
Film Actor

Pranab Mukherjee
Hon. Finance Minister of India

Dr Edward Horton
Professor, Harvard Medical School

Wasim Akram
Former Pakistan Cricket Captain

Dr Anoop Misra
Director and Head of Diabetes & Metabolic Diseases, Fortis Hospital

Dr Manmohan Singh
Hon. Prime Minister of India

Al Gore
Vice President, United States of America, 1992-2000

Arun Jaitley
Hon. Leader of the Opposition, Rajya Sabha

Brinda Karat
Member CPI(M) Polit Bureau

Prof. Pawan Sinha
Assoc. Professor of Computational and Visual Neuroscience, Department of Brain and Cognitive Sciences, MIT

Prof. Drazen Prelec
DEC LGO Professor of Management, Management Science and Economics, MIT Sloan School of Management and Dept. of Brain and Cognitive Sciences, MIT

Prof. Jitendra Sharma
Professor, Radiology,
Harvard Medical School

Dr Ravi Gopal Verma
Professor and Head, Department of Neurosurgery, M.S. Ramaiah Medical College, Bangalore

The Rt. Hon. Gordon Brown
Prime Minister of
the United Kingdom, 2007-10

Dr Kenneth Lieberthal
Senior Fellow, Foreign Policy Studies, The Brookings Institution

Prof. Yasheng Huang
Professor of International Management,
MIT Sloan School of Management

Prof. Richard Rigby
Executive Director, The ANU China Institute, Australian National University

Shobhana Bhartia
Chairperson & Editorial Director,
HT Media Ltd

Contents

Hindustan Times
Leadership Summit

Every year for the past eight years, distinguished speakers including heads of state, cultural ambassadors, athletes, academicians, business leaders and representatives of civil society have come together under the aegis of the Hindustan Times group in New Delhi to discuss contemporary issues and set the agenda for the future.

The 2010 Leadership Summit was held as the world slowly emerged from the economic crisis only to confront new challenges. The threat of global warming has not abated with unexpected droughts and inexplicable floods impacting, among other things, food production. China's spectacular rise reworks old equations and raises new questions. As individual prosperity increases, diabetes and other lifestyle-related illnesses take on a new dimension and unexpected costs.

There has been an irreversible shift in the balance of the world's power towards the Asian region. India's role in world affairs too has undergone a change, both within the region and beyond in striking new alliances and refreshing old partnerships. With its young demographic and rising middle class, India seeks also to find a balance between the environment and development. There has been urgent need to respond to the needs of all its citizens, whether it is by infrastructure development, improving the regulatory environment and parliamentary democracy or ensuring inclusive growth. In the words of Prime Minister Manmohan Singh, 'It is on the foundation of a better educated, more healthy and more skilled people that we must build the edifice of a more entrepreneurial society, and leverage our capacity for innovation.'

In a globalized and interconnected world where developments in one part of the world have implications on another part, problems as well as solutions increasingly call for international rather than national responses. Whether it is climate change or terror, economic crises or health pandemics, the world's borders have begun to blur. It has become imperative for leaders to work together for the greater good – and if humanity is to win in these testing times.

'The world belongs to people, not governments. To change the world, people must play a more active role. Many positive changes of the later part of the twentieth century happened not at the government level and not by violence but through popular, non-violent movements.'

The Art of Happiness in **Troubled Times**

His Holiness, the 14th Dalai Lama

Moderator

Sanjoy Narayan

Editor-in-chief, Hindustan Times

Dalai Lama

His Holiness, the 14th Dalai Lama

His Holiness the 14th Dalai Lama, Tenzin Gyatso, is both the head of state and the spiritual leader of Tibet. He has travelled extensively around the world and met most world leaders and heads of different religions. Since 1959 he has received more than 100 awards, honorary doctorates and prizes – including the Nobel Peace Prize – in recognition of his message of peace, non-violence, inter-religious understanding, universal responsibility and compassion. He has also authored more than 72 books. The Dalai Lama, who describes himself as a simple Buddhist monk, was born on 6 July 1935 to a farmer family in Taktser, Amdo in northeast Tibet. At the age of two, the child, who was named Lhamo Dhondup at that time, was recognized as the reincarnation of the 13th Dalai Lama. Following the Chinese invasion of Tibet, he was forced to escape into exile in 1959. Since then he has been living in Dharamsala in Himachal Pradesh.

BROTHERS AND SISTERS, I AM EXTREMELY HAPPY TO HAVE THIS OPPORTUNITY TO TALK TO AND INTERACT WITH SUCH A SIGNIFICANT AUDIENCE. WE ARE FACED with a number of problems in the twenty-first century. Different religious traditions have evolved each time humanity has faced problems. If the world was a happy place we would not need these traditions. I am a Buddhist. Buddha came in order to reduce trouble and suffering. Others too – Mahavir, Jesus Christ, Muhammad – came to reduce trouble.

There are two levels of pain and suffering. The first is the physical level. The other is the mental level. Physical experience derives from sensorial consciousness. On the mental level, like during dreams, sensorial consciousness no longer operates. In Buddha's time there was a lot of physical level trouble: disease, poverty and violence. With progress and the advance of technology and science, disease and poverty today have lessened. But mental problems have become worse. In ancient times, smaller populations led a more relaxed life, perhaps because of their philosophy. Modern lifestyles are very busy with too much competition. In big cities like Delhi, Mumbai and Kolkata there is more stress compared to rural areas where farmers might encounter more physical difficulties but much less mental stress.

In many ways, mental troubles are more intense. On the physical level we can reduce pain and difficulties by material means. You can take medicines, either allopathic or Tibetan medicine, for instance. But, mental stress entirely depends on one's own mental attitude. Shantideva in the eighth century said, 'Unruly beings are infinite, like space. How can one actually overcome them all at once? But if you are able to overcome your own anger, then that would be like overcoming your enemies or adversaries.'

It is impossible to remove all troubles. Some problems will always be there. But if you develop a right attitude – I usually say, a realistic attitude – then no matter what you are surrounded with, you can keep your peace of mind. Peace of mind is the basis of a healthy body and a healthy mind. Too much agitation on the mental level leads not only to mental suffering but physical suffering as well. A calm mind is therefore, very important for the individual's own peace of mind and also for inner peace to remain undisturbed during times of problems. If your mental state is disturbed and there is too much emotion, it becomes difficult to handle problems; the mind becomes too emotional and biased. You can't see reality. Without knowing reality, every method becomes unrealistic and is bound to fail. You cannot achieve your goals.

There is a method to keep our mind more peaceful. The part of the brain which develops a calm mind enables human intelligence to judge, to investigate and to find out reality. Too much anger, too much fear, too much attachment, means that that part of your brain cannot function properly because there is too much emotion. An American friend who is about eighty-four years old told me that when people are angry they look at things very negatively. But actually, 90 per cent of that negativity is mental projection. Buddhist psychology also mentions this. If you are mentally agitated, then you can't see reality.

The compassionate mind is very important. Fears, anger and jealousy are all based on a self-centered attitude. If you develop more sense of caring towards others, your heart will automatically open. That brings friendship. We are social animals. Individual survival depends entirely on the rest of the community. A self-centered attitude develops distrust, suspicion and fear. No matter what the attitude of others, you must develop concern for their well being. Only then, you can live in peace. Concern for others brings inner strength and self confidence. All social animals, even bees and ants that have no constitution or law, work together. Nature makes them that way. We are also social animals but our intelligence sometimes makes us think of short-term interest, narrow-mindedness and negative emotions. We sometimes forget our basic nature. But a compassionate attitude is the key to developing a calm mind and a calm mind is related to self-confidence.

The second thing I want to talk about is religious tradition. All major religious traditions carry the message of love, compassion and forgiveness. One of my Muslim friends told me that the true practice of Islam is to extend love towards all creatures. There are two kinds of traditions: the theistic tradition that believes that God is the creator and so, asks for total submission to God. If we take the philosophical view that we are all creations of God, we will totally submit to God. That reduces our self-centered attitude. We see God as infinite love and this creates more faith towards God.

The non-theistic tradition is the one followed by Buddhism and Jainism where there is no concept of God as a creator. Buddha is our experienced teacher who showed us the path according to his own experiences. Buddha himself came from an ordinary being. He became the Buddha, not a creator. Things exist because of the law of *causality*. There is a cause and effect, quite like the Darwinian theory. That is non-theistic view point.

Everything depends on action. Karma means action. If you do good things to others, you get benefits. If you harm others, the consequences will be negative. Knowing that sort of law of causality reduces harming others. You must extend yourself to serve and bring happiness to others.

I always tell people that I learned compassion from my mother. I had a very kind mother. All of us come from our mothers. At a very young age we survive on our mother's affection. At that stage the maximum affection we receive is from our mother. That experience is absorbed in every particle of our body. The latest scientific findings and brain specialists tell us that constant fear and anger are actually eating into our immune system. A calmer mind, more compassionate mind increases this positive element which is our body. Our body develops through the mother's affection. Those who receive the most affection from their mother at an early age are safer and feel more secure. Those who grow up lacking a mother's affection or in abusive conditions, always remain insecure no matter how smart they may turn out to be. Their whole life remains a little cold. It is difficult for them to respond with a genuine sense of compassion to other people. But those who receive maximum affection find it much easier to extend love and compassion.

A friend of mine, a Tibetan monk spent about nineteen years in a Chinese Gulag. In early 1980, under the more open policy of Deng Xiaoping, he was able to come to India and join his previous monastery. I met him and since I had known him well, we began to talk. He told me that in the nineteen years he spent in the Chinese Gulag he faced dangers on a few occasions. I thought he meant that his life had been in danger. So, I asked him, 'What kind of danger?' He replied, 'Danger of losing compassion towards the Chinese.'

It is very important to keep a compassionate attitude towards one's perpetrators. My friend is now ninety-four or ninety-five year old and physically very well. He is always cheerful. I casually told some scientists about him and they said they wanted to meet him. They found an extraordinary man with no sign of any sort of traumatic experience. His mind was calm, happy, and compassionate. So, if you keep a positive attitude, the maximum benefit will go to you.

In conclusion, religious believers every day practice to get the immense benefits of reducing stress or worry. The non-believer too, through awareness, through a deeper understanding about emotion can develop warm-heartedness. This is something I try to share with thousands of people. Everybody wants a happy life and a healthy body. But the ultimate factor for this healthy mind and healthy body is within ourselves.

For the past 3,000 to 4,000 years, people have been putting hope on faith and prayer to God. Of course, prayer is very useful for peace of mind. But for the well-being of the community or world, prayers have a limitation. I was invited recently by the chief minister of Bihar for the inauguration of a Buddhist Vihara. The chief minister mentioned in his speech how with Buddha's blessings, Bihar had begun to prosper. But Buddha's blessings had always been in Bihar. So, if blessings can develop a state, then Bihar should have developed much earlier! Buddha's blessings need human action. Without human action, Buddha's blessings are not very effective, are they?

God is merciful but the planet is full of problems. Therefore, action is very important. Action depends on our motivation. With negative emotion we tend to harmful actions. With positive emotion there is constructive action – verbal as well as physical.

Science and technology have developed in the last two centuries. Technology has given us what we want immediately. For thousands of years we had been praying to God but things failed to materialize. Now, with technology, health has improved, economies are more prosperous. So, it is logical that people will now rely more and more on science and technology and forget their inner values.

People are losing some sort of awareness through their own experience. There are limitations to material value. I have a friend who is a billionaire but is very unhappy. He has too much stress and worry. Money cannot bring inner peace. It is very clear. Among Indians also, people are more aware of material development. But material value alone will not solve our problem. It cannot bring real happiness or satisfaction. We need some sort of effort to develop inner values, irrespective of whether we are religious or non-believers.

I believe the world belongs to people, not governments. To change the world, people must play a more active role. Many positive changes of the later part of the twentieth century happened not at the government level and not by violence but through popular, non-violent movements. Already, the first ten years of this century are over. Whether it will be peaceful or whether it will be a century of bloodshed ultimately depends on people. People are a combination of individuals. And any real change begins from the individual. Then it moves to the family, the community and so on. There is possibility of change in this world to make it more compassionate and more peaceful; to make it a world where we solve problems not by force but by dialogue. That is the way to make this a peaceful century. It is in everybody's interest to do so. And each of us has the potential to contribute to it.

Moderator | **Sanjoy Narayan**

Editor-in-chief, Hindustan Times

Sanjoy Narayan: Thank you, Your Holiness for such an inspiring address. If I might ask the first question: many surveys across the world have shown that today's youth is increasingly disenchanted and there is a feeling of loneliness and disaffection amongst them. There is a quest for authenticity in a world which many believe is over-commercialized. In India nearly 50 per cent of the population is under the age of twenty-five. How do you suggest we engage with the youth and address these issues?

Dalai Lama: As I mentioned already, we are relying too much on material values. My generation belongs to the twentieth century, a century of violence. Some historians estimate that 200 million people were killed in the twentieth century through violence, including civil wars, the world wars and so on. There could have been some justification if this immense violence had led to permanent peace and permanent happiness. But it did not happen. We still have problems.

It is the responsibility of my generation to tell the younger generation that material developments and weapons, including nuclear weapons, will not solve human problems. Human problems can be solved only through cooperation, mutual trust and genuine friendship. Any conflict or potential conflict must be solved through dialogue. The twenty-first century should be a century of dialogue.

The younger generation must pay more attention to inner values. But the younger generation is following my generation's way of life – seeking more money, more power, and in order to get these, taking to corruption which has become a normal way of life. Yet, if people do not give serious thought to inner values, there will be no basis for moral principles. The twentieth century failed to bring happiness to the world. We must be realistic. We must accept our failure. We must tell our younger generation of our failure. They now have the responsibility to build a healthy new world. Whether in America or Europe or this country, young people seem more open. From lack of experience they are sometimes a little impatient. They want everything 'now'.

The media, including Hindustan Times, have an important role to educate the younger generation. We are not preaching religion but simply using our common sense and common experience and the latest scientific findings.

Q: In the Indian tradition as well as in many other traditions, we have a concept of 'destiny' or bhagya. When we talk about action in the affairs of human beings, what is the role of destiny and how much of it is action?

Dalai Lama: If you ask me my personal view, then everything depends on its own cause and condition. Among the causes and conditions the main factor for experience of pains and pleasure is karma. Karma means action. From the Buddhist view point, certain destinations are due to our previous karma and karma which accumulates in past lives. But with new action and new karma, we can change. So, ultimately, your destination is entirely in your own hands.

Q: Your Holiness, you have been an apostle of compassion for the world. What are your views on succession planning? Do you have any thoughts about who would be the next Dalai Lama?

Dalai Lama: That for me is not a serious question. The Chinese government is seriously looking for the next Dalai Lama. But I stated as far back as 1969 that whether the centuries-old Dalai Lama institution should continue or not is up to the Tibetan people. If the majority of the Tibetan people (and also Mongolian people and those from the Himalayan range who share the same Buddhist tradition), feel that the Dalai Lama institution is no longer relevant, then the institution will automatically cease. If they want to keep it, it will remain alive. Over the last few centuries, the Dalai Lama institution carried some sort of important role. But things are always changing. So, it is quite silly to think that this old institution will always be present. If I die in the next few days, then people would most probably want to keep this institution. But after twenty or thirty years, then maybe there will be a different situation.

Q: There are more than 4,000 religions today, if you count all the sects and sub-sects. Despite this, there is no compassion or peace. Do you think organized religion has failed society?

Dalai Lama: We can't say there is total failure. At least for me, Buddhism has not failed. My religious life has been very helpful. Millions of people still receive immense benefits from their religious traditions. Sometimes, even among Tibetans, people just carry on with ceremonial rituals without touching upon the real meaning of religion. Religion is also used for exploitation. Whether you accept religion or not, is up to you. But once you accept a religion, you should be serious and sincere and full of knowledge about religious traditions.

My Indian friend recites a few slokas of Sanskrit but does not know their meaning. That is not very useful, is it? I just returned from Japan which is traditionally a Buddhist country. Some Japanese at the time of birth perform rituals according to Shintoism, the native religion of the country. At the time of marriage, they perform a Christian ceremony. Then, at the time of death, ceremonies are conducted according to Buddhism. That is not really serious, is it?

I would not say there is failure of religious teaching, but failure of the person who is supposed to follow that religion but does not implement it sincerely. I usually see major religious traditions like Hinduism with a lot of philosophical views and Buddhism with its texts full of psychology, human emotion and function of the emotion as a Buddhist science, not Buddhist religion. Buddhism teaches about matter and particles. Buddhist philosophy is an analysis of reality on the basis of science.

I like the concept of 'interdependency'. There is no absolute existence; everything is interdependent. The Buddhist word is

Pratîtyasamutpáda which is from Sanskrit and means dependent and arising. Many scientists are fond of this concept. This concept is close to the concepts in Quantum Physics, like the theory of relativity. Unless we know the foundation of these sort of Buddhist concepts, the practice of Buddhism becomes a ritual – not of much use and not effective in our mind.

Many Hindu temples just rely on rituals without much explanation. About two or three years ago, I met some Thai students who were studying in Chandigarh. They had come to see me. Their family background was Buddhist. But, they do not know what Buddhism is. Thai monasteries in Thailand do not explain Buddhism to ordinary people. They simply carry some rituals and chanting. Of course, there are some universities where maybe it is different.

I often describe myself as a messenger of India. That means, wherever I go, I talk about ahimsa and non-violence. Non-violent action is related with the compassionate mind and where there is a compassionate mind, there is also non-violent action. My second commitment is to religious harmony. This country is perhaps the only country on this planet where all major religious traditions live together. Occasionally, there is some problem. That is, of course, understandable. But overall, this is the only country where all major religious traditions have mutual respect.

Once a Chinese reporter asked me, 'Why do you say you are a son of India?' I told him that within my scalp, within my brain, every particle was filled with Nalanda thought. Physically, too, I have lived here for the last fifty-one years – the major portion of my life. I escaped from Tibet at the age of twenty-four. For the past fifty-one years, my body has been sustained by Indian dals and Indian rice. Therefore, I describe myself as a son of India.

So, my Indian friends, you must realize your traditional values. When you see some drawbacks like the caste system or dowry you must address these very seriously. When there is suffering in political spheres, whether it is Naxalites or Maoists, you must understand that there is need for much development in these areas some of which still have no electricity or proper schools. That is why the people here are easy to manipulate. Sending more Indian police is not the answer. You must lift their living standard and provide education and electricity. Only then will the problems reduce.

I am also a son of India because Buddhism comes from India. All the Buddhist masters – Nagarjuna, Aryadeva, Buddhapalita – are the masters of the real texts of our study. I am a lazy student, but I study these root texts. Therefore, I consider Indians my gurus. The relationship between Indians and Tibetans are like the relations between a guru and a chela. I jokingly tell people, 'We are quite reliable chelas.' On occasions when I have a gathering of sadhus and religious leaders, I often tell them that I am really proud to be a messenger of ancient Indian thought. But, in the meantime, within the country, there are still some drawbacks or backwardness in the name of tradition. These must be addressed seriously and changed. Even a 1,000-year old tradition must change when it becomes outdated. This is the reality we must accept.

Going Global:

Prospects and Pitfalls for India Inc

■

Shashi Ruia

■

Nandan Nilekani

■

Moderator

R. Sukumar

Editor, Mint

Shashi Ruia

Chairman, Essar Group

One of India's leading industrialists, Shashi Ruia has steered the $15 billion Essar Group to a premier position in global business. Ruia began his career in the family business in 1965 under the guidance of his father, the late Nand Kishore. Along with his brother Ravi, Ruia was instrumental in Essar's foray into businesses that were the domain of multinational giants or Indian public sector units: shipping, marine construction, steel, power, telecom, offshore engineering, and oil exploration. Ruia's vision saw the Essar Group gain a first-mover advantage in many of these businesses. He masterminded the group's business strategy. Today, the Essar Group is a multinational conglomerate and a leading player across sectors.

IT IS INDEED A GREAT PLEASURE TO SHARE MY VIEWS ON GOING GLOBAL: THE PROSPECTS AND PITFALL FOR INDIA INC. GLOBALIZATION TODAY IS NO LONGER DEFINED AS YOU and I knew it until a few years ago. The way globalization is defined has undergone a change ever since the financial crisis broke out on Wall Street leading to a global recession. Today we live in a very different world but one fact we are all convinced of is that it wasn't market liberalization or capitalism which caused the crisis.

The geographic spread of the crisis affected all the markets. In fact, we live in a more risk-prone world. A crisis in one part of the world has the potential to hurt other regions. We also witnessed massive bailouts of private companies by governments. Their survival was threatened and jobs lost. Government taking over of a private company is unusual but was needed as national interest took precedence over free market principles. It was an interim measure but critically worse was the real possibility of sovereign failure and country defaults.

In the midst of all these, redefinition of globalization led to a resurgence of economic nationalism. At the same time, the lead players of the next phase of globalization also changed. In the aftermath of the financial meltdown, it was clear that the global landscape has what is popularly known as BRIC – Brazil, Russia, India, and China – as the more important players than just USA, Europe, and Japan.

The emergence of the G20 is a clear statement of that group replacing the G8 and OECD. Within Asia, India is clearly the big player after China. India's demographic advantages make it an attractive market which was quite evident during the recent trip of US President Barack Obama. In his own words, India is no longer emerging. It has emerged and today is an equal partner.

Before I talk about going global, I must flag two notes of caution. When it comes to the way the global economy has evolved, one worries about the future commodity price and its inflation potential. There would be huge pressure on the prices of resources like oil and gas to feed the hunger of China and India's growth. This will cause hardships for industry while also adding to the overall inflationary environment. The other worry I have is human resources. The demand for it will continue to rise as skilled manpower moves from one market to another and the cost for advantage gets equalized. While the positive may be greater purchasing power, it will be relative. Higher purchasing power in an atmosphere of high inflation will hardly do any good. For example, a pilot of Indian origin who used to charge $20 an hour now has equal access to a foreign market and knows that he can get paid $81 an hour. No wonder Indian pilots are getting expensive adding to the ticket cost when you and I fly.

Let me come to the topic of going global. I would like to share a different perspective on this issue. There are two ways to define 'going global'. When Indian companies go and buy assets abroad and run them successfully, that's going global. We have seen many examples of this. We at Essar have done some and so have Reliance, Tatas with Corus and Jaguar, the Mahindras, Bharti and many others.

Global India will truly go global when it is able to

There is a reason why this kind of globalization is important and is done because it gives access to markets, resources and technology. But it is a different world out there. We are not exactly flush with funds like the Chinese. Incidentally, the total value of Indian acquisitions abroad is not more than $45 billion and just three or four transactions account for a large chunk of it. There have not been significant greenfield investments by Indian companies globally. I may also add that the value of total global acquisitions has actually declined from a level of $1.22 trillion in 2007 to $250 billion in 2009. This decline reflects the global sentiment.

But today I want to talk of going global in terms of globalizing our economy. Global India will truly go global when it is able to market and sell its own goods and its own services. The global market plays on a much larger scale. According to me, the world should be a greenfield. It is not enough to just produce and sell in India. Well, it allows us to derisk our business. It also allows us to create wealth for those who produce these goods which can be utilized for inclusive growth. But I believe that we have to create wealth before we can distribute it for inclusive growth. Consumer demand in India alone will not ensure India's economic prosperity. It is necessary to reach out to other markets and add to our GDP. Of course, it also makes Indian companies compete with the best and develop world-class products besides honing our skills.

Now let's look at the way the global market place is laid out and who all are occupying important positions. The market today is split in two. One part is dominated by China. It stretches from the east of its border all the way to USA, NAFTA, Australia, and Japan. That's their forte. China is a dominant player in the USA. Then is the market to the west of us: the Middle East, Africa, Europe, and Russia. These are markets where China is not dominant. This is the region where India has to go and occupy its rightful place.

market and sell its own goods and its own services.

With an appropriate strategy, India can be a dominant player in these regions. India has a few advantages – language adaptability, a huge pool of young skilled manpower, geographical proximity to most of these markets and its historical trade relation with these countries. India's entrepreneurial skills are well established. China is handicapped on this front. We are thankfully better at marketing our business. They do it better when it comes to their government but India's soft skill is still an advantage today.

But marketing and entrepreneurship is not good enough. For India's capabilities to grow, for it to go global and for Indian companies to cater to the global market place, India needs to be a leader in manufacturing and infrastructure. You can't build and grow economies without these two essential elements. This is where we have to learn from China. We need to focus on what I call the three S's – size, scale and skills – if we have to build capabilities in manufacturing and infrastructure. On all three counts, China has set standards which India needs to emulate.

If you look at the way an economy grows, you will see that people are pulled up to middle class. China has displayed to the world that it has pulled 400 million people out of poverty. Just to give you an example of scale and size, India today produces 65 million tons of steel; China produces 650 million tons. India consumes 140 million tons of oil; China consumes 380. China has made 11 million cars; we are at 2 million. India's trade with the US is $50 billion while China is at $450 billion. This just reflects the potential for India's growth. India should grow and go global. There is no escaping the fact that we need to hugely step up on scale and size.

On skills, we really need to think how we will train 350 million youngsters who join the mainstream. And really whose responsibility is it? Is it necessary to ensure that this workforce has adequate technical knowledge and world-class skills? We need to address this key issue. If you do some basic calculation on the purchasing power of the majority of India and back it with real life examples, you will realize that exporting our goods and services is as crucial for India to grow and for Indians to do well.

Take the example of Indian IT services. With $50 billion of revenues annually with four or five purchase parity, Indian IT companies led by talented people like Nandan Nilekani and working in Bangalore and Gurgaon captured the global markets. They used that income to buy cars and homes and, as a result, the companies that sold them, the car manufactures and builders did well. Today if every Indian company can replicate that model by treating the world as one market, they can add so much value.

Look at the examples of world-class products which are coming from India and the market potential, if you have scale and size. Nano, a world-class product can sell anywhere. I wouldn't be surprised if President Obama took one home. Who wouldn't want a $2500 car? If President Obama is in awe of it, why can't we flood the world market with it? Going global needs to be seen in this light: how the export of goods can create wealth for Indians working for other markets.

However, there are many pitfalls. Indian companies require the support of government for ensuring an investment climate and world-class infrastructure for businesses to be able to compete. The other huge challenge is the lack of a national vision which should drive this kind of industrialization. Take the example of bullet trains in China which are emerging as the most favoured mode of transport. They travel at 420 kilometres per hour. The train to Lhasa is pressurized. Should India ever dream of this? We need a national commitment, a national movement, a national resolve, a national strategy and a national belief that we can do it. That is our goal and that is good for us. We should have more people with Nandan Nilekani's vision to run critical projects, to achieve scale and size like UID. We have to think big and we have to think now.

The other big problem as we go global is capital. If we are to aim for global scale, size and capacity, Indian companies will need financial support. The government should think of setting up funds and lending money to companies the way Sovereign Wealth Funds function across the world.

Let me conclude by saying that India seems to be on the cusp of realizing its potential but that can only be done if we define globalization by treating the world as one market place. It is time to start now. If we don't, someone else will. We are hurting our own potential for going global. We need to begin today.

Nandan Nilekani

Chairman, Unique Identification Authority of India

After leading one of India's most respected companies, Nandan Nilekani has joined hands with the government in implementing an ambitious project that aims to provide a unique identification number to all Indians. Nilekani, chairman of the Unique Identification Authority of India, was most recently co-chairman of the board of directors of Infosys Technologies Limited, which he cofounded in 1981. He has held various posts at Infosys, including chief executive officer and managing director, president, and chief operating officer. In 2006, he was awarded the Padma Bhushan and named businessman of the year by *Forbes* Asia. *Time* magazine listed him as one of the 100 most influential people in the world in 2006 and 2009.

I WILL FIRST MAKE THE CASE FOR INDIA TO GLOBALIZE, TAKING OFF FROM WHERE SHASHI RUIA LEFT OFF AND THEN TRY TO ARGUE WHY CORPORATIONS SHOULD globalize and therefore what is the kind of acquisitions they would need to do.

The argument for India to globalize is very compelling. We are a young country. In the next twenty to twenty-five years, we are going to have a few hundred million people joining the workforce and we have to create jobs for them. These jobs will have to be created by companies and entrepreneurs. We are also very fortunate that we are the only young country in an ageing world. The rest of the world, including China, is ageing, and we will actually be providing the workforce to the world. Therefore, it is in our interest to keep the world markets open so that our young men and women can work for global markets both in terms of working for companies in India as well as in terms of going out to work in various countries.

When we look at Indian companies globalizing, we have to look at the history of what has been happening. We had for many years a very protectionist environment where Indian companies were operating within the four walls of this country. In the last twenty years, Indian companies have become more and more confident of the world and about their competitive advantage. Today we are in an era where Indian companies are going out and buying companies, and putting their footprint across the world in very diverse sectors whether steel, cars, automobiles, telecom or IT. This is a very welcome development.

Shashi was saying that when India itself has to grow, when India itself is going to be such a large market, how does this globalization contribute? Globalization contributes because companies go abroad for acquisitions follow a number of different strategic intents. First, they go to acquire market access. In a European country, it's worthwhile to buy a local company which gives you market access. Many companies have been doing that to create market access around the world.

Second, they do it to expand their portfolio of production services. For example, in the IT sector many companies who have been going to new areas like infrastructure management and consulting have found that rather than building up that capability from a greenfield start, it makes more sense to do an acquisition and then integrate it into the company. So the expansion of production services becomes a second reason.

A third reason is for the purpose of getting technology. For example, if you are in a field that requires some kind of intellectual capital like patents and copyrights, it is worthwhile to acquire companies that have these patents, copyrights or other forms of intellectual capital which you can then harness in your global portfolio of products and services. So, the third reason for which companies do acquisitions is for the purpose of intellectual capital.

Of course the other big reason for a growing country is to create access to natural resources. Companies have gone abroad

We are the only young country in an ageing world. The actually be providing the workforce to the world.

and bought iron ore mines, coal mines or uranium mines in all kinds of organizations because they feel that they need to have a long-term hold on global resources and, therefore, acquisitions are driven by that.

All these reasons are a compliment to the domestic markets. It's not that this strategy is independent of the domestic market because when you go and buy natural resources abroad, you are actually using these to fund them back or to provide a secure source of resources for your domestic consumption. Similarly, when you go and buy a technology company abroad, you are possibly using that technology to provide services to an expanding mass of customers that you have in India. Clearly these are interrelated and, therefore, you can leverage both the growth of the domestic market as well as global expansion.

There is one very important reason why globalization will continue to happen and Indian companies will become more and more globally competitive. It's what I call the 'exporting of the business' model. What that really means is that the Indian market for Indian companies has actually created a crucible where they have been able to create very innovative business models. We have examples of what Carlos Ghosn calls 'frugal engineering'. Our automobile companies have done a great job in creating low-cost cars whether it's the Tatas or the Mahindras. Mobile companies be it Bharti, Vodafone, or Idea have shown us how to create low-cost factories to create among the lowest cost services in the world.

The Indian market is driven by a large pool of consumers who are essentially very cost conscious and whose purchasing power is limited. This has forced Indian companies to respond by creating new business models that deliver high value at low cost and scale. That business model itself is an exportable business model. The Bharti-Zain acquisition is an example of that where they will take the factory from India and replicate it in Africa.

rest of the world, including China, is ageing, and we will

There are different ways to look at the whole issue of Indian companies going global. There are, of course, risks. To run a distributed company, you need the management bandwidth and you need the management architecture. There are issues of how we manage skills. One of the challenges, for example in the services industry, is that if you buy a company abroad and don't really have a cultural fit with that company, then all those people are likely to leave and all that will be left are tables and chairs. Therefore, making sure there is cultural compatibility and making sure that you are able to retain people becomes very important.

I agree with Shashi that among all Asian countries, India actually has the best ability to do this in a much more global fashion because of our English language skills, our experience with running companies here and the education of our business leaders. Globally, the ability of Indian companies to make acquisitions and integrate them is far better than that of many entrepreneurs from other countries. This again serves as a competitive advantage.

There are certain risks and there are certain pitfalls and there are many examples of acquisitions by Indian companies in the last couple of years which have turned sour. But notwithstanding all that, fundamentally India is going to be a growing economy for many years with this young demographic dividend. We have a wide pool of entrepreneurs who would like to make acquisitions for a variety of strategic reasons be it market access, product access, intellectual property, resources, or to export the business model. This is really setting the stage for a very huge leadership role played by Indian entrepreneurs worldwide to create world-class companies in the coming years.

Moderator | R. Sukumar

Editor, Mint

R. Sukumar: Economic nationalism is on the rise and clearly at some level you can see this as an anti-globalization effort. There are efforts to prevent flow of goods, services, and people. We know that the World Trade Organization has failed. You can't have a multi-lateral organization which is trying to function when countries are going around creating economic blocs on their own and signing bilateral economic treaties. So, what do you see in the future because both of you spoke about opportunities and how India is well poised?

Shashi Ruia: There are a lot of imperatives that all governments have to take care of. First is the employment of its own people. We acquired a steel mill in Canada and have about 3,700 people working there. It was flooded with bright Indian managers at cheaper cost but three years down the line, we only have 12 people from India. We are having to contend with a janitor getting $81,000 a year.

Now there is no way the Canadian government is going to allow me to leave. If you are given this imperative, there is no way I am going to make cheap steel. The relative cost per tonne of steel labour-wise is about $150 a ton in Canada and $4 in India. There is arbitrage available of a huge value. If you see steel, normally the gross margins are about $100 or $150 and you have just this arbitrage of extra $150. But they will not allow you to close down the plant. You can't enter the market. They are going to put restrictions on your coming there. It's because of necessity. The wages in all these countries have grown to a point where they are out of the manufacturing market. But they still, according to me, prevent our goods as much as they can from entering there. It's a reality.

Nandan Nilekani: I agree with Shashi's description of economic nationalism. I think that when the first wave of globalization began twenty or thirty years ago, it looked like it was a good way for global companies headquartered in the West to really expand the market. But what has happened now partly because of outsourcing and partly because of Indian companies becoming global is that the other side of globalization is now becoming apparent to everybody. As long as people feel that globalization leads to loss of jobs, lowering standards of living or some kind of economic insecurity, there is bound to be a reaction. We can't avoid that.

But we have to keep emphasizing that for the entire world keeping the free trade open and encouraging trade is actually going to create jobs and economic growth, even in countries that are now feeling the pressure. When Shashi goes and buys companies in Canada or the US, he is creating jobs. Similarly when India buys planes from an American company, we are creating jobs in Chicago or Seattle.

Today, there was a paper about India investing a trillion dollars in infrastructure in the coming 12th Plan and thereon. That means we are going to buy a lot of things. We are going to buy generators, turbines and all kinds of things which are going to be made outside India. The people who are going to make them are going to have jobs. Our economic growth is going to create large imports of these things which in turn will create jobs in our partner countries. This needs to be emphasized to make it politically palatable to keep the economic alliance of trade open.

Q: I am involved with education and both of you spoke about entrepreneurship problems. But what about India being a global partner in creating new knowledge? In the long run, it is the creation of new knowledge and the centres where new knowledge is created from where everything else will flow. In the US, there are a lot of private-public partnerships, for example, in the area around Stanford, Palo Alto and the area around MIT. Why is it that sort of thing not happening here?

Nandan Nilekani: I think it is part of a process. It will happen. I have been tracking what's happening in the IT industry for the last thirty years. In the last ten years, a number of new companies have come up out of work done in a university. The whole ecosystem is just falling into place. But increasingly, in many areas in IT, in pharmaceuticals and in many industries, it will be innovation-based and innovation-led. It's a timing issue. It takes time for that to happen but when I talk with the people who fund companies, they tell me that they are amazed by the new ideas and innovation and knowledge-based businesses that are coming up.

Q: Both of you have spoken of exporting products and services. But what about Indian culture? How can we use Indian culture to go global and be more competitive on a global scale?

Nandan Nilekani: It's happening already. A.R. Rahman is going to sing in the Nobel Prize distribution ceremony. That's Indian culture going global.

Quality and Quantity in Education:

Can India Achieve Both?

Kapil Sibal

Dipak C. Jain

Chas Edelstein

Moderator

Gautam Chikermane

Business Editor, Hindustan Times

Kapil Sibal

Union Minister of Human Resource Development

A successful lawyer turned-politician, Kapil Sibal has fast emerged as a trusted lieutenant of the prime minister and is today in charge of some of the government's most critical ministries. Busy ushering in education reforms as human resource development minister, Sibal has also been given charge of two additional portfolios – science and technology, and telecommunications and information technology. An alumnus of Harvard Law School and Delhi's St Stephen's College, Sibal is a second-time Lok Sabha MP from Delhi. He has also been a member of the Rajya Sabha.

ISSUES OF POLICY CAN ONLY BE ADDRESSED IF WE UNDERSTAND THE TERRAIN IN OUR SYSTEM OF GOVERNANCE. THE TERRAIN OF INDIA IS HIGHLY COMPLEX and complicated. When we look at an urban agglomeration like New Delhi or Mumbai, the issue of access has different perspectives depending on where you are located. If you are in a posh colony in a posh school, the issue of access doesn't arise. The issue here is the quality of education that is being imparted to students. Even though they might be scoring 90 or 95 per cent, the quality here depends on the quality of the curriculum. How do you want your children to move forward and on what route?

The issue of access is entirely different in a slum or a vegetable market or a mandi. It is different if you go to a rural area, say in a Naxal-affected area. If it's the Northeast, the issue of access becomes different. So that itself is a very complicated thing.

The issue of quality depends on what kind of child you want as he or she moves forward in school to be educated? What kind of value system do you want? Are you looking at people who score well in subjects or are you looking at people who actually think for themselves? In other words, do you emphasize the learning processes rather than the outcomes in terms of rote learning? For that you need to change curriculum. In order to change curriculum, you need quality teachers to teach that curriculum. You don't have quality teachers. Where will you get quality teachers from? You have a million schools in this country in the primary sector. Do you have that kind of quality teachers? You don't. How do you train those teachers? How do you change the exam system to bring quality into the system? And this is only the school level.

The ball game is entirely different at the higher education level. Some 90 per cent engineering colleges in India are set up by the private sector. There are quality institutions in the private sector but by and large it's under-the-table quality. How do you deal with that? You can have eight more IITs or seven more IIMs and four Indian Institutes of Education, Science and Research. But will they deal with the issue of the millions of children who actually go out of the college system? If you don't become an engineer, doctor or IT professional, then in the eyes of the kind of static society that we have, you will be labelled as a good-for-nothing. So, you need to change the mindset of people. Quality will only come if mindsets change to accept other disciplines and consider them also as good careers.

Let me now just give you some facts. Some 220 million children go to school and of these 13 million will reach college. About 200 million will not reach college. The difference between the developed world and the developing world lies in the gross enrollment ratio – every 100 children in the age group of 18-24 who reach college. In India it is 12.4 per cent. But in a developed country it is not less than 40 per cent. The reason why we are underdeveloped is because our gross enrollment ratio is low.

We don't have a critical mass of people going to college and

The US has all the human resources but no jobs. India has of the world today.

university. We don't have critical thinking because it is at the university level in research and development that we have critical thinking which produces wealth – not tangible wealth but intangible wealth in terms of intellectual property. Unless that critical mass of people moves into the college system, the nation will not have the kind of intangible wealth that will then be translated into products by industry. Industry doesn't produce wealth; industry translates wealth. Wealth is in the idea; the mind of the individual, and that wealth is created by the university system.

Our first task as a nation is to ensure that a critical mass of people go to university. The Right to Education Act is fundamental. Every child must go to school. Hopefully, this government in years to come will pass another law for all children to go from elementary to higher secondary education. The result of that will be that by 2020 we must have at least 30 per cent gross enrollment ratio instead of the 12.4 per cent we now have. In other words, the 14 million children who are going to college must move up to 50 million or

45 million. This will create a critical mass of people to move into the university system to create wealth for the nation.

This is easier said than done. You need to change the curriculum in the school system to ensure that creativity is at the heart of education. For that you need to change. You do not need to have 50 different exam systems for children. You need uniformity. All the different state boards must come together for a uniform system of education. Different boards can't have different qualities. That is a monumental job. I will assume that we can do it by 2020. That is our objective.

The 14 million children who go to colleges are served by 800 universities. If the increase in the number of university students is going to be from 14 million to 45 million, in other words if we have an additional 30 million children coming into higher education, then we need many more universities. We need another 1,000 universities in the next ten years. Who is going to provide them? The government cannot. So, what do we need? We need the private sector. We need technology. We need distance learning. We need a self assessment procedure. It's not necessary that children must go to class. There can be self-learning procedures where you can actually reach benchmarks and be able to tell yourself that you have reached a certain level. There will be a teacher down the learning process who will test you.

all the jobs but no human resource. That's the conundrum

Who will make the investments? There will be a mix between physical institutions and online learning. There will be a huge expansion of distance learning. What do we need for that? We need infrastructure, specifically IT infrastructure. We need broadband. Every college, school and institution must be connected. We need huge investment in broadband infrastructure. We have a National Mission on Education through which we are going to connect 26,000 colleges in this country and 800 universities in the next two years by broadband. Any child can take any course anywhere in India. As we move along, the bandwidth is going to be so wide that we can include many more institutions into the system.

That is the only way you can deliver quality. Children should have the right to choose. They should have the right to choose which professor they want even if they are sitting in Delhi and the professor is in Mumbai. A credit transfer system must take place which is why we are saying all universities must move to the semester system. If you move to the semester system, you have credits. If you have credits, you can transfer credits. You can take any course anywhere.

Now this is all about academics. But there will still be 150 million children who won't go to college. We are only talking about 45 million even in 2020. This is very important. Even if we achieve gross enrollment ratio of 30 per cent, some 150 million children still won't go to college. What about them? You need quality for them. That means skills. That means the nature of education in school must change. We must start vocational education from class eight onwards.

If CBSE gives an academic degree, CBSE should also give a vocational degree. We are going to put in place before next year the National Vocational Qualification framework under which in the next three years children will get CBSE vocational degrees in whatever vocation they choose. Then we move into ITIs and polytechnics. We work with industry and tell them, 'Come and do my programme on vocational training in hospitality or automobile engineering, refrigeration, geospatial technologies, financial management, paramedics or paraclinics.' There are a host of vocations for which a job market is available.

We need a holistic vision that involves civil society, NGOs, industry, academics and state governments. This is a national enterprise. It is not about political parties. Education is empowerment. What is happening in the United States? The US has all the human resources but no jobs. India has all the jobs but no human resource. That's the conundrum of the world today. By 2050 India will be providing jobs to the world. This is the greatest global opportunity India has and if we don't set it right in five years, it will not happen. The nation must come together on education to empower India.

Dipak C. Jain

Dean Designate, INSEAD and Dean Emeritus, Kellogg School of Management

Marketing is Dipak C. Jain's forte and for more than a decade, the Kellogg School of Management (Northwestern University, US) has been his academic home. Since 1994 he has been Sandy and Morton Goldman Professor in Entrepreneurial Studies and professor of marketing and, from 2001 to 2009, dean of the school. Jain's teaching interests are in areas such as strategic marketing, marketing research, new products and services innovation and pricing policy, while his research interests are spread across topics such as customer life-time value analysis, new product innovation, market segmentation and product positioning, and cross-cultural issues in global product diffusion.

BEFORE I START MY REMARKS, I WANT TO SHARE WITH YOU WHAT I DESCRIBE AS THE POWER OF INDIAN EDUCATION. I WAS NAMED DEAN OF THE KELLOGG School of Management in 2001. It was the first time in US history that a person of colour had been nominated to be the dean. One day Philip Kotler, the marketing guru and a colleague of mine came to see me. He said, 'Dipak, I need your help.'

I replied, 'What can I do for you?'

He said, 'Dipak, I have been invited to give a talk at a summit and they are expecting about 1,200 people but I am not going to be able to make it.' His son-in-law had been involved in an accident and was scheduled for surgery on the day of the talk. 'Will you substitute for me?'

I said, 'Prof Kotler, why do you want to put me in such a big trouble? The audience is coming to listen to you, the guru of

Education is not just about teaching but creating the flame which will continue to glow over the years

marketing. Why do you want to put me in that spot? Why don't you call the conference chair and see if they can either postpone or cancel it?'

He said, 'Dipak, I will try.'

So he called the conference chair and the conference chair said, 'It's too late to postpone because almost 880 people have already registered and now to give back the registration fee would be a logistical nightmare. So you just send anyone.'

So I flew off in his place. The seminar was at 9 in the morning and at 8 o'clock I was supposed to have breakfast with the chair. When he saw me, he almost had a heart attack. He must have thought to himself, 'Is this guy going to speak to 1,200 people?'

So he asked me, 'What do you do?'

For some reason, Prof Kotler hadn't briefed him on who I was. I told him that until recently I was a professor of marketing and since 11 September, which was my date of joining the Kellogg deanship, I had been dean of the school. Now, he didn't know what it meant to be the dean. So he asked me, 'What do you do as the dean?'

I said, 'As the dean of the school, I am responsible for setting the vision of the school, creating new innovative programs and also designing the global initiative for the school. When faculty members are asked to go and speak at various conferences or go as visiting professors to other institutions, they have to take permission from the dean.'

I said that in some sense the dean of a business school is like the chief executive officer of a corporation. Now being a businessman, he understood this language. So he said, 'Now I know how to introduce you.' Until then he hadn't even asked me what my name was. Anyway I didn't have any business card and neither did he.

So he came to the podium and he began with 'Good morning.' Then he said, 'How many of you have heard the name Philip

desire to learn. Our role as academics is to spark the to come.

Kotler?' All hands went up. He replied: 'Today I present to you the boss of Philip Kotler!'

Who would have imagined that when I left a small town in Assam called Tejpur to go to the US to study that I would one day be referred to as the boss of a guru? This is what I describe as the power of the education system.

I would like to pay tribute to the minister for his excellent education system. People talk about creative capitalism. The time has come for people like us, and all of us in this room, to start distributing education wealth which is enduring. Physical wealth may disappear but we are privileged today because of the foundations we have had in this country. We have set a new model of leadership in the US and now my next job is to do the same in Europe which would be another journey for me, but again I am very grateful for all the teachers I have had over the years.

What really keeps us going on the academic front is the unique advantage of India and the dedication of Indian parents to education. This is going to be our brand for the future. Today you see one Dipak shining. I am sure a day will come when there will be a lot of Dipaks all over the world in leadership roles. With all the changes in policy that we are seeing in this country, the best is yet to come.

What is education? Education is not just about teaching but creating the desire to learn. Our role as academics is to spark the flame which will continue to glow over the years to come. What are the roles and responsibilities that we must play in order to make this happen? We have recently established a chair in Florida International University in the name of Bhagwan Mahavir Swamy called the Mahavir Swamy Chair in Jainism studies. The inauguration on 25 October had two speakers, His Holiness the Dalai Lama and myself. At the inauguration, His Holiness took me in his arms and said, 'Dipak, Buddhism and Jainism are like twins. You talk about non-violence; I talk about compassion.' I thought that this is a good way for us to promote Indian values and cultures. Now there will be courses on Jainism at Florida International University. That is how we can increase what I call the gross national happiness index all over the world.

As academics we have a three-fold mission: knowledge creation through research; knowledge dissemination through programmes like master's, PhD, and high school; and the third is knowledge certification. Academic institutions have the power to grant degrees whether it's a bachelor's, master's or PhD. That is where the brand of the institution gets spelt out.

If you look at the late-eighteenth century, the entire theme in the world was colonialism. Countries came and acquired land. In the late-nineteenth century, we moved towards capitalism. But the coming century is going to be a century for human capital. You heard from Shashi Ruia that human talent is going to be the key and hence we need to focus on competencies. I have a colleague in India who says, 'Our education system is what I describe as reproduction.'

You teach something and the exam system tests how well you can reproduce. We need to move from a reproduction system or testing of facts to what I describe as testing competencies.

There are a lot of institutions in India but there is a huge quality variation. The topic today is very pertinent: how can you have quality education for the masses? If a person from the town of Tejpur can become the dean of a top school, then we have quality in our DNA. It's only a matter of how we scale it. The resources are there.

In the US, you have public universities and private universities. The privates are known for profits – Harvard, Stanford, Northwestern, Yale, Chicago. We need to think about a similar structure here and I am seeing lots of people willing to do that part. The second is partnerships – we created the Indian School of Business between Wharton and Kellogg. The third is Foreign Direct Investment. INSEAD went and invested in a full campus in Singapore. The fourth is creating knowledge cities like the one in Doha, Qatar.

We need to think about the right models for us. My first suggestion is that we need to develop physical training places where students can come and we can use technology as a way to deliver that message. We also need to teach teachers. We need to have 'train the trainer' programmes. Finally, instead of having more IITs, we need more ITIs or industrial training institutes.

People say the challenge ahead of you is never greater than the force behind you. If you have good people and good teams behind you, you can rise to any challenge.

Chas Edelstein

CEO, Apollo Group

Chas Edelstein, director and co-chief executive officer of the Apollo Group, has more than twenty years of industry experience in proprietary higher education. The Apollo Group is a leading provider of higher education in North America. Edelstein's focus as a leader in the industry is to expand access to cutting edge, innovative models of higher education. He has focused the Apollo Group's resources on delivering quality, innovative and distinctive educational programmes with the goal of providing today's working adults the tools to compete and thrive in a changing global economy.

THE APOLLO GROUP IS A HOLDING COMPANY FOR A NUMBER OF EDUCATION INITIATIVES INCLUDING THE UNIVERSITY OF PHOENIX, WHICH IS OUR LARGEST company where we have about 470,000 students currently in post-secondary education. Apollo Global is looking to bring some of the methodologies we have used more broadly. I have been involved in education for over twenty years out of the belief that if we can provide a fair return for investment dollars to come into education, we can get more activity in education. I want to spend a short time talking about a model that we have seen in the US and the applicability that has a potential in India.

When you look at the 1950s in the US, only about 20 per cent jobs required a degree. Most jobs were unskilled. The post-secondary education system was created at a time when only a small proportion of people needed a college education. Today in the US, 65 per cent jobs require a degree. In the next ten years most new jobs will require some sort of degree. The growth in new jobs is going to be degree-oriented. This has created a real need. In the US, for example, we currently have about 30 or 35 per cent of the workforce with degrees where 65 per cent need degrees. This has created a chasm and a real need to provide education to many more people.

What Dean Jain spoke of earlier is delivering quality education to many more people. It requires creative solutions to be able to do that. How do we think about delivering quality and quantity, and is it possible? Part of this is defining what we mean by these terms. Is 'quality' robustness from an institution's standpoint of education or is it from the student's standpoint of getting services and experience that they need? Or is it the outcome that students get from education? It's certainly all of these.

What are outcomes? Is it getting a better job? Is it increasing your income? Is it increasing your academic capabilities? When you think about the type of institution, these might be different and there might be different ratings. All institutions of learning don't have to have the same mission. Rather, the richness of an educational system is one that provides a broad range of opportunity and choices for students, provides an experience that is very academically focused but also can provide opportunity and access for people to reach education. Quality might also be things that are unconventional. Recently I met one of our students at one of our campuses and I asked her what she was studying. She told me about her studies and then I asked her, 'What do you want to do with your degree when you graduate?'

She replied, 'I'm not sure yet but I have already accomplished what I came here to accomplish.'

I said, 'What do you mean?'

She replied, 'Well, I'm the first one in my family to go to college and now my kids will want to go to college. So if you ask me, I have already changed history by being here.'

Today in the US, 65 per cent jobs require a degree. In of degree.

That, in a sense, is quality. In the case of one individual, it has changed the course of history for her and her family and many families. So when you think about the various definitions of quality, keep in mind that it can be different for different institutions and the most robust education system provides a choice of many different options.

When you think about quantity, think not just about how many people we reach in terms of quantity but think of access. Quantity means a great number of people should have access to education. Access is really a function of cost. Cost can be keeping the price of tuition down. It can also be making education available if you are in a remote area through technology or allowing you to keep your job when you go to school. That would provide access if you can have the flexibility to study at night or on weekends.

The challenge that we face in the US which would be similar here is that students have risk factors. In the US, only 27 per cent students in the college system go straight from high school to college. Another 73 per cent are non-traditional in some sense, working adults and so forth. You can address the risk factors by providing services or flexibility that helps get over a major hurdle to many people. Other challenges lie in access technology and finding available teaching labour. For teachers, the solution that we found is to use part-time teachers to supplement full-time faculty.

Lastly there is the issue of financial resources. Think about the range of financial resources that can be brought to bear – charitable, corporate and students contributing. By addressing this range of challenges, we can address a very large problem.

By 2025, over a quarter of a billion people will demand a college education. We need to have flexible solutions, technology, access and cost cutting driving many of them. We have hopefully found

the next ten years most new jobs will require some sort

some of the solutions. We hope to find more together with you in the wonderful rich history that India has in education.

Moderator | **Gautam Chikermane**

Business Editor, Hindustan Times

Q: My name is Vani Tripathi and I am the national secretary of the BJP and an actor by profession. My question is to the minister. Taking a cue from the debate in the country on the Right to Education, a lot of academics are of the view that the way that the Right to Education is being viewed will probably kill public school education in the country. There is a huge deficit of teachers at the primary and high school level. The other issue is of investment in higher education in terms of global collaboration. How do these two connect? In terms of job generation, a lot of academics feel that the public school education will take a beating because of the cost of education going up in the country. What do you have to say to that?

Kapil Sibal: I don't understand how public school education will take a beating. The Right to Education Act provides for free education to the people of this country. The private sector only occupies 7 per cent of the space of this country. The remaining 93 per cent is occupied by the public sector, which is free. So how will cost of education go up?

Q: I am Samyak Chakrabarty and I run a youth marketing company in communications. I work with young people. I have a two-part question to the minister. First, how do you plan to ensure that the education system and its content is inclusive of the opinion and aspirations of all students? Second, is with reference to what you called 'mindset'. I think it's very important that the government bring about the mindset change so that students look at education more as a resource than a compulsion because even when there is access people don't utilize it.

Kapil Sibal: Absolutely right. As far as mindset change is concerned, we must reach out to people. The most important role to be played is by the media. It's the media that can actually bring about a change of mindset. As far as the aspirations of young children are concerned, that is our whole focus. We must ask children. We must get feedback from them. We are interacting with children to find out what is it that they want and I can assure you presently the children say, 'We don't want people on our backs. We want to learn. Just give us the tools to learn.' Children don't want rote learning anymore. Ultimately, society is going to be empowered if you allow children creativity for solutions and that's the way education must go.

Q: My name is D.K. Jain and I am in the field of writing instruments. Do you have any plans to incentivize the industry to come forward and invest into education as Uttarakhand is doing by excise exemption for ten years and five years for income tax benefit? Do you have any plan where hundreds and thousands of crores can come into education and can build this quality education that you have been discussing?

Kapil Sibal: I am deeply disappointed by the question that industry is asking for incentives to invest in our children's future.

Q: My name is Reena Chandran. I represent an American company and my question is to the panel though I would love it if Mr Sibal can also answer. At this point of time, many of us here are spending an inordinate amount of money on sending our children overseas for higher education. Is this education going to really help them in the long run if the jobs lie in places like the BRIC countries?

Chas Edelstein: The way that we have been able to roll the way is to have connections to industry. We have people from corporations and people who are doing the hiring on advisory boards to help us understand where the needs are. The key to a successful institution is to be responsive as needs are changing. We have to be able to develop a curriculum that is relevant and meaningful for the jobs out there.

Dipak Jain: I agree with Chas. We need more experiential learning. Traditionally, we have focused on the classroom but we need to bring a component of experiential learning, which is a balance of rigour and relevance. I am just completing a book called *The Browning of the West and the Creaming of the East* which talks about how we are going to capture the Western world in terms of jobs and how lots of people from the Western world are interested in coming to India to experience what is happening here. We need to bring academic rigour with business relevance to our education system. Students need to be included in co-creating the educational experience. Power must go to students rather than just teachers.

Kapil Sibal: Let me put a different spin: it's the rusting of the West and the shining of the East. I will tell you why. The solutions for the world are going to come from our part of the world in the years to come. They have to. The problems are in this part of the world. You find solutions where the problems are. You don't go 20,000 miles away or 10,000 miles away to solve a problem which is at your doorstep. So you are going to have people coming back to India or not wanting to go abroad because the new solutions for the world – in energy and sustainable development – will be high quality and low cost. You cannot get high-quality, low-cost solutions anywhere else in the world but in India.

Q: This question is for Chas. Do you propose to do some initiatives in India on behalf of the Apollo Group?

Chas Edelstein: We would love to be able to help in India. I think there is a long process with that in terms of understanding where the needs are, where we can help and who the best partners are. So we will see what that brings but we would love to help if we can.

Gautam Chikermane: I would like to end with one question. We have been talking a lot about education in the context of economic welfare, jobs and so on. But what is the final objective of education? Is it to get a job? Is it to make money? Or is there some higher goal that we are probably not seeing today?

Dipak Jain: The goal of education is definitely to educate people but the main thing is what the minister here said and that is to empower people. We need to make the best use of context rather than complain. When I became dean of the school, I made a presentation to a group of 600 students who were looking to go to an MBA programme on why they should come to Kellogg. There were students who had admissions from Harvard, Stanford,

MIT, other places. One student raised his hand and he said, 'Dean, I hear all about Kellogg. What are you going to do about the Chicago weather? Nine months of the year, it's so cold.' I thought to myself as a dean of the school, I have control over many things but I don't control the weather. But I thought I should not end the presentation on a depressing note like the Chicago weather. So I told this person, 'I have one piece of advice for you. In life, you should believe in the principle of a refrigerator. Things kept in the cooler environment stay fresh for a longer time.' So, India is what it is, and we have to make the best use of it.

Chas Edelstein: My personal philosophy is that the role of education is to improve your life. It was the reason why I told the story about the woman that I met on campus because to her a better life meant a change of direction for her children and her children's children. For many people, a better life means a better job and more money. I think that's totally fine. I think that the educational system should be flexible enough to be able to help people with different goals toward what it takes to improve their life.

Kapil Sibal: Education is all about self realization because I think each individual has a genius or a talent which many times is not allowed to mushroom for reasons that are environmental. So we must create an environment where you can actually realize yourself. As a societal issue, education must have two objectives with an underlying purpose. The first objective is to create new kinds of wealth through new ideas. I don't mean wealth in tangible terms. In other words, new theories, new solutions through nano technology, through cutting-edge technologies, and cutting-edge ideas that's the level of research which we need as a society.

The second for self realization is to be able to get a job and realize your immediate need. These are the two different levels but underlying these is the purpose of education to make us able to deal with each other in a reasonable, fair and equitable way and to have a peaceful environment around us. Therefore, the ethical aspect must underlie each aspect of education and this is what is missing in our country. We are looking for jobs. We are looking for research-ships but we don't have an ethical attitude towards any of these things. Ultimately, unless ethics is integrated into the education system, we will have the kind of problems that we see across the world.

Environment vs Development:

Striking the Right Balance

■

Jairam Ramesh

■

Sunita Narain

■

Moderator

Bahar Dutt

Environment Editor, CNN-IBN

Jairam Ramesh

Minister of State for Environment and Forests

As environment and forests minister, Jairam Ramesh has given new direction to India's environment concerns and brought the country into the forefront of global climate negotiations. An alumnus of IIT, Mumbai, Carnegie Mellon University and the Massachusetts Institute of Technology in the US, Ramesh has taken tough decisions on balancing environmental concerns with developmental needs, not hesitating to show the red flag to projects that have violated green norms. Ramesh led developing countries in taking a strong stand on greenhouse gas emissions by the developed world during the world climate change conference at Copenhagen in 2009.

THIS WAS SUPPOSED TO BE A SESSION ON ECOLOGY VERSUS DEVELOPMENT OR CONSERVATION VERSUS DEVELOPMENT, BUT I FIND MYSELF A REFLECTION OF the changed climate: Sunita Narain and I are actually on the same side on many issues whereas we ought to be on opposing sides. I think something has gone wrong and I'm sure both of us are trying to live down the substantial areas of convergence between our positions.

There is an episode of *Yes Minister* in which Jim Hacker begins to take his job very seriously and so, Humphrey Appleby becomes very concerned. He goes to Hacker and he says, 'Minister, you can't let us down.'

Hacker says, 'What have I done, Humphrey?'

Humphrey replies, 'Well, you're beginning to take your job too seriously, Minister. That's bad for us.'

Hacker never gets the better of Humphrey, but this was one occasion where I think he did. He tells Humphrey, 'Well, Sir Humphrey, you'll be pleased to know that the fact that I'm taking my job seriously should not cause any fear. The fact that it has become newsworthy is a commentary on the society in which we live.'

I'm really in the same position right now because nothing that I have done is actually newsworthy. All that I have done is to take the laws of the land – the Forest Conservation Act of 1980, the Environment Protection Act of 1986, and the Forest Rights Act of 2006 and a variety of other legislations like the Coastal Zone Regulation, which is now in the news in the post-Adarsh scenario – and made them stick. All that I'm doing in this ministry is saying that the debate is not between environment and development. The debate is not between conservation and growth. The debate is simply: are you going to stick to the laws of the land? Are you going to navigate these laws like you have navigated them for the last thirty years? We all know what navigation means in our system. Are you going to manage the regulatory process as you have managed over the last thirty years or are you going to follow the laws of the land in letter and spirit?

This is really the first and most important objective that I set for myself. I am not standing in the way of growth. I am not an activist. In fact, I'm embarrassed by the encomiums activists pay me. But the fact of the matter is that when the laws of the land have to be implemented in all seriousness in letter and spirit, then some tough choices have to be made.

This brings me to my second point. In the trade-off between environment and development, in this perceived conflict between conservation and growth, I see three options as alternatives for getting out of the conundrum. In 95 per cent cases, we say 'yes'. That never gets reported by Bahar Dutt and her company. In a couple of cases, we say 'yes, but...' and in a tiny miniscule of cases we say 'no'. It's this 'no' that hits the headlines and drives the news cycle. It's this 'no' that leads people to call me a Demolition Man. But the fact of the matter is that 95 per cent approval rate for any

In any regulatory system it is not the nature of the in which the decision is taken. People will respond to confidence they have been taken in a transparent and

ministry is not something that we should be defensive about.

The real challenge for us is to increase the proportion of the 'yes, but...' cases – to say that you can go ahead but subject to safeguards and conditions – and also have the courage to say 'no' on occasion. I see the resolution of this conflict between conservation and development as yielding a large majority of solutions where the answer is 'yes' and increasing number of solutions where the answer is 'yes, but...' and also a number of instances and examples where the answer necessarily has to be 'no'.

We should have the courage to accept the fact that in many cases there will be a 'no'. Vedanta was an example of a clear, categorical, unilateral 'no'. The Navi Mumbai Airport will soon be an example of the 'yes, but...' category. I would say that in the months to come, as long as I'm there, you will see more and more of 'yes, buts...' more and more of 'nos' and fewer plain vanilla 'yes' because it is this category of projects for which clearances have been given that has caused much of the disillusionment of civil society with the track record of governments.

In any regulatory system it is not the nature of the decision that you take that is as important as the manner in which the decision is taken. People will respond to decisions provided they have the assurance and the confidence they have been taken in a transparent and accountable manner. Therefore, it has been my endeavour to ensure that the reasoning behind all decisions, whatever the controversy that may surround it – BT Brinjal, Vedanta, Posco, Navi Mumbai or Jaitapur – must be put in the public domain and the public, the larger constituency, must have an opportunity for holding the minister and the ministry accountable. I am not saying that I am right on every occasion. But people must have an opportunity to address their fears and concerns through this process of public interaction.

decision that you take that is as important as the manner decisions provided they have the assurance and the accountable manner.

One of the main tasks that faces me today is the reform of the environmental governance system. The governance system as it relates to the environment, has suffered from many pitfalls, many inadequacies and many shortcomings. We are taking some baby steps. We have set up the National Green Tribunal, which is a specialized environment court. We are on the way to setting up a National Environment Protection Agency, which would be an independent professional body for the clearance of projects. A number of such governance systems and reforms are on the anvil. We are also looking at more market-friendly ways of implementing regulations because I have often said that in our system, regulations are good but regulators are bad. We need more regulations, fewer regulators. Can we think of new market-friendly systems of implementing environmental laws and regulations that do not necessarily involve an army of civil servants who only add to the harassment and compliance costs for the corporate sector?

In conclusion, I would say that this debate between environment and growth, between conservation and development is a bogus debate. The real debate is between following laws scrupulously or doing bypass surgery on these laws. I have to say that the large majority in this country get a great thrill from doing bypass surgery on the laws. The time now is for them to get equal thrill by following the law.

Bahar Dutt: Just this morning we heard that there may be a red light given to the Posco project. Posco is the biggest foreign direct investment in the country. So, how would you assure corporates that you're not starting a license raj in this country and there is a genuine implementation of laws which is taking place?

Jairam Ramesh: I don't want to comment on Posco right now. But all I can say is that it goes back to the point that I had made earlier. If decisions are made transparently, if the reasoning behind the decisions is put in the public domain at a fairly early stage and if all the relevant facts and figures are brought out in a proactive manner, then much of the suspicion on the manner in which decisions get taken will evaporate.

Of course there is criticism that I am favouring Congress states over non-Congress states, and red signalling projects in non-Congress states while green signalling projects in Congress states. Statistically, this is not a good comparison, but nevertheless even after accounting for the numbers that there are more Congress states than non-Congress ones, the criticism does not hold water when you consider the number of projects in Congress states that have got the red signal.

The main criticism is that the wrong signal is being sent to investors and growth is being adversely affected. All I can say is that truly intelligent investors would rather follow the law than circumvent the law. They have a guarantee that if the laws are followed, they do not have to come and meet the minister. I have not met a single industrialist in the last eighteen months that I have been on this job. I don't see the need to meet them. Nearly 95 per cent of the applications that come to our ministry get approved, without my meeting anybody.

If we build confidence in the probity and transparency of the system, many of these fears on the adverse effects on investor sentiment would evaporate. Yes, there are negative headlines and negative feelings on what is happening. Let me give you one example. We spent ₹ 2,000 crore on a hydel project on the river Bhagirathi. The project would have destroyed the entire ecology of the Himalayan upstream areas. It was a tough decision to take. Everybody said, 'You cannot stop a proposal on which ₹ 2,000 crore has already been spent.' But the project should never have come up in the first place. Yet, it did. When we considered its long-term devastation – and Sunita played a very important role in the advocacy phase of this decision – the Government of India bit the bullet and decided to scrap this project.

We must take a long-term view of many of these situations and not get mesmerized by figures of investment or growth. This will happen, but if they cause long-term devastation and long-term destruction, then we're not in the game of sustainable development.

I just want to very quickly make two points. The first is on Green Accounting. It is a fact that today's economic accounts do not reflect the full environmental costs of economic growth. Sir Partha Dasgupta of Cambridge University, perhaps the most celebrated economist of the world who has worked a lot on environmental economics, some years ago estimated that between 1970 and 2000, over a thirty-year period, the per capita GDP as conventionally reported for India went up by 3 per cent per year. But if you take the full environmental and resource costs of that growth, then the per capita natural wealth actually went up by only 0.3 per cent per year. So Green Accounting is a very important and powerful concept and I am hoping that by 2015, India will be a world leader in reporting not just GDP as conventionally defined, but in terms of its environmental impact as well.

The second point I want to make is that it is important to recognize that the environment is no longer an elitist, urban, middle-class past-time. Too often environmentalism was dismissed as a

NIMBI (not in my backyard) syndrome. Then it became dismissed as the BANANA (build absolutely nothing anywhere near anyone) syndrome. Today it's neither NIMBI nor BANANA. It's a public health issue. In city after city, town after town, people are raising not environmental issues but public health issues: the causes of contamination of water, air, and land. In Bhatinda, which has emerged as the cancer capital of India, nearly all cancer incidents are attributable to pollution caused by a variety of factors. In all the polluted parts of India – the industrial clusters – the increase in respiratory diseases, cancer and other public health emergencies are directly on account of the environment. So, the environment is not an external issue. It is an issue of public health. If you don't address the environmental issue as a public health issue you will always be in danger of having the environment condemned as a middle-class-elitist issue.

Sunita Narain

Director, Centre for Science and Environment

Writer and environmentalist Sunita Narain is the director of the Centre for Science and Environment. She is also publisher of the fortnightly green magazine *Down To Earth.* Narain conducts research with forensic rigour and passion, believing that knowledge can lead to change. In 2005, 2008, and 2009 she was included by US journal *Foreign Policy* as one of the world's 100 public intellectuals. In 2005 she was awarded the Padma Shri by the government. She has also received the World Water Prize for her work on rainwater harvesting. In 2005, she chaired the Tiger Task Force set up by the prime minister. She is a member of the PM's Council for Climate Change, and the National Ganga River Basin Authority.

LET ME SAY I AGREE WITH WHAT THE MINSTER HAS SAID. IT IS ALWAYS AN EMBARRASSMENT FOR HIM WHEN I SAY I AGREE WITH HIM, BUT LET ME SAY THAT I DO agree with him on this issue.

It is important for us to put this debate in a different context. I would argue that the debate is not environment versus development. It is really a debate of development versus development. Why do I say that? Look at Niyamgiri. On one side you have a very powerful corporate asking for a bauxite mine, a sign of progress. On the other side are poor, primitive tribals arguing that their God lives in that forest. This was an important issue for us to understand. This was development as we saw it, and development as they saw it. There are other big fights happening. In Nirma, Gujarat, people are fighting against a cement plant. In Sompeta, Andhra Pradesh people fought against a thermal power plant. What was the fight there? People said, 'This is our water. We need it for our survival. If you take away our water for building a thermal power plant what will it do to our agriculture? What will it do to our livelihoods?'

Environmentalism demands that we celebrate limits to frugality is not poverty, where cars are not mobility

This is what is happening across the country. It is something that we have to recognize. It is what I call a million mutinies because of pollution. But we are listening to what people are trying to tell us. They are telling us that they are very poor. But they are also saying that our 'development' will only make them poorer because the development that we are bringing destroys their jobs, livelihoods and water systems and does not replace them.

In some sense what you are beginning to hear is the biggest indictment of what we call development. This is happening across the country. It is not just about one struggle here or there. It is across the country and this is what the minister is responding to. We have to step back and understand that this is the emerging voice of what I would call the environmentalism of the poor. The poor are saying that for them the environment is not a luxury. It is their survival base. If the forests are cut, their livelihoods and their water systems are destroyed, they cannot survive. What they are demanding is a change in the way we do development. They are actually teaching us a lesson that the world has not learnt yet. They are teaching us that we have to do more with less. This is what we have to understand against the environmentalism of the rich.

The environmental movement of the Western world grew after affluence and after they had created wealth. I tell my friends in the Western world that they are nothing more than a waste manager's movement. What they are constantly doing is staying behind the problem. They keep creating new technologies to fix the problem and every new technology has a fallout that cannot even be predicted. Emissions from a country with a small population like the US are putting the entire world at risk. This is not to say that US is bad, but we have to understand that small populations have massive impacts on the environment.

growth. The issue really is to reinvent politics where and where growth is not consumption.

The big challenge, therefore, is how do we reinvent growth without pollution? That is what the poor of this country are demanding from us. We need to rethink agriculture and we need to rethink the role of forests.

The minister and I are constantly debating and fighting on how to make sure that forests are put in the hands of the community so that they can build livelihoods. We need to think of technologies for water and energy and, most importantly, we need to change the indicators of how we measure growth. One quick example: can we reinvent mobility without cars because that is one of our big challenges? When we started our air pollution campaign in the mid-1990s Delhi was choking under pollution. One person was dying every hour because of pollution. We put out an ad saying, 'Roll down the window of your bullet-proof car Mr Prime Minister. The security threat is not the gun it is the air of Delhi.' We published the prime minister's home phone number and fax number – Mr Atal Behari

Vajpayee was the prime minister at that time – and we made sure that he got woken up very early in the morning every day.

The question we were asking at that stage was whether Delhi had to take the same incremental route that the rest of the world had taken. The solution was to move to CNG which gave us a huge leapfrog advantage over cleaning diesel or petrol over the years. Today, can we think of another leapfrog to reinvent mobility? We know transport-related emissions are growing. They are the key contributors to climate change. We also know that the world continues to look for small solutions like fuel-efficient cars, hybrid cars and, bio-fuels, but none of these are working. In the UK, as cars became more efficient, emissions are only increasing for the simple reason that people are buying more, driving more. So it is not about efficiency. It is really about sufficiency.

This is where the opportunity exists in our world. In no city of India have cars replaced the bus. They have only marginalized it. If you look at the statistics that the Government of India recently put out, 40-60 per cent Indians still take the bus. Another 10-20 per cent cycle. But even in rich cities, 20-30 per cent walk because they cannot even afford to take a bus. We cycle or take the bus because we are poor. The option for the future is to take the bus or cycle not because we are poor but because we are rich. That is the big challenge that is being posed to all of us today. Only 10 per cent of Delhi actually drives. The question that the world has is the same that Delhi has: can we provide a car to every citizen? Is the American lifestyle not negotiable? And in Delhi, the question is: if only 10 per cent drive and we are already congested and polluted, can we provide for the remaining 90 per cent? If we cannot, then how do we reinvent mobility?

Finally, for me, the challenge really is to listen to the voices of the people which I believe the minister is listening to. He is implementing the laws, but through the implementation of laws he is actually beginning to make a big change in this country where if we listen to the people, we will set limits and those limits will set new conditions for technology innovation.

Environmentalism demands that we celebrate limits to growth. The issue really is to reinvent politics where frugality is not poverty, where cars are not mobility and where growth is not consumption.

Moderator | **Bahar Dutt**

Environment Editor, CNN-IBN

Q: My question to the minister: yes or no to Endosulfan?[1]

Jairam Ramesh: Wait for a few days.

Sunita Narain: No, absolutely no. There have been devastating results from the use of Endosulfan in Kerala. I don't understand how when a whole community is suffering and you can see the effects of Endosulfan on those communities, you can have a debate. I am from Kerala. I have seen it myself.

Bahar Dutt: So why are you not banning Endosulfan?

Jairam Ramesh: My ministry is soon going to be renamed the Ministry of Bans and Moratoriums. I am well aware of this issue. I do not want to get into specifics and particulars because that is not the objective of this session. This is a public issue with multiple viewpoints that have to be reconciled and multiple voices that have to be heard. For every MP from Kerala who meets me for a ban on Endosulfan, two MPs from Gujarat meet me against the ban on Endosulfan. I have to listen to everybody. There are scientific issues involved here. There are epidemiological issues involved here. There are issues of cost-effective substitutes for Endosulfan. By and large, every environmental issue that comes up for public debate has these manifestations: multiple voices, multiple interest groups, differential impacts and scientific background which is questioned by many. Under these circumstances one has to take a decision and whatever gets taken is going to be an unpopular decision. Some constituency or the other is going to be unhappy. But one thing I

---

1 Endosulfan is an off-patent insecticide that has been banned in more than 63 countries. India is the world's largest user and a major producer and, along with China, Argentina, Brazil and the US, is opposed to a ban, saying that there is no evidence that it causes health hazards as claimed by the EU.

can assure you is that a decision will be taken. What that decision is and when it is going to be taken is another matter.

Sunita Narain: Endosulfan for me signifies a larger issue of how you move from one toxin to another toxin. The issue for us has been that this is one place where there is huge corporate power. When it comes to Endosulfan you can see the huge corporate power of companies who are filing cases and strategic lawsuits against public participation and against individuals. You're seeing the worst corporate behaviour imported from countries like the US. This is very important for us to understand that it should not happen because if those voices have to be heard and if the minister has to do justice to all those voices then all voices must have equal space.

Bahar Dutt: Why do you want this pesticide banned?

Sunita Narain: The case in Kerala exemplifies how toxic it is. All over the world there is increasing concern about its toxicity and of the fears that the use of Endosulfan will lead to health problems. The larger issue for me is the danger of industry in refusing to listen to the kind of risks posed by new technology. Diesel is another issue on which the minister spoke about recently. We have been saying to the diesel industry: this is a toxin and there will be increasing pressures to have fewer diesel cars. But industry does not listen. It goes ahead and invests and then later on cries and says, 'But my industry will be shut down if you shut this down.'

Q: Sunita Narain said 'frugality is not equal to poverty'. This is a very powerful statement. But this is not a decision that can be legislated. It's a societal decision. Society has to decide whether it wants to have its cake and eat it too. Therefore, this is not a political debate or a corporate debate. It is for civil society through its democratic process to take decisions.

Bahar Dutt: So the problem of environmentalism is really a change in our own lifestyles, something we are not willing to do.

Sunita Narain: I agree totally. What the minister represents is the element of the democracy that we have in India. The changes that you are seeing in India are because we have a vibrant democracy where the poor can still make their voice heard. The tribals against Vedanta could still be heard even though they are poor, impoverished and marginalized. Corporate power here is still not as powerful and rapacious as in other parts of the world. My entire effort as an activist is to make sure that we can work our democracy, to deepen our democracy. As we listen to people I am sure new solutions will be found.

Jairam Ramesh: All societal decisions have to be in the political arena. My objective has been to make the environment a political issue; not a technocratic issue or a scientific issue or an activist issue, but a political issue. We must bring it into the public domain and political parties must engage with such issues, genetically modified crops, for instance. Scientists can advise and carry out tests. But the ultimate call has to be taken by the political system of the day. What you say is true that these are societal issues – frugality, consumption, and so on – but the political establishment and the political discourse has to deal with these issues, which they have not done so far. Environment has been seen as sort of side issue. But I think we have to mainstream many of these issues in the political agenda.

Bahar Dutt: Is there a dichotomy within the UPA government? You have a prime minister who states that the environment is important, but not at the cost of development. Congress party President Sonia Gandhi says the environment is the most important issue of our times. So, are we hearing two voices within the UPA government? And who would you listen to more: Sonia Gandhi or the prime minister?

Jairam Ramesh: I don't think there is any dichotomy between the two. The prime minister represents a point of view which believes that at today's point of time economic growth must have primacy. The statement that the Congress president has made reflects a point of view that says that in the drive towards 9 per cent growth, environmental concerns must not be sacrificed. I don't think they are mutually exclusive. It is perfectly possible for us to have both. This, in fact, is the essence of Indian civilization. For 5,000 years when confronted with a choice, we have taken both. We have the ability to reconcile two parts. There will be occasions where choices have to be made and we must make those choices upfront with courage and learn to live with the consequences of that decision.

Bahar Dutt: Have there not been instances where, for example, the prime minister's office has put pressure on you for the Navi Mumbai project or the Posco project? Is there no pressure from the prime minister's office?

Jairam Ramesh: We are in a democratic system. We are not working in a regime in which my voice is the only voice or another minister's voice is the only voice. There are multiple voices and multiple interest groups. I see no reason why there should not be an agitation for an airport in Navi Mumbai as much as there is an agitation against the airport. These are all natural reflections of our democracy.

Q: Mr Ramesh, I would really like to know how many SUVs[2] are being sold compared to the number of tractors on the field or number of trucks on the roads. Your comment on SUVs has succeeded in bringing the debate to the forefront, but don't we have a larger issue at hand?

Jairam Ramesh: Tractors and trucks fulfil a larger social purpose than SUVs. I used the example of SUVs only as a reflection of a certain trend in our automotive sector which causes me grave concerns. Cars are becoming more fuel efficient. Fuel is also becoming better. But cars are becoming heavier and bigger. When you look at the cars on Indian roads you would think that we are an oil-surplus country. You would not get a signal that we are importing 80 per cent of our oil and that we are going to continue to import 80 per cent of our oil. That is what bothers me.

We must have better fuel efficiency standards and these are being legislated. We must have better fuel quality. Indian refineries have spent ₹ 40,000 crore in the last fifteen months to improve the quality of diesel. But at the same time, the cumulative impact on emissions is not very visible. Today, the transportation sector accounts for 7.5 per cent of our greenhouse gas emissions. The way we are going, by the year 2020 the transportation sector will

---

2 Just days earlier, Jairam Ramesh had said the use of sports utility vehicles that consume subsidized diesel and contribute to air pollution was 'criminal'.

probably account for almost 14 per cent of our emissions. We are showing to the world that we are an oil-surplus country and that we are not serious about moving away from a dependence on fossil fuels. That is what bothers me. Why can't we have better, more fuel-efficient or smaller cars?

Sunita Narain: Even in Europe they are struggling to clean up their air. They are struggling to deal with greenhouse gas emissions because they are finding that as car fleets are getting bigger and heavier, they cannot control CO2 emissions. They have set standards but are slipping on standards. So, it is right for us to talk about it today. Sixty per cent cars sold in India are what are called the Alto-model cars, which are far more fuel efficient and far better than heavier cars. The question we have to ask ourselves as we get richer is can't we find that leapfrog? If we want to buy a Mercedes Benz then why do we want to run it on cheap fuel which is reserved technically by the UPA government in the name of socialism for the poor?

In Conversation with Vir Sanghvi

■

Rishi Kapoor

■

Ranbir Kapoor

■

Moderator

Vir Sanghvi

Advisory Editorial Director,

Hindustan Times

Rishi Kapoor

Actor and Film Director

Rishi Kapoor made his memorable debut as a chubby boy in his father Raj Kapoor's labour of love *Mera Naam Joker* forty years ago. More than 120 films later, he could well go down as the most indefatigable romantic hero in Bollywood history. *Bobby* (1973) instantly turned Rishi into a superstar. Some twenty-five years and 150 films later, Rishi turned to direction with *Aa Ab Laut Chalen* (1998). He continues to work as an actor in such films as *Hum Tum, Namastey London, Delhi 6, Love Aaj Kal, Luck By Chance,* to name some recent hits starring him. This year, the veteran actor teamed up with his wife, Neetu, in a leading role for the film *Do Dooni Chaar*, perhaps his finest performance ever.

Ranbir Kapoor

Film Actor

In a very short period, Ranbir Kapoor has taken on the glowing initials RK, once synonymous with his grandfather Raj Kapoor. Ranbir's first film was Sanjay Leela Bhansali's *Saawariya* (2007). It bombed in theatres, but did wonders for Ranbir's career. He was signed on immediately for several commercial endorsements by leading brands. Commercial success in cinema followed, as did critical acclaim with films such as *Wake Up Sid* (a coming-of-age romantic comedy) and *Rocket Singh* (a scathing take on boardroom politics). *Ajab Prem Ki Ghazab Kahani* (2009) and *Raajneeti* (2010), both Ranbir starrers, ranked among the top three hits of the year. The actor is currently working on three films.

VIR SANGHVI: WE HAVE HAD FILM SESSIONS BEFORE, BUT WE HAVE NEVER, IN THE EIGHT YEARS OF THE SUMMIT, HAD A FATHER AND SON TEAMED TOGETHER. YOU HAVE fathers who are successful and you have sons who are successful. But, it is very hard to find two people who have been so successful at such a young age in such a competitive industry. I'm going to get right into this conversation by asking you, Rishi, the caricature of the Kapoors is that of you are all larger-than-life characters who are extroverted, love food, don't mind the odd drink and so on. Is this an accurate caricature?

Rishi Kapoor: It is. We like life. We love work. We work hard. We love to entertain. We like smiles. We like tears and we are entertainers. Those are perks for us. I don't know how it is with the new generation but it worked for me.

Vir Sanghvi: You are pretty much a chip of the old block, right?

Being a star son also comes with a lot of baggage. People have a lot of actor relatives, so it can be an uphill task for into the film world. After that you are on your own.

Rishi Kapoor: I think we all are, and we all like to be. As they say about my family, we have blue eyes and Black Label. Unfortunately, I didn't get the blue eyes but I did get the Black Label (laughs).

Vir Sanghvi: Ranbir, in terms of talent and success, you are very obviously a Kapoor. But in terms of the habits I spoke about – love of food, extroverted, outgoing, love of the odd drink – you are not really a Kapoor, are you?

Ranbir Kapoor: Well, I love the movies. I love food. But there is a misconception that the Kapoors are all about alcohol and eating. They are just very passionate people.

Vir Sanghvi: Is that true? Is that how people talk about the Kapoors?

Ranbir Kapoor: You just said so yourself. But really, they are just passionate people – passionate about the movies, food, family, their dogs. They are passionate about everything.

Vir Sanghvi: I didn't know that. You are passionate about dogs?

Rishi Kapoor: Yes. I have two of them.

Vir Sanghvi: You don't drink very much, do you Ranbir?

Ranbir Kapoor: I am a social drinker but not really a Kapoor drinker.

Vir Sanghvi: You are also not extroverted; not larger than life. You strike me as being relatively introverted. When your father enters a room, he commands the room. When you enter a room, you strike me as being slightly more measured. You have a look that implies you are assessing what is going on, and then make your moves. Is that true?

Ranbir Kapoor: It is not something that I have cultivated. It's just the personality that I have been born with. If I enter a room, I don't want to be the centre of attention. As an actor you become the centre of attention anyway when you enter a room. If people like you, if they like your work, your personality, then they will make you the centre of attention. I don't have to go and make a big noise to make my presence felt.

compare you with your predecessors, and in my family I an actor like me. Being a star son gives you an entry pass
– Rishi Kapoor

Vir Sanghvi: Are you an introvert?

Ranbir Kapoor: Yes, I think so.

Vir Sanghvi: Explain that. In what way are you an introvert?

Ranbir Kapoor: I guess it is a bit of a contradiction because you don't expect an actor to be an introvert. We go out there and bare ourselves. Nobody will connect with you if you don't give something of yourself to your performance in a movie. But yes, I am a little private where my life is concerned. And, I don't think any of you guys will believe me, I am also shy to go up to a girl and talk to her.

Rishi Kapoor: Really? I didn't know this.

Vir Sanghvi: Is he as introverted as he says he is?

Rishi Kapoor: Thank God, he didn't take my nature. He's gone on his mother, both in his looks and in his nature.

Vir Sanghvi: Ranbir, were you closer to your mother while growing up?

Ranbir Kapoor: I guess so because my dad was really busy, constantly shooting. At that time, actors worked on several films together. When I was growing up, a lot of films were being shot in Bangalore and Chennai. So my dad was always away. My mum was the only parent at home and my sister and I are both close to her. We could speak to her about anything. She was our friend. When my dad used to come back, we were scared of him even though he never shouted at us or hit us.

Rishi Kapoor: *Humein shaitaan bana diya tha yaar, kaam kar rahe the;* you're making me out to be some kind of demon. I was only working.

Vir Sanghvi: Did you ever get angry with Ranbir? Do you have many memories of that?

Rishi Kapoor: Oh, I have many memories of getting angry with him but when he was much younger. The only time I actually gave him a *tappu* – rather a hard *tappu* – was at a Diwali puja at RK Studios when he was up to some mischief or the other. The panditji was there and there was the usual chaos and I just happened to give him one tappu and he just started crying. I felt so bad. I am sorry Ranbir about that and I openly say this, I am very sorry.

Vir Sanghvi: Do you remember this Ranbir?

Ranbir Kapoor: I do.

Vir Sanghvi: Was he a strict father?

Ranbir Kapoor: He wasn't strict. The perception was far stricter. If we were on the dining table and I wasn't eating my vegetables, all he had to do was look at me and say, "Move your vegetables." That was enough to make tears come to my eyes. We were just so scared of him.

Vir Sanghvi: Was your relationship with your father different, Rishi, or was it similar?

Rishi Kapoor: I couldn't talk with him. I don't know why but, perhaps he was my father, my guru and mentor. We started getting a little friendly only much later when I became an actor and just before he passed away. He used to say, "Come and have a drink with me." And I'd have a drink with him. Then he would talk about films. Otherwise, we were never really friendly. It was the same story, I guess. When we were young he was working all the time.

Vir Sanghvi: But also this generation is different. I don't think Ranbir is ever tongue-tied in front of you.

Rishi Kapoor: I would say that he is very respectful and thank you Ranbir for that.

Vir Sanghvi: I wanted to talk about the parallels in your careers. You were both launched at a relatively young age in romantic films. The film wasn't quite the hit it was expected to be in Ranbir's case, but it was in your's. What was it like to become a star when you were so young?

Rishi Kapoor: In 1973 I was twenty or twenty-one years of age. Those days teenagers and young people didn't have so many opportunities. They didn't have the kind of exposure that today's kids have. *Bobby* was a big, successful film at that point of time but the film industry was not ready for me. I couldn't work with the likes of Hema Maliniji or Rekha or Zeenat or Parveen. The only person I could work with was either Neetu, who became my wife, or some new girl, which is why I worked with so many new girls.

I became boisterous, mad, crazy. I was earning rupees two to two-and-a-half lakh per film. That was a lot of money in those days. I bought a red sports car. I was an absolute brat, so to speak. But with time you mature and mellow down. I went through a rough patch. My films didn't do well. So, I had to pick up the threads and really work hard. That's when I found my own ground.

Vir Sanghvi: When *Bobby* was made, your father was in quite a bad way financially. He had gambled everything on *Joker*. Producers were saying this is the end of Raj Kapoor. Distributors were walking away. RK Studios was mortgaged. And then he came back, famously, with a film starring his son and an unknown girl. Were you conscious of the pressure?

Rishi Kapoor: Let's take it by one by one. Raj Kapoor was in a mess because he was a very passionate film maker and he lost everything with *Mera Naam Joker*. He had to make a film again but his ego did not allow him to work with the big stars of that time. I wouldn't like to name the stars but every famous actor was ready to give his arm and leg to work with Raj Kapoor as the film director. But he chose to make a film with newcomers.

Vir Sanghvi: There is a story that Rajesh Khanna and Sharmila Tagore

had offered to make Bobby with him. Is that true?

Rishi Kapoor: We will have to check it out.

Vir Sanghvi: I will take that as a yes. The story then goes that he said no and went with you.

Rishi Kapoor: Raj Kapoor was inspired by the first chapter of *Mera Naam Joker*. He wanted to make a typical love story with teenagers and have teenagers as lovers. *Bobby* was a female-oriented film. *Bobby* was Dimple Kapadia in the film, not me. I got to play the lead by default. So my father did not launch me in films so to speak. I was just lucky to ride on a film which was a huge box-office success.

Vir Sanghvi: But there was no pressure? No sense that this is your father's tough period?

Rishi Kapoor: We were so young. Dimple was an industrialist's daughter and used to travel in a Chevrolet. She used to say that if she became a star she would buy a Mercedes. But if she hadn't made it, she would still have been travelling in a Chevrolet. It didn't make a difference to her. But for me, it did. If the film hadn't worked, I don't know which way I would have gone.

Vir Sanghvi: Were you surprised when she got married before the release of the film?

Rishi Kapoor: Well, yes, she did get married and we missed her at the time of the film release.

Vir Sanghvi: Ranbir, you had potentially a similar beginning with *Saawariya* which was much hyped. You had one of the greatest directors of current Bollywood, Sanjay Bhansali and yet the film was a complete disaster. How did that feel?

Ranbir Kapoor: I was twenty-four when it released in 2007.

Rishi Kapoor: So much more mature than your father in many ways.

Ranbir Kapoor: Yes, of course. I come from a generation that has way more exposure than my father's generation. I have also grown up in a film family. I have seen success and I have seen failure around me. So when *Saawariya* did not work, of course, I felt gutted. It was my first film. I had worked so hard. But I did not really take it badly. I did not go into depression because I knew that I had at least begun. I had taken my first steps into something that I love doing; my first steps into acting which I would like to do for the rest of my life.

Vir Sanghvi: So there was no self-doubt?

Ranbir Kapoor: No. I am quite detached that way.

Vir Sanghvi: In what way?

Ranbir Kapoor: I don't get affected by success or failure. I have never really celebrated a successful film my head. I have never felt like a star. I have never felt like a youth icon or any of these titles that people keep giving you. It's all created. It is just temporary. I might have a successful patch but at the same time I have also had failures in the form of *Saawariya* and *Rocket Singh, Salesman of the Year*. Now that was a film I truly believed in. I love the character. He comes from a world I can connect with. It represents the thoughts and notions of my generation. But a film like that does not work. So, it confuses you. At the same time, that same year, a film like *Ajab Prem Ki Ghazab Kahani* worked. It's a more dated film but it reached out more because it was mass and commercial. It had songs, dances and it celebrated Indian films. But it confused my notion about which direction to take. I don't really have a method. I don't really think things through. It is just what organically comes out. It is instinctive.

Vir Sanghvi: People say that you have deliberately chosen different roles. *Rocket Singh* and the role you played couldn't be more different from, say, *Raajneeti* and the role you played. Was this deliberate or did it just happen?

Ranbir Kapoor: It's just that I've been in the right place at the right time. I can't take the credit for this. Even after a debacle like *Saawariya* I got such films that I would have been foolish not to take them. They were characters I connected with and characters that I loved. There was no plan.

Vir Sanghvi: There was no grand plan: I will do a comedy then I will do a love story and then I will play a sinister character?

Ranbir Kapoor: No. It just came naturally. If I like something, I will instinctively say yes. There is no plan to do a romantic film now and a comedy or action film later. It doesn't work in my case.

Vir Sanghvi: So people come to you with proposals and if you like the film you just take it. Rishi, you also played a huge range of roles, didn't you?

Rishi Kapoor: No, we were all one dimensional. In our time, the audiences were very forgiving. Every actor had four films based on the lost-and-found theme: separated at childhood, then in the climax when the villain has tied up the heroine, everyone is reunited. The audience used to accept this. Today with the advent of the internet, Twitter, Facebook, television exposure, the audience cannot take the nonsense of these films.

Ranbir has a tough time choosing his films but in our time it was very easy. You either worked in a romantic film or in an action film where all you had to do was beat up the bad people. The times now are different. It is more challenging for Ranbir. That is the difference.

Ranbir Kapoor: We always say it is easier now or harder then,

I have never really celebrated a successful film my head. youth icon or any of these titles that people keep giving successful patch but at the same time I have also had

or harder then and easier now. But today actors are more fearless. They have the opportunity to play different characters. There are no preconceived notions that I will have a slow motion introduction shot or I will run around trees in Ooty and then in the climax, I will have blood running down my face. Now it is more real; more relatable. Films can be made on a conversation between a boy and girl where he wants to break up and says, "I want to break up because I think you are commitment-phobic." And she says, "Ok. I think we should break up." Back then you couldn't do that. There were way bigger problems, more social norms that they had to deal with.

Vir Sanghvi: And the audience wasn't that sophisticated either.

Rishi Kapoor: Exactly. We got one-dimensional roles. Today the audience is more receptive to watching different kinds of cinema.

Though I must say, I am not one to say that no good movies were made in my time. But personally I feel we are making the best films now technologically.

Vir Sanghvi: Bollywood makes much better movies now?

Rishi Kapoor: Perhaps. We have fewer stories. Ranbir rightly said you could make a film based on a conversation or an isolated incident. You don't need to have a full story with a definite beginning and a definite end. Today audiences are, with the advent of good digital sound, willing to watch a movie that is engaging. Personally, I miss the music of my period, the golden period of the 60s and 70s. That was real music. I do miss the music but I would say that on the whole films are much better now.

Vir Sanghvi: Both of you grew up as sons of big stars. What was it like for you, growing up as a star kid?

Rishi Kapoor: We were all normal kids. We went to normal schools with normal friends.

I have never felt like a star. I have never felt like a you. It's all created. It is just temporary. I might have a failures. – Ranbir Kapoor

Vir Sanghvi: You were Raj Kapoor's son! How could you have been a normal kid?

Rishi Kapoor: Sure, we were recognized. But we didn't take advantage of the situation of being Raj Kapoor's children. We had friends. We had everything. The only perk that we probably had was that when we went to a restaurant, the waiter would give us a better table.

Vir Sanghvi: You didn't take your friends for shooting and that kind of stuff?

Rishi Kapoor: That is not a perk yaar. I owned the studio. I could walk in any time to see my father work.

Vir Sanghvi: You also had this reputation, correct me if I am wrong, of being a little pampered when you were young.

Rishi Kapoor: Pampered? No.

Vir Sanghvi: There is a story that you were sent to boarding school at a youngish age.

Rishi Kapoor: You have done your homework (laughs).

Vir Sanghvi: Tell the story. What happened?

Rishi Kapoor: I was sent to boarding school. Actually, I wanted to go because all my friends were in Mayo college, Ajmer. They played cricket and hockey. I was fascinated. So, I insisted that I wanted to go as well. But I went there for just one term. In those four months I lost about 30 pounds. From a chubby Kapoor I became a normal kid. But when I got off the train when I came home after the first term, my mother started weeping at the station. She said, "My God. He has lost so much weight." That was it. I wasn't sent back.

Vir Sanghvi: So you were pampered.

Rishi Kapoor: Is that pampering?

Vir Sanghvi: Yes, I think for most of us, it is.

Rishi Kapoor: Well, then, yes I was.

Vir Sanghvi: You grew up as a star kid too, Ranbir. What was that like?

Ranbir Kapoor: I didn't know any other life. I have grown up around films. Yes, in school you get attention because you are a celebrity child and you are famous with girls because of that. But my parents did not spoil me. I actually got less pocket money than most other kids. My mother was really strict. So, I valued money. I valued my family. I knew I had a responsibility on my shoulders. It wasn't pressure. It wasn't a burden on me. I didn't feel that I had to behave in a certain way because I came from a certain family. But, yes, I had a very normal childhood.

Rishi Kapoor: You didn't. When you were three years old, you broke a refrigerator in London.

Ranbir Kapoor: I was three years old! I didn't know better.

Rishi Kapoor: Then, when he was four years old, he made me walk in the rain from Soho to buy him a small guitar.

Vir Sanghvi: Sounds pretty pampered to me. The other interesting thing about you, Ranbir is that when you joined films rather than being launched by your father as a hero, you went and worked as an

assistant director to your father and then as an assistant director to Sanjay Bhansali.

Ranbir Kapoor: While growing up, I was never taken to film sets. I did not know how films were made. My sister and I used to eat dinner and watch our parents' movies but for us it was entertainment. When I decided that this was what I wanted to do, I thought of going to a film school or acting institute. But these places teach you theory. It's only on a film set where you actually feel a movie; where you see the world come alive and how that world comes alive – how the director instructs an actor, how the actor takes instructions and how he performs, what are takes, what a set director does, what a costume designer does. I thought this was the way to open the window to films. Of course, I have an immature dream to direct a movie one day.

Vir Sanghvi: Why is it immature? A lot of young people direct movies.

Ranbir Kapoor: I have been busy as an actor. But directing is something I aspire to do one day. I want to tell a story and make a film but only when I have something to say. Right now, I really don't have anything to say. There is no story that I really want to relay to an audience.

Vir Sanghvi: When you were growing up, were you conscious that you were going to become an actor?

Ranbir Kapoor: I didn't make an effort to become an actor. A lot of people were offering movies to me. I was a star son. There was curiosity about me: how will he be once he comes into films? Also, there is a constant dearth of actors. So, really, it came to me.

Vir Sanghvi: Rishi, did you know he was going to be an actor?

Rishi Kapoor: I certainly wanted him to be one, but I didn't know that he wanted to be one too. Then one day he said to his mother that he wants to be an actor. So, I said that he would have to go to a film school because there is no point sending him to a business administration school and telling him to become a doctor and engineer when he is going to join films. I said to his mother that even if he fails as an actor, eventually he is going to do something in film. He will either be a producer or director or spot boy. But he was going to be a part of films, so there was no point sending him to do any other kind of a course. It was never a question that if he failed as an actor, he would become an engineer. That does not happen in cinema. It has never happened and it will never happen because the passion of cinema is such that when a kid grows up around cinema, he is going to be in that field in whatever capacity. He may become an editor. He could become a director. But a failed actor is not going to leave.

So, this was going to be his field. I said, "Let's groom him in this world." I was lucky enough to be groomed in the University of Raj Kapoor. My father had a studio. When we were kids we used to hang around the sets and see how make-up was done, how people acted, how people reacted, how lighting was done. Ranbir didn't have that facility or opportunity.

Vir Sanghvi: Do you enjoy being an actor, Ranbir?

Ranbir Kapoor: I love it.

Vir Sanghvi: What part of the job do you like the most?

Ranbir Kapoor: The working. I don't really get affected by the perks that come with being an actor. But it's waking up every morning and going to a film set that is most fun. It's a lot of good, hard work. It is not as glamorous as a lot of people think. A lot of people have this misconception that if they build their body or do horse riding classes or gel their hair, then they can become actors. But it is way more than that. It is about exposure in life. It is about how much you have taken, and how much you can give of yourself. Everybody is hard working and passionate and you have to be a good person; there has to be a likeable factor which goes with actors. Your audience has to like you. If your audience does not like you, you can never be successful as an actor. But basically, the perfect life for me is just working every day: waking up in the morning, brushing my teeth, going to the film set, coming back, eating dinner, going to sleep.

Vir Sanghvi: And the money?

Ranbir Kapoor: While growing up I never saw any dearth of money. I grew up in the lap of luxury. So money was never my driving force. I didn't want to do well in life so that I could buy myself a plane or a big apartment. I just love films. I want to be part of lot of films. I want to be the biggest star and, at the same time, I want to be the greatest actor.

Vir Sanghvi: Is being the biggest star an ambition?

Ranbir Kapoor: Absolutely. I have so many achievers in my own family. To make a name for myself, I have to break benchmarks that my father or my grandfather have created.

Vir Sanghvi: So the money does not matter as much as fame.

Ranbir Kapoor: No the work matters.

Vir Sanghvi: We were mobbed on the way in. What about the babe factor?

Ranbir Kapoor: The babe factor? The babe factor is always good. Look, if it didn't happen, you would probably start worrying: why isn't it happening? I am young. If girls didn't like me then...

Rishi Kapoor: ...then you are in trouble!

Ranbir Kapoor: Yeah.

Vir Sanghvi: So you don't get embarrassed by all the female attention.

Ranbir Kapoor: I don't. I am shy so sometimes the compliments can make me turn red. But, when I go home and think about it, it makes me smile that people actually love what I do and that people love me for what I love.

Vir Sanghvi: Isn't there an apparent paradox? You are shy and yet you have this reputation of being a ladies' man. How do you reconcile these two?

Ranbir Kapoor: I am twenty-eight. I am an actor but I do have a life of my own, which is apart from movies. If I am dating a girl, I will be open about it. I guess most superstars in movies right now are married. Those who aren't, are seriously dating women they talk about. I am single. So, I'm like a *bakra*. When people have nothing to write about they link me with a new girl. I just want to clarify that it is not true.

I come from a family which lot of people respect. I don't take advantage of that. I don't take advantage of my position as an actor. It's not that I only have to marry an actress, but actresses are the only women I meet. So, if I meet a glamorous person and because I am well-known, people write about it. It's an occupational hazard. I just have to learn to live with it.

Vir Sanghvi: Do you mind all the controversy and gossip that surrounds your love life?

Ranbir Kapoor: I used to. Now I mind it only when it overrides my work. If I am going to promote a movie and if I want to talk about a film that I have spent one and half years working hard on, journalists will just want to know where I had dinner last night. I feel bad but I have to get used to it. I have to take it with a pinch of salt and just let my movie release. If it does well then I can say, "Ok, it's been worth it."

Moderator | **Vir Sanghvi**

Advisory Editorial Director,
Hindustan Times

Q: My question to Ranbir Kapoor: you have a big influence over the youth of today. Do you feel the pressure?

Ranbir Kapoor: No, I don't. As I mentioned earlier, I love what I do. I am not trying to put up a façade. I do wrong things myself.

Vir Sanghvi: Like what?

Ranbir Kapoor: My father is here. I can't talk about it! What should relate to me, is the kind of movies I do; not what people write or sources claim that I do. If the youth like me or look up to me, they should follow my films because that is something which I honestly give to them.

Q: I am from South America, probably the only Latin Indian here. You have a big fan base in the Caribbean, Ranbir. Would you be up for a music video with Shakira?

Ranbir Kapoor: Absolutely. With Shakira I will be up for anything.

Rishi Kapoor: Ranbir and I once flew with Shakira in the same aircraft between London and Los Angeles.

Q: We are lucky to have a father-son duo here. The question is to both of you: how did Ranbir become so focussed in life and what influence did Rishi have in making him so focussed? Is good parenting an accident or by design?

Rishi Kapoor: When Ranbir was growing up, I was away working so I will give credit to my wife Neetu who had all the time to look after the children. There is a misconception that the Kapoors don't want their wives to work. But when Neetu and I decided to get married, we decided that one parent would work and the other would look after the family. God was kind enough to make this arrangement work. After my daughter got married and Ranbir was doing pretty well, I asked Neetu to work in a film with me after thirty years. Why would I want her to work after thirty years, if I didn't want her to work at all? We shared our responsibility and we were lucky that we could do it in the way we had actually perceived.

Q: There are twelve living actors of the Kapoor family including Aditya Raj Kapoor, Sanjana, and Karan. When are you all going to work together?

Rishi Kapoor: When we have stories to make with them.

Q: Rishi, would you have been successful had you not been a star son?

Rishi Kapoor: Yes, I was a star son. It gave me a good launch, an easy launch because people try and recognize you or identify you *ki ye uska beta hai*. But being a star son also comes with a lot of baggage. People compare you with your predecessors, and in my family I have a lot of actor relatives, so it can be an uphill task for an actor like me. Being a star son gives you an entry pass into the film world. After that you are on your own. I worked in *Bobby*, yes I was Raj Kapoor's son. Then what? I was down in the pits after that. I had to fight to get back on my feet.

Vir Sanghvi: Did you find that as well, that as a star son you had advantages even though your father did not launch you?

Ranbir Kapoor: There are advantages. But after the first easy entry into movies, after that it is the work you do. I think I was given a very good opportunity, even though I wasn't launched by my father or by RK Films. I was launched by one of the greater directors living today, Sanjay Leela Bhansali. Although the movie failed, I was given opportunities by other filmmakers and I am really grateful for that. I think partly it had to do with my family's contribution towards cinema and the goodwill people have for them.

Vir Sanghvi: Let me ask you a slightly controversial question. Many people say that the film industry has become like politics; it is dynasty after dynasty and to make it you have to be born into a film family. Is that accurate? There is no entry for people from outside.

Rishi Kapoor: There are so many actors who have no lineage in films. It is pure talent. Why only actors? We can talk about singers, music directors, they are all artists, performers and gifted people. It's not necessary for them to have a relative in the film fraternity. It is only their talent.

Q: You, Rishi had a start very similar to that of Kamal Hassan, your co-star in *Sagar*, as a child artist. He has completed fifty years in film and is still going strong. Why do Bollywood actors have a comparatively shorter shelf life?

Rishi Kapoor: Good question. Why do Hindi film actors have a shorter shelf life? Hindi cinema is very youth-oriented. We have a lot of song and dance and obviously when you cross a certain age, you don't really look your best singing songs. That's the time when you have to hang up your boots. I was lucky to have worked as a romantic hero for twenty-five years, from *Bobby* in 1973 to *Karobaar* in 1998. I introduced about twenty-three to twenty-four new girls and I am very happy to have set that kind of a record. Kamal Hassan has been my colleague and a great actor. Unfortunately, I wasn't as young as he was when he started. Incidentally, this December is going to be forty years since I released *Mera Naam Joker*.

Vir Sanghvi: Wow! And you're still standing!

Rishi Kapoor: Well, at least I am not tottering. I started off as a young boy, playing my younger father in that film and I am still lucky enough to get some work even today.

Q: I pose my question to Ranbir Kapoor. Did you like your role in *Raajneeti* or was it too controversial for you?

Ranbir Kapoor: *Raajneeti* was a hugely successful film for me. But I honestly understood the character only after I finished working in the movie, when I was dubbing for the film and seeing the scenes. I think it went a little beyond my experience. Yes, I got a lot of appreciation for it. But like I say: it's a question of being in the right place at the right time. If the film works, if it's a hit, then *sab* fit *hai*.

Vir Sanghvi: Did the rave reviews for that performance surprise you?

Ranbir Kapoor: I got a little lazy with my work method and the way I was approaching movies. I realized with my last two releases, *Raajneeti* and *Anjaana Anjaani* that I was very comfortable in my roles. So when people say they appreciated my performance, I always wonder: are they making fun of me or are they actually appreciating me?

Rishi Kapoor: That is actually the insecurity of an actor. It's a trait that you must have. An actor always wants to be appreciated. Healthy criticism is, well, a very healthy thing.

Vir Sanghvi: What did you think of his performance in *Raajneeti*?

Rishi Kapoor: I saw the film in London before it released and I have to say that I really can't relate to Ranbir's films. I don't like any of his films. When I see them, I am asking all the time, "Why he is not doing this? Why did he do this?" His mother fights with me and says, "You better chill and learn to see his films in a healthy way."

Vir Sanghvi: Do you have a favourite among his films?

Rishi Kapoor: Not really. He has worked so little. His body of work is very small. It doesn't really measure up to anything.

Vir Sanghvi: That must be really encouraging!

Ranbir Kapoor: I always say that in my own house I have my biggest fan in my mother and my biggest critic in my father. He will always call a spade a spade. I realize that I have really not done anything special yet. I have been lucky. I have sailed through and I have been successful.

Rishi Kapoor: Vir, let me tell you a story. There used to be a street performer. He had a big pole on which he used to balance his two-year-old child. It was, of course, a very dangerous thing to do. The kid could have fallen down. But the child used to take great pride in his work and would always ask, "Dad, how was my performance?"

And the father would reply: "You're getting there."

My grandfather, Prithvi Raj Kapoor, once told me that I will often be tempted to ask him and my father, "How was my performance?" And that they would always tell me, "Son, you're getting there."

Q: You have a tremendous following in Pakistan. Successive generations, starting from your father have made various attempts at joint Indo-Pak productions. A number of Pakistani actors have come and performed in films here. But somehow this concept has not taken off in films the same way it has in music, where singers like Rahat Fateh Ali Khan come and perform in India. Do you see that there is some potential in this and can one can go forward and have some joint productions?

Rishi Kapoor: Just after my father's demise, we made a film called *Henna* where the lead player was a Pakistani girl called Zeba Bakhtiyar. I should also tell you that Nusrat Fateh Ali Khan performed for the very first time for my wedding. My father brought him here. So, yes we welcome a joint production and we welcome healthy working conditions. We definitely want to work with some of the great talent in Pakistan. We would love for them to work with us, given the right opportunities and the right stories.

Vir Sanghvi: *Henna* was your father's dream project, though it was your brother who completed it.

Rishi Kapoor: Yes.

Vir Sanghvi: Alright, we are at the end of our time. Ranbir, your father said he is not so keen on your movies because he is too critical of them. Are you keen on his movies?

Ranbir Kapoor: Absolutely. I have been his biggest fan. He has been my favourite actor.

Rishi Kapoor: I didn't say I have not been his fan. He's made six films. What can I assess with six films? I made 150 films yaar.

Vir Sanghvi: Two favourites?

Ranbir Kapoor: *Zamane Ko Dikhana hai* and *Sargam*.

‘An enabling government does not try to directly deliver to its citizens everything that they need. Instead it creates an enabling ethos so that individual enterprise can flourish and ordinary citizens can, for the most part, provide for the needs of one another.’

Balancing Reforms with Inclusive Growth:

The Agenda for the Future

■

Pranab Mukherjee

■

Moderator

Nik Gowing

Main Presenter, BBC World

PRANAB MUKHERJEE

Finance Minister of India

The most experienced minister in the UPA government, Pranab Mukherjee is regarded as the ace trouble-shooter for Congress President Sonia Gandhi. Besides his current portfolio, the finance ministry, Mukherjee has handled such key ministries as commerce and industry, defence and external affairs in a political career spanning four decades. He was the deputy chairman of the Planning Commission between 1991 and 1996. Known for his negotiation skills and knowledge of government functioning, Mukherjee was the pointsman for dealing with the Left allies in the UPA government's previous tenure, 2004 to 2009. Mukherjee is a trained lawyer and has authored five books on politics

I AM VERY HAPPY TO SEE THAT THE HT SUMMIT IS GRADUALLY EVOLVING INTO AN OCCASION FOR SOME SERIOUS THINKING ON ISSUES THAT HAVE CONTEMPORARY relevance to India.

The topic of my speech is an issue which the Indian polity has been engaged with for over two decades. The current phase of globalization had shrunk the world and made boundaries between countries truly irrelevant. At one level, it reduced us to a single entity such that developments in one part of the globe have implications on the other part. As a result, the challenges and opportunities of development in general and of sustaining high growth over an extended period of time in particular have become more complex.

Moreover, the process of change is not linear nor is the outcome uniform everywhere. There are always choices to be exercised from competing alternatives and objectives. The process is indeed challenging. This could not have been better demonstrated than by the unfolding of the global financial crisis. This crisis has suddenly exposed before us the pitfalls of an unquestioning dependence of liberal markets to sustain and enhance human wellbeing. In a sense, it has reinforced a belief that has always been close to every policy maker's heart in India.

Yet, we have also seen how these very markets have been the means to bring unprecedented prosperity to a large part of the world over an extended period of time. They have opened up possibilities for many of us in the developing world to make progress in addressing the persistent problems of poverty, livelihood, health, education, and security.

In an ideal case there should not be any conflict of economic development, reforms for sustaining high growth and ensuring that growth is also inclusive. These objectives should be mutually reinforcing and an integral part of the development strategy. However, in reality that is not always the case.

In India, structural factors like poverty, literacy, deprivation and lack of adequate connectivity have created segmentation in our markets and among our people. As a result, while some of us have been able to ride the wave of prosperity that economic reforms have ushered in the country, there are others who are struggling to stay afloat as they can barely participate in the markets.

With development and economic reforms, the focus on economic activity has decidedly shifted towards the non-governmental actors. In fact, the need of the hour is to have an enabling government. Let me elaborate. An enabling government does not try to directly deliver to its citizens everything that they need. Instead it creates an enabling ethos so that individual enterprise can flourish and ordinary citizens can, for the most part, provide for the needs of one another. At the same time, the government steps in to help those who do not manage to do well for themselves. The government has to safeguard the interests of citizens who are left out of the growth process. It is this balance in policy that we have tried to evolve ever since the UPA government led by the Indian National Congress first came to power in 2004.

The 11th Five Year Plan endorsed a need for inclusive growth to ensure equality of opportunity for all. A multipronged strategy was adopted. This included rapid growth for reducing poverty and creating employment opportunities, improving access to essential services in health and education, empowerment through education and skill development, and creating employment opportunities supplemented by the Mahatma Gandhi National Rural Employment Guarantee Programme. The Rashtriya Krishi Vikas Yojana was launched with a view to improve agriculture productivity and ensure food security. We outlined a strategy for taking the Green Revolution to the eastern part of the country. We also renewed the thrust of our development in physical infrastructure.

For our government, inclusive development is an act of faith. In the last five years, our government has created entitlements backed by legal guarantees for an individual's Right to Information and his or her Right to Work. This has been followed up with the enactment of the Right to Education in 2009-10. As the next step, we are working on a draft Food Security Bill which is presently in the public domain for discussion.

To fulfil these commitments, the spending on social sector has been rapidly increased and now stands at 37 per cent of the total Plan in 2010-11. Another 25 per cent of the Plan allocation has been devoted to the development of rural infrastructure. With growth and the opportunity that it generates, we hope to further strengthen the process of inclusive development.

We recognize that the success of this strategy rests on sustaining high growth over an extended period of time. Growth of income is important in itself but it is also important for the resources that it brings in. These resources provide us with the means to bridge critical gaps that remain in our developmental efforts particularly with regard to the welfare of the vulnerable segments of our society.

It is equally important that these resources are effectively used. We are conscious that if these resources are to bear fruit, we will have to tackle issues of governance and service delivery. We have taken up an ambitious programme of providing unique identities to the people, focussing initially on the poor. Provision of identity will enhance the access of the poor and marginalized to public services and enable efficient delivery of benefits directly to targeted populations.

The government is striving to improve the regulatory environment in the country. There are no off-the-shelf solutions available to the regulatory dilemma facing any developing country. Each country has to chart its own path on the regulatory reformed road based on its native genius and the conditions on the ground.

The 11th Plan set a target of an average 9 per cent GDP growth for the country as a whole. That we have been able to average nearly 9 per cent growth in GDP in the four year period from 2004-05 attests to the fact that we have the capacity to do it. Moreover, the success in managing the economic slowdown in the wake of the global financial crisis and engineering a quick turnaround shows a growing maturity for policy management in a globalized world. It has highlighted the importance of pursuing reforms to make the economy more competitive and the oversight system more efficient and sensitive to the new developments.

We have to build and sustain an economy where the growing capabilities and rising aspirations of individuals can be matched with an expanding set of opportunities for people to enjoy. The economy should be able to support productive employment for all those who enter the labour force. It requires a massive scaling up of our physical and social infrastructure and skill upgradation. Then alone can the benefits of economic growth percolate down effectively to the most marginalized and vulnerable segments of the population.

Looking ahead, I am very hopeful that we will be able to create the right balance between the need for reforms to sustain high growth and, at the same time, deepening the inclusive character of our development process. There are several factors that have emerged for the performance of the economy in the last twelve to eighteen months, combined with performance over the last couple of years. Savings and economy investment rates have reached levels that even ten years ago would have been dismissed as a pipe dream for India. As the demographic dividend begins to pay off in India, the savings rate is likely to rise further, provided we are able to create productive employment opportunities.

Moreover, the arrival of India's corporations in the global marketplace is an optimistic prognosis of the economy in the medium-to-long term. I am confident that we are in a position to sustain high economic growth in the coming decades and create a more inclusive outcome for our society. I have faith in the Indian entrepreneurial spirit and we have the political will to do the needful to sustain this momentum.

Moderator | **Nik Gowing**

Main Presenter, BBC World

Nik Gowing: Minister, you've talked about the new optimism that you have about inclusive growth. But let me quote you a report from CII, literally a few weeks ago, that India faces considerable challenges from its growth aspirations. Poverty remains high, human development indicators are poor, malnutrition and infant mortality rates are at unacceptable levels. The recent Human Development Report talked about a widening of the position at the economic prospects in your country that suggests that even after six years of your coalition government, you are not achieving what you believe you are achieving.

Pranab Mukherjee: In fact, the reasons for which higher growth is needed are exactly the same which I have also identified in my observations. To eradicate poverty, to remove imbalance, to improve quality of life, we must have high growth; growth not merely in statistical terms but growth in terms of creating wealth which can provide strength to the government to intervene effectively where it is needed.

I will give you just one example to illustrate this. In the 1980s, I had the privilege of being the finance minister. At that time my tax-GDP ratio was little less than 8 per cent. I could not provide relief to indebted farmers which we could do in 2007 when my tax-GDP ratio improved from less than 8 per cent to more than 12 per cent. It is because of sustainable growth of around 9 per cent for the period of 2003-04 to 2007-08 compared to the GDP growth of less than 5.2 per cent in the early 1980s. Therefore, my short point is that one does not contradict the other. As long as there is poverty, illiteracy, deprivation, lack of quality life, we shall have to emphasize more on achieving higher growth to create more wealth so that effective intervention by the government in desirable areas is possible.

Nik Gowing: But you accept that there is now this growing gap between the vast numbers of people in India who are not being included,

according to the latest statistics. You are talking about inclusive growth. Do you accept that there is an even greater challenge, even though the growth figures that you are quoting are extremely positive for India?

Pranab Mukherjee: You should keep in mind that the standard does not remain the same. To determine poverty in the 1960s, the major criterion was calorie consumption. Poverty and backwardness today are not confined to calorie consumption but have extended to areas that include access to many more facilities. Therefore, if in absolute terms, somebody says that in the 1960s, the people below the poverty line were, say, 30 per cent and after forty years it is more or less 36-37 per cent, it will not be correct to conclude that the incidence of poverty has increased. It is that the ingredients of poverty determination have altered.

We have to keep in mind life expectancy, rate of child mortality, rate of literacy. In absolute terms with a billion plus people, this will always be a huge number. Even in terms of percentage, because we have higher standards, 20 million people have been added to the poverty line.

Nik Gowing: There are a quite a few questions being raised here about the credibility of the government. To sustain growth, there must be good governance. The fundamentals of inclusive growth are now under challenge. The reputation, behaviour and credibility of the Congress-led coalition and governing system is increasingly being challenged and doubted because of current events in your country. Liz Mathew of Mint has a question about the government's reputation and the image that is taking a beating because of current events which in turn is going to affect the public perception of the achievability of inclusive growth.

Pranab Mukherjee: To achieve inclusive growth, of course, the credibility of the government, transparency and honesty and integrity are the most important factors. If there has been a misdemeanour in certain areas, people will naturally be agitated and expect corrective steps to be taken. The strength of our system is that we have the capacity to take these corrective steps.

Nik Gowing: But what about the reputation of your government taking a beating at the moment?

Pranab Mukherjee: In a Parliamentary system, these things happen sometimes. It is nothing new. It has happened earlier. But in course of time what is damaged can be restored. Confidence can be built up.

Nik Gowing: I have a question from Raj Kumar who asks: "When will policy makers in India do something to bring back black money, estimated at $1 trillion, for use for productive purposes?"

Pranab Mukherjee: I don't know the actual estimations of unaccounted money and black money stored in other countries. If I remember correctly, there was only one study conducted in the mid 1980s by some government-sponsored experts. Thereafter, various studies have been undertaken by individuals, experts and economists and they have made some estimations. But in so far as there is a substantial quantum of money parked in foreign countries in tax havens, what measures we are taking?

We have double taxation avoidance agreements with 78 countries. When India became a member of FATF (Financial Action Task Force) in July 2009 we did so after obtaining a requisite number of votes in that organization. Before that, we accepted the OECD (Organisation for Economic Co-operation and Development) code and we started revising the avoidance of double taxation agreement with all these 78 countries.

Until now, we have been able to amend [agreements with] eight countries and with certain entities which are not sovereign jurisdictions but have their independent jurisdiction for taxing and banking purposes – with them we are entering into an exchange of tax information, not an avoidance of double taxation agreement. We have entered into such agreements with about four countries, including Bahamas and Virgin Islands.

My conclusion is that it would not be possible for us to get the necessary information and thereafter raise a tax demand on defaulters. In one case we have done so; we have raised the demand but could not make a public disclosure because the country concerned put an embargo saying we could collect tax from the defaulting tax payer but could not make it public. So by making this commitment we have served notices and are trying to realize the tax.

Nik Gowing: There are a lot of questions about corruption. Does inclusive growth include accepting corruption and fraud, inappropriate corporate and political behaviour and other issues on multiple fronts? Is that part of inclusive growth? Or given that what is happening now in public life, is this now a turning point when you hear Ratan Tata telling us why he didn't setup an airline; when you hear Rahul Bajaj saying bribing by big business is common; and an NDTV poll recently talking about corruption as the one big issue that could block India's greatness potentially as a superpower? In other words, the issue of corruption is probably more on the political agenda and the public agenda than it has ever been in this country.

Pranab Mukherjee: I don't know whether it is current or whether it has been continuing for a very long period of time. Recently, one study made a comment that from 1948 to 2008, in sixty years, there has more than $640 billion outflow of money from India. One of the study's revelations was that in terms of percentage it has increased after the 1990s when we adopted liberalized economic policies which is broadly termed as economic reforms. We are in touch with the people who conducted this study to find out their methodology by which they arrived at this figure. After obtaining the report, the department is examining it to see what corrective measures are possible.

The short point which I am trying to make is that allegations are there. Allegations in public life are not new. But that does not mean that they can be justified. The short point is you shall have to fight it out. It definitely is a matter of concern, and unless we address this issue properly and nip it in the bud, it would be difficult for us to achieve the desired level of growth.

Growth cannot be seen merely in economic terms or having access to certain facilities. Growth is in the overall improvement of human life, character and its values. Therefore, the fight against corruption must take institutional measures to improve the system in a transparent manner.

Nik Gowing: You are talking about nipping it in the bud but there are several cases which are well known to everyone in this room which are impacting public life day after day, on every front page on every

news channel at the moment. It comes again down to the issue of what you are able to do. The prime minister, after all, does have a stated determination to act more firmly against the corrupt. Is there frustration within your government that you have not made the impact that you wanted on corruption, given the kind of revelations there are at the moment with the number of public figures who have been forced to resign?

Pranab Mukherjee: First of all, whenever questions are raised and doubts expressed, we take preventive measures. We take corrective measures and thereafter we analyze the situation. I will give you just one example which will tell you why I don't feel frustrated. Before this decade began, similar types of charges of corruptions and allegations were brought against the government of which I was also a part. We had a Congress-led government between 1991 to 1996 and the judiciary made major observations on the discretionary power of the highest executive or ministers. We took remedial measures after that. We have established independent regulatory mechanisms, whether it is in the case of banking, financial institutions, insurance, stock markets or pension funds. We even had a regulatory mechanism for telecommunication.

Sometimes, when these mechanisms fail to function then we find some distortions taking place. But that does not mean that we are complacent or we are not looking into these aspects. Whenever such aberrations take place, we analyze, find out the cause and take corrective measures and that is the way we have to deal with them.

Nik Gowing: You talk about distortions and anomalies and really that does raise the issue of the 2G Spectrum crisis. You spoke about the need to spend on the social sector and the need to increase spending on vulnerable sectors of society. But there are many who say that the government probably lost up to ₹ 1.76 lakh crore from spectrum which could have been sold at a much higher price. That money could have gone into social investments. What is your response as finance minister?

Pranab Mukherjee: Of course, if I had got that money I could have spent it on social response. But, I would like to request you to pause for a minute. When we are evaluating the 2G Spectrum's valuation in the context of the 3G Spectrum auction, the money which we have got perhaps worked at the back of our mind. But when I myself as finance minister projected the budget and showed that I expected to realize ₹35,000 crore from the auction of 3G spectrum, I don't think anybody disputed that figure. Nobody said, 'Mr Minister you are grossly undervaluing the money which we will realize on spectrum.' Later, when the auction was conducted in a transparent manner, the auction began at ₹ 35,000 crore. Now if somebody says that I had deliberately made an undervalued projection in my budget, then it would not be correct.

So, yes, if we had got this money, it would surely have helped us. But please remember, these calculations are sometimes made in hindsight, after seeing experiences in other areas. In our system, we take in the Comptroller and Auditor Generals' (CAG) report. That report is examined by the parliamentary committee. The parliamentary committee then re-examines all the issues raised by CAG, sees the clarifications from the concerned ministry, examines them, and when thereafter they submit their report that become the final observation of the Public Accounts Committee. That is the finally recognized document.

Right now, it has been examined by the Public Accounts Committee. The CAG's job is to point out financial irregularities. I am not raising any doubt about their bonafides. They have done a good job. They have done their mandated job but that is not the end of it. It will have to be re-examined by the Public Accounts Committee. Further evidences will be called for and only after that will the final report of the CAG come out.

Nik Gowing: Was it really a transparent process? After all, the prime minister wrote on 2 November 2010 questioning transparency. The CAG report talks about fraudulent means to get access to spectrum applications that were either incomplete, wrong or had suppressed facts. You are talking about transparent processes but I am coming back to the original question about inclusive growth and the credibility of government. This kind of language from the CAG is really denting public confidence at the moment.

Pranab Mukherjee: This is my twenty-first year in a ministry and I have dealt with so many CAGs reports. It is my official duty to deal with them. You have arrived at a report which has been received as the final report. Let it be examined by the Public Accounts Committee. Let the Public Accounts Committee reach its conclusion. These audit paragraphs are yet to be analyzed by further evidences given by the officers before the Public Accounts Committee and only then will a final report be submitted. So far as the language is concerned, I have no comment. It is a free country. Everybody has the freedom to express their view the way they want to. I can only explain the system.

Nik Gowing: What is your view of what is happening in Andhra Pradesh with regard to Microfinance Institutes (MFIs)? What is the impact on the microfinance business, where it seems to almost be threatening the chances for inclusive growth because of the credibility of microfinance companies being put into the public spotlight? Do you believe you should be in a position to rescue them, and swiftly, with clear legislation?

Pranab Mukherjee: I am afraid the concerns expressed by a large number of people are genuine and I am equally concerned. This is one of the instrumentalities through which we are trying to reach the people and provide them with banking services. I had analyzed the Andhra Pradesh government's ordinance when it was introduced. We have made certain suggestions to them and when the ordinance will be replaced by an act in the state Assembly, I do hope those will get reflected.

In addition, the governor of the Reserve Bank of India has already appointed a committee[1] to look into microfinancing in all its aspects and asked for it to submit its reports within three months. After obtaining this report, I will take appropriate measures in consultations with the RBI.

---

1. The Malegam Panel to regulate India's Rs 22,000 crore microfinance industry was appointed in October 2010 after the sector plunged into a crisis following the Andhra Pradesh government restricting operations. Andhra Pradesh accounts for more than a quarter of India's total microlending loans. The state law barred weekly collections and made government approval mandatory for every second loan to a borrower. This resulted in a sharp fall in collection rates, leading many MFIs to stop fresh lending.

My idea is not to strangulate but to regulate the interests that they charge and to see that these are not exorbitant and that the method of realization, under no circumstances, should be questioned. The rate of interest should be moderate. Lending banks are being instructed to be in touch with them, provide them with necessary guidelines observe whether these are complied with. I would not like to strangulate the system because it is not possible for banks to reach large numbers of people through their regular banking services.

Nik Gowing: I have to ask one final question: when are you going to become the prime minister?

Pranab Mukherjee: Why should I? I am quite happy with what I am doing.

The Diabetes Pandemic:

Challenges and Solutions

▪

Dr Edward Horton

▪

Wasim Akram

▪

Dr Anoop Misra

▪

Moderator

Sanchita Sharma

Health Editor, Hindustan Times

Dr Edward Horton

Professor, Harvard Medical School

Edward S. Horton, professor of medicine, Harvard Medical School and head of the clinical research section at the Joslin Diabetes Center in Boston, received his medical degree from Harvard Medical School in 1957. His major interests include obesity and insulin resistance as they relate to diabetes mellitus and cardiovascular disease, and the regulation of energy balance and metabolic fuel homeostasis. He has received several awards, including the Banting medal for distinguished service awarded by the American Diabetes Association.

I AM HONOURED TO HAVE BEEN INVITED TO PARTICIPATE IN THIS LEADERSHIP SUMMIT AND, PARTICULARLY, TO BE ABLE TO DISCUSS WITH YOU DIABETES, WHICH IS truly becoming a worldwide epidemic and a major public health problem.

At the 2003 International Diabetes Federation Congress in Paris it was estimated that there were approximately 194 million people worldwide with diabetes – about 90-95 per cent of these had Type 2 diabetes or what used to be called Maturity Onset Diabetes and the remaining 5-10 per cent had Type 1 diabetes or what we used to call Juvenile Onset Diabetes.

Those terms are not pertinent anymore because Type 1diabetes can occur at any age and Type 2 diabetes is occurring younger and younger in our population. But back in 2003, the projection was that by 2025 the number was going to increase to 330 million or about a 72 per cent increase in diabetes worldwide.

There were certain hot spots around the world. One of them was Southeast Asia, particularly India where it was projected to double within that period of time. I can tell you that we are ahead of schedule. India has reached the status of having more people with diabetes than any other country in the world. So, you are number one in that regard. It is becoming a major problem for society.

In the US we have a dual epidemic because diabetes is closely associated with the development of obesity in our population. It is currently estimated that about two-thirds of adult Americans are overweight, if you use the measure of Body Mass Index being greater than 25. In this part of the world, 25 is probably already overweight. But in the US, 25 is the cut-off point between what is considered normal weight and overweight. If you are interested in calculating your own BMI, it is your weight in kilograms divided by your height in metres, squared.

Obesity is defined as a Body Mass Index of greater than 30 and it is currently estimated that one-third of the US population is obese. Twenty four per cent, or one in four people, have what is called metabolic syndrome, which is a cluster of obesity, elevated blood pressure, abnormal lipids in the blood and elevated blood sugar. This is considered to be a very high-risk condition for cardiovascular disease and for the development of diabetes.

There are currently an estimated 24 million people with diabetes in the US or about 7 per cent of our population. Another 57 million have a condition called Impaired Glucose Tolerance, which is a grey zone between completely normal glucose metabolism and diabetes, but a group that is at very high risk for developing diabetes.

The particularly frightening statistic is the life-time risk of developing diabetes for people born in the year 2000 or children who are now ten years old. This is estimated to be 33 per cent for men and 39 per cent for women. For Hispanic women, a particularly high risk group, it is as high as 50 per cent. In this population, cardiovascular disease is a major cause of mortality.

In the US currently there are 50,000 deaths directly attributed to diabetes. It is the number seven cause of death in the US. But this

The most critical factor in developing diabetes is to do we pay for economic growth and progress throughout

is probably under-reported and there could be as many as 193,000 deaths linked to diabetes, moving it up to the number three cause. It is the third or fourth leading cause of death in African-American women, the third leading cause in Latino women and the third leading cause in Native-American women in the adult population.

What is the impact of this on our healthcare system and economy? One in every seven healthcare dollars spent in the US goes to caring for diabetes and its related complications. The estimated total cost attributed to diabetes, which includes both direct medical care cost and indirect cost, has gone from $98 billion in 1997 to $132 billion in 2002 and $174 billion in 2007. I hate to think what it is going to be in 2010 because I don't know that figure yet.

What is driving this diabetes epidemic? There are multiple causes, and I just want to mention briefly a few of them. First, we know that there are inherited genetic factors in diabetes. Unfortunately, most of us cannot choose our parents, so we are stuck with the genes we have inherited. But there is a rapidly rising field called Epigenetics, which is modification of genes by environmental factors. We know that both low-birth weight and high- birth weight children are at increased risk for developing diabetes. Low-birth weight children are probably related to maternal under-nutrition, particularly protein malnutrition, which can be a major problem in a country like India. Over-nutrition is related to a mother having gestational diabetes or high blood sugar levels during pregnancy. We also know that exposure to certain environmental toxins is contributing and there is now very good evidence that air pollution is actually a factor in the development of diabetes. But by far the most critical factor in developing diabetes is to do with changes in our lifestyle. This is one of the prices we pay for economic growth and progress throughout the world.

A friend from Amsterdam recently sent me a photograph of a street corner in New York city. He sent it to me with a note that

with changes in our lifestyle. This is one of the prices the world.

said, 'This is why you have so much diabetes in the United States!' In the picture each one of the stores in the background is a fast food outlet. There is a Middle Eastern deli, a Dunkin Doughnuts, Taco Bell, Pizza Hut. Then there is a gentleman in the centre of the photograph, obviously obese, eating while he is talking to his friend. An individual in the foreground has a potbelly – that is abdominal obesity which turns out to be a major risk factor for diabetes and for the metabolic syndrome. He is going down a one-way street, and my friend said: 'This is clearly a one-way street to diabetes.'

The challenge that we face is how to turn that slide around and reverse the process. There have been many trials around the world looking at the strategies for the prevention of diabetes. I have been very fortunate to be a part of a programme called 'The Diabetes Prevention Programme'. This is a large multi-centred study that involves 27 different centres in the US funded by the National Institute of Health. It is studying more than 3,000 people at high risk for developing diabetes because they have Impaired Glucose Tolerance.

There were three groups in this study. One group was treated with the drug Metformin, which is usually the first line drug we use for treating people with diabetes. The second was treated with an intensive lifestyle modification programme focusing on a healthy diet and weight reduction – we asked everybody to lose and maintain 7 per cent of their body weight and increase physical activity consisting of at least half an hour of walking or other equivalent moderate intensity exercise most days of the week. And then there was a placebo control group.

The control group developed diabetes at a rate of about 11.5 per cent per year. Those on Metformin had this rate decreased by 31 per cent. But lifestyle changes turned out to be the most effective treatment, reducing the development of diabetes by almost 60 per cent – the actual number was 58 per cent risk reduction in this intervention. We also found several other things: high blood pressure that was present in 30 per cent of the subjects was significantly decreased in the lifestyle group. The second thing we found was that triglycerides were decreased in this group. The third was an improvement in lipid profile. We know that there was much less use of medication in this group. We have now followed these people for ten years and we are still seeing the long-term effects.

I want to point out that prevention strategies are critical, but once people develop diabetes, we have to focus on global treatment. Fortunately we have new medications for managing this. A number of medications have become available since the 1950s for treating high blood pressure. For diabetes we had only had insulin and a few agents for a long time. But now we have many agents that are coming and several that are in development.

Diabetes is a major global health problem which is increasing at an alarming rate. The underlying causes are multiple. The economic burden is a major concern for society and stopping the epidemic will require considerable efforts by many elements in society including public education, governmental programmes, community planning, and better health care.

But the bottom line is that this is a societal problem and not just a medical problem. I want to leave you with a message that I think it is time for all of us to get together to develope strategies for dealing with this global epidemic. It is clearly time to act because we are losing the battle and the numbers are going up even as we speak.

Wasim Akram

Former Pakistan Cricket Captain

Wasim Akram is regarded as the best left-arm fast bowler in history and one of the greatest cricketers of his generation. He was the first bowler to claim more than 400 wickets in Tests and One-Days and is the only one with two hat-tricks each in both forms of the game. It was magical to see Akram running in and hurling thunderbolts at batsmen from that short run-up. He could bowl six different balls in an over. He forged a deadly pair with Waqar Younis and, in their prime, the duo formed one of the most potent fast bowling combinations cricket has seen. That Akram accomplished all this while battling diabetes – he was diagnosed with the disease at the peak of career – makes his achievements all the more heroic.

I WAS DIAGNOSED WITH DIABETES IN 1997. I WAS ONLY THIRTY-ONE YEARS OLD AT THE TIME AND AT THE PEAK OF MY CRICKETING CAREER. I WAS LOSING WEIGHT RAPIDLY and I was sleeping a lot. I was thirsty and hungry all the time and yet, I was losing weight. I thought I was getting fitter. I knew what diabetes was. I knew that it was associated with obese people who don't exercise. But my job was to exercise; to run around all day long. I used to go to practice at 9 in the morning and come back at 5 in the evening every day.

Obviously, I was stunned when I was diagnosed as a diabetic. I didn't know what to do. My wife really helped me a lot. The doctors helped me a lot but it took me one month to come out of that mental phase where I thought, 'My cricket is finished. My life is finished and I won't be able to play anymore.'

I went to a doctor in Lahore who told me that I would have to go on insulin right away. That was a huge shock for me – to inject myself, I thought, who will do this for me? Will I be able to carry on with my cricketing career after having three jabs a day? But the doctor said, 'If you look after your sugar levels for a month or so, you can play cricket.'

It took me a month. And then in November 1997, I got picked for the Pakistan team again. I rested for a month. It took me about six weeks to get my insulin going. First, I thought it would be painful. But I got used to it. And then I learned that in diabetes you can be your own doctor if you know what exactly is happening with you. I learned that I had to make a huge difference in my lifestyle. I had to carry chocolate with me to prevent hypos, which is when your blood sugar goes down.

Then I went to South Africa to play the series. It was a bit difficult. I started putting on weight and everybody else told me, 'If you are diabetic you will get tired faster than any other normal person.' I began to read about diabetes. With my wife's help, I realized what it meant to have my sugar levels in control, take my insulin on time, check my sugar levels randomly, early morning, under stress, or if I am happy

– all of these could trigger off all sorts of fluctuations in my sugar levels.

I started playing again. I have got 250 wickets in One-days after my diagnosis. I have 200 wickets in Test cricket after that. It all has to do with learning about the disease; learning to live with the disease. I was exercising a lot more than anybody in the Pakistan team at the time. If they did five laps, I would do seven. So, I broke the myth that diabetics get tired faster. I didn't because I was looking after my health. I learned that if I had to bowl after lunch, I have to skip my insulin because I will be exerting myself. In the beginning I used to have four or six units of insulin and then I would get a hypo. After a month I realized that if I'm going to be bowling after lunch, then I shouldn't be having insulin. That is how I have controlled my diabetes.

I do go through phases as a diabetic. There are days when I don't feel like checking my sugar levels. Sometimes I feel like

In diabetes you can be your own doctor if you know what make a huge difference in my lifestyle.

having biryani. But I've cut down on food. I eat healthy food. I try to have less oil and, of course, I exercise. I have been retired for six years now, but I exercise regularly. I go to the gym in the morning and I try to do cardio in the evening. I try to be stress-free at all times.

Sanchita Sharma: When you were playing for Pakistan, weren't you tested and screened? Didn't you undergo regular health tests?

Wasim Akram: We never had our doctors with us. We never had regular check-ups. I hope they do it now. But until 2003, there was no regular or routine check-up for players. There was no awareness about the disease – not just this disease, but any disease.

Sanchita Sharma: So, the only time you went to a doctor was when you pulled a muscle or had an injury?

Wasim Akram: Yes, when I pulled a muscle or had an injury, but never otherwise. Our Pakistan Cricket Board has never had a doctors' panel that can review the players' physical and mental health.

Sanchita Sharma: You mentioned earlier that you travel for six months in a year. How do you manage your food and exercise regimen then?

Wasim Akram: The timings may be different but there are 24 hours in a day. Sometimes it takes a couple of days to get the timing right. I have breakfast at 9 o'clock at home. So, say, I am travelling to England, I will make sure I have breakfast for the first day at 6 in the morning to get my timing going. This is something you learn with time and experience. I have learned with fourteen years of diabetes that to manage time, to manage insulin and, of course, exercise is very important.

Nowadays our younger generation in India and Pakistan tends to have a very laidback and easy going lifestyle. When I was young, in class six or seven, my mother used to literally kick me out and say: "Go play." Now kids come back from school, they

exactly is happening with you. I learned that I had to

have Playstation, they have Xboxes, and they don't go out. One of my sons is like that, but hopefully he will get around to playing outdoors sooner than later.

Sanchita Sharma: What really works better for you: diet management or exercise? And what kind of exercise, aerobic or weights?

Wasim Akram: Both. I do weights in the morning and cardio in the evening. I go for a run or a brisk walk for at least 45 minutes or an hour. That makes me feel better mentally and physically.

Sanchita Sharma: Have you discussed diabetes with your sons?

Wasim Akram: I am a known diabetic worldwide and particularly in our part of the world. My younger son is nine and is very healthy. He wants a six-pack already, so that's a good sign. My elder son is over thirteen. He is bit overweight and that's where I am trying to teach him. I say, "Go out, play for 30 or 40 minutes and then do whatever you want to do."

Sanchita Sharma: Do they play any sport? What about cricket?

Wasim Akram: They have no idea about cricket, but they do play soccer, badminton and tennis.

Dr Anoop Misra

Director and Head of Diabetes & Metabolic Diseases, Fortis Hospital

Anoop Misra is director of the department of diabetes and metabolic diseases, Fortis Hospitals, New Delhi and director of the National Diabetes, Obesity and Cholesterol Foundation. He has been on the faculty at the department of endocrinology and human nutrition at Southwestern Medical Center in Dallas, Texas. Dr Misra has over twenty-five years experience in teaching, service, research, and community health intervention programmes. He is a recipient of the Dr BC Roy award (2006) and the Americare Award for outstanding contribution in tackling diabetes in India. In 2007 he received a Padma Shri. Dr Misra has been personal physician to two former Indian prime ministers.

TEN YEARS AGO THERE WAS A MAN WHO HAD A MERCEDES, A BIG MANSION, INDUSTRIES, LOTS OF MONEY, AND DIABETES. TODAY, DIABETES HAS BEEN taken over by another man – younger, middle class or even from the low socio-economic strata.

I open with the story of such a person who is thirty-six years old and lives in New Delhi. He started by having a severe pain in his right foot. This quickly developed into gangrene. His foot had to be amputated and it was at this stage that he was discovered to be diabetic. He didn't even know what diabetes was; he had never heard the word. He was a farmer who had moved to Delhi four years ago. From a diet of simple roti and dal he started having deep fried and carotid-dense food. He got a job in a shop. His physical activity levels decreased. He gained weight. And was tired all the time but never went for a check-up.

India is at the epicentre of a diabetes quake. The problem diabetics in the world, 50 million people. And the tide

After his amputation, he now works part-time and spends ₹ 1,000 per month on his medicines. His total family income is ₹ 5,000. He told me, 'Now I depend on my wife for my livelihood. If something happens to me, who will look after my two children?'

This is the new phase of diabetes in India. India is at the epicentre of a diabetes quake. The problem is as big as global warming. We have the most number of diabetics in the world, 50 million people. And the tide is still rising. That is the most worrisome part of it. We have more people with diabetes than Australia and UK. This year it will kill one million people in India.

Who are these people who will die? They are young diabetics. Asians are getting diabetes sooner and dying younger. The first barrier, steeply increasing from twenty years onward, is the cholesterol line. Then comes obesity. At thirty-five years of age, they are hit by diabetes. The age of onset of diabetes among Indians is a decade earlier than the Western population. Many are in their late twenties, working in burgeoning new businesses. But in life's journey, these young people will stumble and fall because they will have blindness, they will have nerve damage, and, as you have seen with our protagonist, amputation of the foot.

This is the type of burden that diabetes in India carries because of complications like heart disease, kidney disease, eye disease, nerve disease, foot problem, and infection. Every year 200,000 amputations are done in India because of diabetes. This is one fifth of the global total. The occurrence of kidney, eye and heart complications are two to four times more than other races because of our genetic code. The cost is a whopping ₹ 1,500 to ₹ 1,800 billion in 2010.

Why is this happening? Is there something wrong with our bodies? Yes, there is. We may not be as fat as many Western people. Yet our body fat tends to be located around the abdomen. Even our fat cells are fatter than those of the Western population. Insulin

is as big as global warming. We have the most number of is still rising.

doesn't act on these fat cells. White populations have fat cells which are smaller and thinner where insulin can act. What is the reason for this? Is it genetics, as has been outlined earlier, or is it something which has been handed down by our forefathers over the centuries, or is it something which happens during pregnancy?

In times of plenty, as is happening now, our body engines are running on famine mode. This is our body's survival ploy which occurs during famines. During this time, energy gets stored as fat. Fat is the most efficient form of energy – one gram of fat is nine calories versus carbohydrates which is only four to five calories, and this is mostly stored over the abdomen. That is the most efficient form of storing energy. Our survival adaptation has now become a liability. Excess calories can neither be stored nor metabolized by the small amount of muscles that we have. This spills over in the blood and causes high sugar and diabetes.

Something is occurring during pregnancy as well. It is often said that diabetes in India is born in the womb of mothers. During pregnancy, if proper nutrition is not given, there is dysfunction in the development of the pancreas and arteries. Such children are born with low-birth weight, a common scenario in India. Then during childhood, they are fed in excess by anxious mothers and they become obese. Along with the pancreas and blood vessel dysfunction, excess fat during childhood leads to diabetes and heart disease.

How do we prevent this? Prevention has a long and binding role. It starts with primordial prevention, when we nip diabetes in the womb by providing proper nutrition to pregnant women. But there are number of pot holes and road blocks. Chief among these is lack of awareness, particularly among the low socio-economic strata where 90 per cent people are unaware about diabetes – what causes it and what it can cause. Even the upper and middle socio-economic strata are not well aware of the problem. This is where we can educate and empower people and, thus, prevent diabetes. This is what is called primary prevention of diabetes.

Physicians are not doing a particularly good job of this. Barely 10 per cent patients are given proper diabetes education. Only 8 per cent are told about the dangers of smoking. Only 50 per cent get nutritional and exercise counselling. If we do our job properly we can prevent many complications. This is what is called secondary prevention.

Prevention is a life-time job. Let me tell you about another case study. A patient who was given inadequate care and nutrition during pregnancy gave birth to a low-birth weight child. Then the child was made obese. Between the ages ten and twenty, insulin resistance occurred. By the time the child turned twenty-six, there was diabetes. A heart attack followed at the age of thirty-eight and death came at forty-seven years of age.

We could have acted at each point of time. We could have acted by providing good nutrition, and thus preventing low-birth weight. During childhood, over-nutrition and physical inactivity could have been corrected and in doing so, diabetes could have been delayed from twenty-six years to, say, seventy years. The heart attack could have been delayed until eighty and death could have occurred maybe at 100 years. But most of the preventive strategies have to be in early life – during pregnancy and during childhood.

These are worst of the times. But these are also the best of times because we have new ideas, new energy, new enthusiasm, new drugs and new concepts. Who are the people who are going to do this – physicians or the government? It is all of us. There are multiple stake-holders. You have the government, non-governmental organizations, media, hospitals, scientists, corporate hospitals and pharmaceutical industries all who can work on primordial prevention by providing adequate nutrition in pregnancy, primary prevention, spreading awareness, identifying high-risk individuals, secondary prevention by diagnosing early, providing the right kind of education, providing drugs which are cheap and widely available, providing new drugs, providing insulin which is cheap and also better devices to deliver that insulin. Hospitals need to be more diabetes-centric. We need diabetes referral and research centres which have a wide area of coverage.

We have new programmes, new guidelines and new treatments. We have hope. It is time to tackle all the challenges. Diabetes control programmes that target rural areas are a government initiative. We have one of the largest childhood obesity programmes where we teach children about the right kind of diet and exercise. This spans 900,000 children in north India.

The government has announced that glucose testing chips are to be made cheaper. These are new and very important initiatives. We have some new regulations on trans-fats in our food, we have new regulations about exercise – we need to exercise 60 minutes every day, seven days a week to prevent diabetes. Obesity guidelines have been lowered for the Indian population so that we can act earlier and in a more appropriate manner. New drugs like Sitagliptin have been identified. This is an excellent drug. Other new drugs are coming.

What can I finally say? We have great hopes in the future to curb this epidemic. But the time to act is now.

Moderator | **Sanchita Sharma**

Health Editor, Hindustan Times

Sanchita Sharma: Before I invite questions from the audience, I am going to ask a couple of question to our experts. Dr Horton, what do you think is more important when it comes to diabetes management and control: exercise or diet control?

Dr Edward Horton: Both together are critically important. The vast majority of patients with Type 2 diabetes are overweight. For them we recommend a heart-healthy diet, focusing on decreasing fat intake, particularly animal fat, and increasing vegetables, fibres and fruit in their diet. Losing weight is really critical; most people can lose anywhere from 5 per cent to 10 per cent of their body weight.

About the exercise component, we have very good data showing that exercise such as walking for a half an hour or more a day on most days of the week has very beneficial effects not only on sugar control but also in reducing the risk for long-term complications, particularly cardiovascular, heart and stroke which is the major cause of mortality.

So, I wouldn't say one is more important than the other. They have to go together and they are both very important as the fundamental thing we do before or in addition to the use of medications that we have.

Sanchita Sharma: Dr Misra you mentioned several drugs for diabetes that have come up over the last decade – how affordable are these? Can people in developing countries afford them?

Dr Anoop Misra: Some of these drugs have been available in India for the last three to four years. Their prices are at the upper end, but these drugs have several properties which have never been seen with other drugs. So, I think these are important but need to be used judiciously – for the average diabetic the old traditional drugs will work.

Q: Wasim, I am wondering if you were able to fast during Ramzan and keep your rozas?

Wasim Akram: I don't fast because I am on insulin. So, I cannot take a risk. People with Type 2 diabetes should consult their doctors.

Dr Anoop Misra: As far as fasting is concerned, there are certain guidelines which we have to follow. We usually use drugs which do not cause too much low sugar. For people who are on multiple doses of insulin – whether they are Hindus observing Navratas or Muslims during Ramzan – we tell them not to fast. But, still, many people do and then we switch them to some other drugs which are more appropriate during that period.

Q: My question is to Dr Horton. What is your view on the preventive aspects of diet on diabetes and has Harvard identified any specific foods that could reduce the incidence of diabetes?

Dr Edward Horton: There have been a lot of studies looking at dietary composition, many of these look at restricting carbohydrates in diet and have shown that you don't get as much fluctuation of blood sugar with a low-carb diet. Clearly, once you develop diabetes, we have to manage both the quantity and the quality of carbohydrates in diet to minimize fluctuations in blood sugar. But for preventive strategies there is some evidence that people with low carbohydrates diets tend to be somewhat protected. But it is very difficult to separate that from weight control and caloric restriction.

Dr Anoop Misra: I would just like to add that as far as Indian diets are concerned, there are multiple factors. Carbohydrates are one, saturated fats are another and fibre content is a third. But the most important are trans-fatty acids which are present in partially hydrogenated vegetable oils like dalda, vanaspati and so on. These directly attack the pancreas. They are present in commercially available food in many hotels and have been traditionally used in India for centuries.

Q: According to Indian tradition there are specific foods, for instance, bitter gourd, that are regarded as medicine. What is your take on these?

Dr Anoop Misra: Since you are asking for specific constituents as far as traditional Indian diets are concerned, at least two stand out. One is fenugreek which is methi and the other is cinnamon. These have been found, in research in India and abroad, to have some effect on blood sugar. But at most, they can be used as an adjunctive therapy to the main therapy.

Q: Dr Misra, have there been studies in India to determine whether genetic factors that influence diabetes in the South Asian subcontinent are similar or dissimilar from those that pertain in the West?

Dr Anoop Misra: No particular gene will ever be found for diabetes. It is a combination of genes and an interaction of genes with the environment. If you ask about the Indian population, there are several genes which have been identified which show that Indians have a propensity to diabetes. But if you ask me about the quality of the study, well we need better studies. There is a consortium of geneticists from UK working with us in India who are dealing with this question.

Dr Edward Horton: I would just like to make a brief comment. The work looking at genetic predisposing factors, as Dr Misra pointed out, is polygenic. I work fairly closely with a group at MIT, so these consortiums are all around the world. Now, there are at least twenty-one different snips that have been associated with an increased risk for diabetes. But in aggregate it does not explain more than 5 per cent of the risk of diabetes. So, we still have a lot to learn in this area.

Q: Do you think the screening of diabetes, recently announced by the health minister, can be effective? My second question to Professor Horton is that Dr Misra talked about prevention in the womb. Can we do this in the form of pre-marital counselling, especially in India where we have families in which both sides have diabetes?

Dr Anoop Misra: More important than screening is spreading awareness about diabetes. This is very, very clear. Screening is costly and screening, as some studies have shown, may not achieve a decrease in the death rate due to diabetes. But in the background of lack of awareness, screening is a good idea because it does a dual job. First, it makes a person aware that he may have diabetes. And second, it will enable that person to get early treatment.

Dr Edward Horton: In the US it is standard practice to test women during pregnancy, generally in the 24th week of gestation for what we call gestational diabetes. If it is picked up at that time it is treated very aggressively to avoid increased glucose levels affecting the growth of the foetus. We know that having large gestational-sized babies is an increased risk factor for children developing diabetes later on.

What we don't test for is protein malnutrition and I am really concerned about low birth weight child because it's very clear that a mother who is malnourished or smoking or consuming alcohol during pregnancy can impair the development of the foetus who then is at increased risk later on for both obesity and diabetes.

Q: Dr Misra, you have worked at two excellent centres – AIIMS and now Fortis – with a different spectrum of diabetic patients. Was the progress of complications very different in these two hospitals?

Dr Anoop Misra: The scenario is quite different in both hospitals. I worked for thirty years at AIIMS and have been with Fortis for the last four years. Your question is very relevant because at AIIMS, patients are from the middle and low socio-economic strata where the problem often is a marked unawareness of the disease. Patients do not realize that if they don't come in quickly or if they come in through a circuitous route via a quack, they are at serious risk of developing complications. They seek medical intervention when they are in an advanced stage of complications, AIIMS patients have advanced complications, some of which we cannot correct or they cannot afford, like laser for eyes for blindness or dialysis.

As far as the corporate sector is concerned, the patients are in their twenties and thirties who are working in the IT industry and so on. Even these people lack awareness, but at least once they are detected they are able to tackle the disease.

Q: Dr Misra, you rightly said that there are certain foods which will help in control of diabetes. However, if somebody already has diabetes and switches to these foods, would it be possible to get rid of medication just with good diet control?

Dr Anoop Misra: If that person is in the early stages of diabetes, say within one or two years, and this person is very obese, we would tell him to diet and exercise. If he loses 30 kilograms we can take off all medication. We have a number of such cases. So this is possible in the early stages of diabetes.

But once diabetes is beyond five years, the pancreas are gone. Then doing diet and exercise can control sugar but you cannot switch back to the normal state. Bariatic surgery for diabetic patients who are very obese totally reverses diabetes because people lose 40 to 50 kilograms of weight.

Q: How do you educate schools and parents to pay attention to health and fitness because their concern really seems to be just education?

Wasim Akram: We have to create awareness, awareness of the need for kids to play some sport every day. We have to get our kids off the couch and go out and play. What I have learned in my fifteen years as a diabetic is that lifestyle matters and, of course, food matters. You have to get outdoors and play with your kids.

Dr Anoop Misra: We have been working with schools and using a module that has shown that if you educate children you can change their metabolic profile and decrease their weight within six months.

Q: Dr Misra, what exactly are the initiatives for stem cell therapy?

Dr Anoop Misra: There are three areas in stem cell research that are being worked upon. The first is for Type 1 diabetes where the pancreas is totally destroyed. There are some US studies which show that by giving stem cells, insulin treatment can be delayed or avoided altogether in Type 1diabetes.

Type 2 diabetes is more difficult because it is a heterogeneous disorder and mostly lifestyle related. But one study from PGI Chandigarh (Postgraduate Institute of Medical Education and Research) has shown some improvements with stem cell therapy, but this has been far from satisfactory.

A third area is diabetic foot ulcer which is highly resistant to treatment. It just goes on and on, getting infected time and again, produces gangrene and then amputation has to be done. Here local injection of stem cells – that is what we are doing at the moment – can help improve increase the blood supply and help heal the wound. So, these are three areas, all of them are experimental, and nothing available commercially at the moment.

Welcome Address

■

Shobhana Bhartia
Chairperson & Editorial Director
HT Media Limited

■

YESTERDAY WE HAD THE PRIVILEGE OF LISTENING TO HIS HOLINESS THE DALAI LAMA SPEAK INSPIRINGLY ABOUT THE ART OF HAPPINESS IN Troubled Times. We had a session on the challenges we face in spreading education and one on striking the right balance between economic developments and protecting the environment. In another session, experts discussed ways to battle the scourge of diabetes, a disease that if unchecked can affect 435 million people across the world – more than the current population of North America – in another twenty years. And we had business leaders debate the prospects and pitfalls for Indian companies to go global in a world fraught with uncertainties.

Today we have another rich array of speakers who will share with us their thoughts on more issues that will impact us and our future. We will hear from former US Vice President Al Gore about climate change, former Prime Minister Gordon Brown will speak about what we have learned from the last global crisis, and we will hear from a panel of the world's leading neuroscientists about how the human brain is evolving.

Last year when we gathered for the Summit, the world was a very different place. The global financial crisis and the economic slowdown had led to an air of uncertainty. Questions were being asked about the stability and future of the world's financial systems. India was still recovering from the 26/11 terrorist attacks and our neighbourhood seemed like a more dangerous place.

The world is now limping back to normal, though many Western economies still struggle with unemployment. And whilst there are questions about the failures that led to the economic crisis, we all agree that the global economic system has survived. The future is always an enigma, but one of the lessons of the crisis – and one we heard repeated at the recent G20 summit – is that if the world is to avoid a repeat of that terrible time, we must all work together.

Whenever I travel abroad, I am often asked why India was able to escape the worst ravages of the crisis. After all, we are an economy that ended decades of relative isolationism to plug itself into the global system. How did we enjoy some of the advantages of globalization without suffering the terrible consequences of the crisis? It is a complicated question, but it is one that has a simple answer, and that answer is here in the hall with us: Dr Manmohan Singh. It is because of Dr Singh's deft handling of India's liberalization and globalization programmes that India approached the world economy on its own terms, enjoying the undoubted benefits of globalization while cautiously guarding against the excesses that would cripple so many other countries during the crisis.

The success of the visit of President Barack Obama demonstrates India's new importance in global affairs, showing us America's willingness to finally accept that India must be a permanent member of the Security Council. President Obama said that India was no longer an emerging power, it had now emerged.

But many significant challenges remain. The prosperity of the last decade must reach all Indians, not just a lucky few. The inequalities that are historical legacy within our society must be reduced, if not eliminated all together. Much of India's current success has been predicated on our status as a knowledge power. To maintain that position we must ensure that quality education is freely available to all. And we must continue to battle against infant mortality and guarantee health care to all our citizens.

These are issues that the prime minister has addressed before us very often on this platform. At a time when the world agrees that India's time is coming, Dr Singh serves as a symbol of the new India eager to forge ahead but simultaneously also wise and cautious.

'We live in an era of rising expectations. We live in an era of multiple contestations. But we are no longer fatalists. We no longer see our destiny as pre-ordained. The youth of today are taking their destiny into their hands and are seeking to shape their future.'

Winning the Next Decade

Dr Manmohan Singh

Moderator

Sanjaya Baru
Editor, Business Standard

Dr Manmohan Singh

Prime Minister of India

Manmohan Singh, the Oxford educated economist, is the longest serving prime minister after Jawaharlal Nehru and Indira Gandhi. Singh is the first Congress leader outside the Nehru-Gandhi family to have led the party to victory after he was declared prime ministerial candidate for the 2009 general elections. Known for the economic reforms during his tenure as finance minister in 1991-96 and for clinching the India-US civilian nuclear deal in his first stint as prime minister in 2004-09, Singh has kept political pundits and analysts busy trying to fathom what his big-ticket step would be in this term. Singh has been a member of the Rajya Sabha since 1991 when he became finance minister to steer India out of an economic crisis. A soft-spoken person who initially appeared to be a reluctant politician, Singh has emerged a popular leader both at home and abroad.

IT IS OFTEN SAID THAT THESE ARE TESTING TIMES. IN FACT, I CANNOT HELP FEELING THAT WE IN INDIA ARE ALWAYS LIVING THROUGH TESTING TIMES. INDEED, AS prime minister, I sometimes feel like a high school student – going from one test to another.

The good news is that despite all difficulties we have to go through and for which we are being tested, we as a nation are winning. Indians are winning. Our children and grandchildren are winning. Our youngsters are optimistic, and their optimism gives me a strong dose of hope. We must be doing at least some things right.

We in India face diverse challenges on many fronts. We live in an era of rising expectations. We live in an era of multiple contestations. But we are no longer fatalists. We no longer see our destiny as pre-ordained. The youth of today are taking their destiny into their hands and are seeking to shape their future.

In my childhood, I lived in a village without potable water, without electricity, without a school or hospital. But we had faith in our future and that motivated us. We walked miles to go to school. We studied in the dim light of an oil lamp and I, therefore, know what it is like to be poor in a country as big as ours.

Today, the percentage of our population that lives in those conditions is much lower than it was at our independence. But the absolute numbers are still very large and that is an unacceptable proposition. Millions of our citizens are still deprived and we cannot rest content if that situation is not ameliorated. Every day is a test for millions of under-privileged children, men and women in our country.

Yet, India is on the move. The rise of India is the rise of a nation of over a billion people fighting poverty, ignorance and disease, battling social prejudices, living with inadequate infrastructure, dealing with corruption and misgovernance. It is one of the great adventures of our times. This adventure, within the framework of a plural secular democracy, is a phenomenon, I sincerely believe, of great historical and global significance. If we succeed, as I believe we shall succeed, it will have profound consequences for the evolution of humankind in this blessed twenty-first century of ours.

I am told that in the Chinese language, the character for the word 'crisis' and 'opportunities' happens to be the same. We in India have seen in every problem the opportunity to seek novel solutions, and I salute that spirit of our people.

Consider the very creation of this blessed Republic of India. India was an imagined idea. We were a sub-continent divided at the time of independence. But through hard work, through wise leadership, we have become a nation united.

We are a multi-religious, multi-ethnic, multi-lingual country. We made plurality and diversity the essence of our society and polity. We broadened and deepened democracy to be the platform to reconcile differences among various groups of people. We gave the idea of difference itself a positive value.

Today, in an increasingly homogenizing world, India is able to challenge stereotypes because differences do not upset us. In fact, we thrive on them and we see them as contributing to, and refining the larger national purpose.

Our freedom movement best illustrates this unique trait of our nationhood. The leaders of our freedom movement led by Mahatma Gandhi devised an entirely new repertoire of weapons like satyagraha to which even the mightiest had no answers.

After independence, our leadership had to contend with limitation of resources on the one hand, and the new rising aspirations that had been unleashed, on the other. We built an industrial structure that put us on the road to self-reliance. When we came to the end of that particular road and there was a crisis, we grabbed that as an opportunity for the management of change.

Looking back at how we have handled crises in the past, I am struck by the brighter side of things. Each time we have been able to turn a crisis into an opportunity. And I salute that spirit of the Indian people. An early example of this was the manner in which we used the agrarian crisis of the mid-1960s to launch a Green

Revolution that turned India around; from a nation living from hand to mouth to becoming self-sufficient in food grains.

We won in testing times again when we unleashed the new wave of economic growth in the 90s. The reforms of the 90s did not follow any external recipe. They were home-grown and calibrated to suit the Indian situation. Initially, many were sceptical of the changes being initiated. Looking back after two decades, one can see that we did manage to do reasonably well.

We built a strong economy more integrated with the world economy but also able to cope with external shocks and difficulties. This resilience has helped us to negotiate the global meltdown of the last three years fairly well. I will not say that we have not been affected, but we were among the few countries that recovered quickly from the after-effects of the global financial crisis. Last year our economy grew at the rate of 7.4 per cent. This fiscal year I am confident that the economy will grow at the rate of 8.5 per cent. And next year we do hope to return the economy to a sustained growth path of 9-10 per cent of GDP.

In celebrating our economic success, we must look beyond the success of our large and visible corporate entities. We must also salute the spirit of adventure and the spirit of enterprise and the creativity of the small businessmen and women, the first generation entrepreneur and the small farmer, each of whom has to deal with a difficult world environment – often including an unresponsive, inefficient and corrupt government.

It is the individualism of the Indian, the entrepreneurialism of our people, the energy of every student preparing for one test after another and the dreams of our young men and women in our small towns that is taking this country forward and that will take this country moving once again.

A challenge that tests us all the time is that of making our growth process more inclusive; of improving our social and economic infrastructure; of reducing regional imbalances; of increasing the social and economic opportunities for the disadvantaged sections, the scheduled castes, the scheduled tribes, other backward classes, our minorities, women and children. We are determined to address these problems. Indeed, our effort has been, and will be, to walk on two legs to accelerate economic growth, on the one hand and to make that growth process more socially inclusive, on the other.

We have to work hard to maintain and accelerate growth. We can get to 9-10 per cent growth but it will not happen automatically. We need to invest massively in modernizing our infrastructure – in more and better infrastructure. We need to invest in education and health, in employment-generating industrialization, in more productive and eco-friendly agricultural development.

We must also address the new challenges we face. There is threat to our environment arising from inadequate regulation. We need new thinking to prevent the degradation of our land and water resources which endanger the livelihood of millions of our people living on the edges of subsistence. We need to deal effectively with the threats of corruption and crony capitalism not only in India but all over the world.

There is no magic formula, no magic wand, and no rabbit that can be pulled out of a hat. Nor can we assume that we are that proverbial tortoise that surprised all by overtaking an energetic hare. You can choose what you like to describe India: hare, tortoise, and elephant, whatever. The simple truth is that India is a nation of over a billion people eager to realize their destiny.

Our government has a great deal to do to make the future happen, and what it does must be innovative and must spur innovation. Our government has dedicated the decade 2010-20 to be a 'decade of innovation', and it is putting together a road map for innovation.

Albert Einstein once said that in the times of challenge, imagination is more important than knowledge. As times get more challenging, we must leverage our unique advantages to make India a leader in global innovation.

First, the young population that we have is a great potential advantage as the young are by nature innovative. They want to break away from the 'dreary desert sand of dead habit'. Using those eloquent sentences from Tagore, if we can educate and provide skills to our young population to realize their full human potential, they would innovate through every challenge that we may face.

Second, diversity is considered another great resource for innovation, and India possesses this too as a great advantage.

Third, we are becoming a much more connected society thanks to the information revolution, the spread of the internet and mobile technologies, and this has truly transformational potential in many areas of innovation and it can enable us to leapfrog in the race for social and economic development.

It is on the foundation of a better educated, more healthy and more skilled people that we must build the edifice of a more entrepreneurial society, and leverage our capacity for innovation. It is our hope that the second decade of this century can be won by us if we invest in the capabilities of our people. It can be won if we invest in education, in health and skills of our people. As a government, our effort should be to create an eco-system of rights to development that empowers our people and enables them to realize their full potential.

To make this happen, we also need to put in place a macro-economic policy framework which encourages savings, which ensures fiscal discipline and which supports the spirit of adventure and entrepreneurship which is so widely prevalent in our country.

The world as a whole is now interconnected and integrated as never before. If we look at humanity at large, it is quite clear that the world as a whole cannot win in these testing times unless we act as responsible global citizens. Winning the next decade globally means reducing inequalities in the world. It means removing unacceptable poverty and denial of human rights. It means allowing every citizen in the world to maximize his or her human potential. It also means creating a world that is environmentally sustainable and which we can proudly leave behind for our next generation.

In each of these battles, humankind can fight and win together. The greatest battles of our times are not ones in which humans will win over humans, or a nation over a nation. The greatest tests of our times are ones in which humanity, actively together and as a whole, will have to fight and win together. These will be our collective fight against hunger, against poverty, against terrorism, against disease, against tyranny, against corruption, against bigotry, and against extremism of all hues.

Such are the testing times, such are the tests before us to fight and win.

Moderator | **Dr Sanjaya Baru**

Editor, Business Standard

Sanjaya Baru: I have before me a list of questions and I have summarized them into three sets. There are questions on what the prime minister has just said. There are questions on the current crises or problem that you face in government. And there are questions about the important initiatives you are taking in the area of foreign policy, the visit of President Obama and your dialogue with Pakistan.

The first set of questions is about what is next in government. You said that every crisis is an opportunity. In what way would you like to turn the current crisis the government faces into an opportunity and what is your agenda for the next four years or so of your term in government?

Dr Manmohan Singh: As I said in my opening remarks, we have to walk on two legs. We need a macro-economic policy framework which will enable our economy to grow at the rate of 9-10 per cent per annum. The material basis for that is now in place. Our savings and investment rates are today close to 35-37 per cent of our GDP. With a capital output ratio of 4:1, I think we can easily sustain the growth rate of 9-10 per cent per annum that would enable us to create wealth which we can plough back to redistribute to help those who are at the margins, to help improve the quality of our education, the quality of our health, the quality of our people's lives in rural areas. This is enshrined in the concept of inclusive growth which the Planning Commission has been talking about.

But it is not merely technical work which will determine whether India achieves this growth or not. It is very much a function of how our polity is managed, how our politics is managed, how we deal with the divisive tendencies in our country – whether these are communal tensions, social tensions or extremist pressures of all kinds. There is a great challenge for the management of political system.

I am today more and more convinced that we have unleashed in our country a whole new era of entrepreneurship. Indian entrepreneurs have shown their mettle and I salute them. Our task is to create an enabling environment which, while giving hope to all those who are at the lowest rung of the social and economic ladder, also enables those who have the critical spirit of adventure and enterprise to make their full contribution to the enrichment of our nation. That's my vision. That's the challenge. That's what I hope the 12th Five Year Plan will elaborate on.

Sanjaya Baru: There is a question from the husband-wife team of Rajdeep Sardesai and Sagarika Ghose. They want to know whether to do all of what you just said, you need a new team and a younger cabinet. Are you are going to use this opportunity to reshuffle your cabinet? And is coalition management an issue which you need to take better control of?

Dr Manmohan Singh: I am not able to tell you what I am going to do by way of a cabinet reshuffle. When that happens, all of you will get to know about it. Yes, we must reduce the average age of people in power. We should bring younger people into our system of government. With that general proposition, I am entirely in sympathy.

Sanjaya Baru: Very understandably, there are lots of questions on the current crisis – the impasse in Parliament, demand for a JPC and the handling of the Telecom 2G Spectrum issue. This audience would like to understand what your thinking is.

Dr Manmohan Singh: I would like to appeal to all political parties to let Parliament do its work. We need Parliament to function regularly to pass motions and to pass laws which will have a bearing on improving the lives of our people which will enable us to pass supplementary demand for grants for important sectors of our economy – education, health, and rural development. We are ready to discuss all issues in Parliament. We are not afraid of discussion. It is my humble request to all political parties to let Parliament function. We can discuss everything.

As far as the allocation of the 2G Spectrum is concerned, Parliament is in session. I would not like, therefore, to make any detailed statement. But I can state that various aspects of this are being looked into by respective investigating agencies in their domain of interest. There should be no doubt in anybody's mind that if any wrong has been done by any one, he or she will be brought to book. But, for all this to happen in a democracy, we have to allow Parliament to function so that we can through reasoning and debate arrive at nationally acceptable and viable approaches to deal with our differences.

Sanjaya Baru: What is your assessment of President Obama's visit and where are we going as far as our dialogue with Pakistan is concerned?

Dr Manmohan Singh: In the last six and a half years that I have been prime minister, my effort has been to give the greatest importance to improving our relations within our neighbourhood and that includes neighbours in south Asia, particularly Pakistan, and also South East Asia. We have succeeded in our 'Look East' policies. I was in Japan and Malaysia recently. We have agreed to work together in the form of comprehensive economic partnership agreements with Japan and Malaysia. Our relations with the ASEAN countries have improved enormously. We are now the founding members of the East Asia Summit.

In the Middle East, our relations with the kingdoms of Saudi Arabia, Qatar, Kuwait and other Gulf countries have also improved considerably. We are now reaching out more effectively to countries of central Asia. Simultaneously, our effort has been to work to improve and have the best possible relations with all the major P5 countries and you will have a unique example this year in India where all the top leaders of the P5 countries from President Obama, President Sarkozy, prime minister of the United Kingdom and the premier of China will be visiting us. This is a tribute to the goodwill which India enjoys today.

Everywhere I go, there is great admiration for India. People marvel that this country of 1.2 billion people with all the complexities, diversities, religions of the world represented among its citizenship is committed to the rule of law, respect for fundamental human freedom, and yet manages to produce growth rates of 8-9 per cent. The world wants India to succeed and we have been able to create that sort of environment.

With regard to Pakistan, I have said before, we are neighbours. We can choose our friends but we have no choice with regard to our neighbours. Our efforts have been to normalize our relationship. Our efforts have been to convey to Pakistan that we are willing to discuss all outstanding issues provided the terror machine is brought under control.

I have always believed that South Asia is a region of enormous capacity to grow at a much faster pace than we have done. But it cannot become a living reality unless there is peace and tranquillity. These are my priorities. These are the efforts which our government has been engaged in and will be engaged in.

With regard to the United States, President Obama's visit was a great success. What the president has said in his address to our Parliament, what is reflected in the joint statement which was placed in the Parliament, are public documents. Anyone of you who is interested can look into them.

'This is an economic issue, a geopolitical issue, a national security issue, and an environmental issue, but it is also a moral issue. It gives the greatest opportunity to reduce poverty and to fight off extreme diseases. It also gives the opportunity to safeguard the future for the next generation.'

Climate Change:

What's to be done?

■

Al Gore

■

Moderator

Rajdeep Sardesai

Editor-in-Chief, CNN-IBN, IBN7 and IBN-Lokmat

Al Gore

Vice President, United States of America, 1992-2000

The world's most influential voice on climate change, an adviser to leaders in Congress and heads of state throughout the world, former US Vice President Al Gore offers a unique perspective on national and international affairs. Gore is co-founder and chairman of Generation Investment Management, a firm that focuses on a new approach to sustainable investing. He is also co-founder and chairman of Current TV, an Emmy- award winning, independently owned cable and satellite television network for young people. He is the author of *An Inconvenient Truth*, a best-selling book on the threat of and solutions to global warming, and the subject of a documentary film of the same title. In 2007, Al Gore and the UN's Intergovernmental Panel on Climate Change won the Nobel Peace Prize.

IT IS A GREAT HONOUR TO SPEAK FROM THE SAME PODIUM THAT YOUR PRIME MINISTER JUST OCCUPIED. I HAVE ENORMOUS RESPECT FOR DR MANMOHAN SINGH. I HAD the pleasure of meeting with him and the rest of your leadership, including Opposition leaders, and I have been uniformly impressed. As an American, I am very happy at the success of President Obama's recent trip to India. I want to pay my compliments to my long-time friend, our very talented ambassador Tim Roemer for his great work in making that trip a success.

I would like to point out that the warming of relations between the United States and India is not a partisan initiative in any way. We have had three administrations of two political parties over an extended period of time pursuing a very determined commitment. As Americans we are very pleased at the cross-party, society-wide receptiveness and warmth in return. I think it is truly a historic development and one to be welcomed.

It is always so amazing to me when I come to India, as I do fairly often these days. I was in Chennai just recently. With every visit I make, I am impressed anew at the rise of India, the economic dynamism of India, the confidence and hopefulness of your people. It is really a wonderful and inspiring feeling that you now give to the rest of the world and somewhat in contrast, I might say, to the global mood coming out of this deep recession.

I was talking to someone recently about the recovery and asked him, 'How do you feel about the economy?' And he replied: 'I feel fine.' It made me think of an old story that I first heard thirty-five years ago when I was a young Congressman in my home state of Tennessee, which is the home of country music. One Saturday I was driving back home from some Town Hall meetings, listening to a music programme on my car radio. A comedian came on air and told about a farmer who was involved in an accident. The farmer had sued the other driver for damages in court and the lawyer for the other driver was cross-examining the farmer and asked: 'Isn't it true that immediately after this accident you said, "I feel fine"?'

The farmer said, 'Well, it is not that simple. You see, I was taking my horse to town in the back of my truck and this man came driving down the centre of the road...'

The lawyer said, 'Wait a minute. We don't want to hear a long story. We are in the middle of a trial here. Just answer the question: yes or no. Did you or did you not say after the accident, "I feel fine"?'

The farmer said, 'Well, I was leading up to that. You see, I was taking my horse to town and this man driving down the centre of the road, ran right into my truck and knocked it over, threw me out and threw the horse out. I was on one side, the horse was on the other. A policeman came up and took one look at the horse and said, "Oh-ho, she is suffering," and pulled out his gun and shot her right between the eyes. Then he came around to my side of the truck and asked, "How do you feel"? So I said "I feel fine".'

I think that there is something of that feeling in India's attitude looking at what has been going on in the rest of the world.

I want to talk to you this morning about the climate crisis and to begin with there is a startling paradox when we speak about the climate crisis because the crisis itself is getting worse rapidly. In spite of the change in public perception in some quarters, this problem is not going away. It is getting worse. We have to deal with it. The evidence derived from the science is ever clearer and, thankfully throughout the world the grassroots awareness of the reality we face is also growing very strongly.

There are many signs of hope. However, at the same time, political progress has been paralyzed – most of all, I must acknowledge, in my own country – but also in much of the world. The Copenhagen process has joined the Doha process as another zombie, a creature that is neither alive nor dead. Yet we move toward the meeting in Cancun with hopes muted and realistic prospects for perhaps some progress on some important parts of what needs to be done.

The world must sooner or later, and hopefully sooner, acknowledge that this crisis demands bold action and the solutions are not that complicated. We have to put a price on carbon because the routine decisions made a billion times over the world every hour are decisions that reflect the economic signals that we get from the marketplace. So long as the 90 million tons of global warming pollution that we put out into the atmosphere every day is invisible to the economic system, we will continue to drive blindly toward the edge of a cliff. We need to eliminate subsidies for carbon-based energy and instead reflect the true cost of the risks we are posing to our future by continuing to rely on this energy so heavily.

The climate crisis, because it is so linked to our heavy dependence on carbon-based fuels, is linked to other problems as well. In the world as a whole, 85 per cent of our energy comes from oil, coal, and gas – and that is where the 90 million tons of global warming pollution comes from every 24 hours, dumped into the atmosphere as if it is an open sewer. Some 150 years ago, scientists discovered that CO2 traps heat and the heat has been building up. But there are other risks that we face due to our dependence on carbon-based fuels.

This audience knows well that India has less than one-half of one per cent of the world's oil supply and yet its consumption of oil is growing. Seventy-five per cent of your oil is now imported and 75 per cent of that comes from the Persian Gulf and the Middle East, arguably the most unstable regions of the world. Most of that comes through the Strait of Hormuz and the supply is at risk. Your dependence on imports, as your own governmental experts have pointed out repeatedly, will rise to 90 per cent dependence on imported oil within fifteen years and 66 per cent dependence on imported coal.

In 2008, the International Energy Agency – a conservative body that was set up in the wake of the OPEC war crisis of the early 70s – had said that peak oil[1] in the world might not be arrived at for another twenty-five years or more. Just last week they radically

1. According to Wikipedia, peak oil is the point in time when the maximum rate of global petroleum extraction is reached, after which the rate of production enters terminal decline.

revised their projections and said, in fact, we already reached peak oil in 2006 and that the world is unlikely to ever again produce 70 million barrels per day. The prospect of replacing that conventional oil production from unconventional sources like tar sands is highly uncertain and is, of course, associated with an even larger impact on the problem of global warming.

The oil price rollercoaster is already headed back up again with oil at $82 a barrel and predicted by the IEA to reach $135 a barrel in the next several years. Who knows where it will go? But as production from conventional sources declines and as the substitute forms of oil are uncertain, the demand is certainly growing.

India's demand for oil is expected to rise from last year's total of about 133 million metric tons by 40 per cent in the next decade or so, according to your own government. China is also increasing its demand and many other countries that do not get as much publicity as China and India are also increasing their demand. The IEA has said that in order to stay on the current course, we would have to discover five new Saudi Arabias within the next two decades. That is not going to happen. So this rollercoaster is headed for a crash and India is in the front car.

The word 'crisis' as I use it in the phrase 'climate crisis', conveys a sense of alarm both in English and in Hindi. The word 'sankat' is a single word, but as many of you know in Japan and in China the word 'crisis' is written with two symbols together and the first one by itself means 'danger' the second one by itself means 'opportunity'. I have often thought that is a better way of thinking about a crisis. It is the most dangerous crisis we have ever faced, but also the greatest opportunity we have confronted.

There are three causes in general. The population explosion worldwide has quadrupled human population in less than 100 years. Family sizes have come down with the education of girls, empowerment of women, availability of fertility management and, most importantly, increased child survival rates, but it has already meant that the human impact on the environment is much larger.

A more serious cause is the technological revolution, particularly internal combustion engines and coalfired generating plants and many other technologies that automate the conversion of carbon into energy with its byproduct of CO2. The impacts are now increasingly clear. This year, nineteen countries had all-time high temperature records. Russia had the worst drought in its history. Its wheat was pulled from the market, sending prices up – and then the fires began.

The historic flooding in Pakistan touched all our hearts and the suffering was just unbelievable: 20 million people rendered homeless with many Pakistani scientists accelerating their research into the connections to global warming. Many cities and towns throughout the world have experienced historic downpours. My own home city of Nashville, Tennessee had a one in a 1,000-year rainfall in the beginning of May. Thousands of my neighbours lost their homes and businesses and had no flood insurance because there had never been flooding in the areas that were affected. That city lost an entire year's budget.

Throughout the world developing countries in particular are facing unprecedented expenses for infrastructure repair because of the extreme downpours and associated flooding with the hydrological cycle being disrupted. As the warmer air pulls more moisture out of the warmer oceans, average humidity has already gone up 4 per cent worldwide. Because of the way the atmospheric phenomenon produce storm shells, the water falls not only from the clouds above, but pulls in moisture from a wide radius all around.

This is responsible for the now well-documented phenomenon that the percentage of rainfall coming in one-time large storm events has been increasing quite dramatically and the warmer air also pulls more moisture out of the soil. So we have the irony of increased flooding and increased drought both at the same time.

A newly published 'Vulnerability Index'[2] looks at forty-two

2 Climate Change Vulnerability Index released by global risks advisory firm Maplecroft calculates the vulnerability of 170 countries to the impacts of climate change over the next thirty years.

social, economic and environmental factors affecting vulnerability to the climate crisis. It lists India as the second-most vulnerable country in the world, the most vulnerable being Bangladesh. Nepal is at number four. Myanmar is also in the top ten. Several other Asian countries are in the 'extreme risk' category including Pakistan, Vietnam, and the Philippines.

These impacts are continuing. Today, many developing countries are facing increased costs from infrastructure repair. Many are facing increased costs in the form of food imports because the disruption of the hydrological cycle is also changing the timing of the rainy season and dry season, making it very difficult for farmers to know when to plant. Yet, after they plant, their crops are often ruined. This is happening throughout the world.

Let's look at other impacts. Two months ago in Northern Greenland, a block of ice four times the size of the island of Manhattan broke off and slipped into the sea, continuing a pattern that is now accelerating both in Greenland and in Western Antarctica. A revised assessment of sea level-rise now predicts that there will be a minimum of a three-feet rise in this century with the risk of significantly higher rises.

India has a coastline of 6,400 kilometres and cities like Kolkata and parts of Mumbai are at the top of the list of the places in India that are vulnerable. Bangladesh has already started sending refugees inland from the coastal areas as big storms and floods are more frequent there. Your own environment minister just made comments about the risk to India of increased flood events.

Of the Arctic icecap, 40 per cent is already gone. It has for almost three million years been twice the size of India and now 40 per cent is gone and the rest is predicted to completely disappear during the summer months within the next one or two decades – some scientists say sooner than that. So these impacts are really only the beginning.

The Food and Agriculture Organization produced a study recently on the impact of the climate crisis on food prices. Of course this is a sensitive issue, but one that is worth focusing on. There is also increased vulnerability to diseases like dengue fever, malaria and cholera, and also plant diseases like more virulent forms of wheat rust. Ocean acidification is a particular problem both in the Bay of Bengal and the Arabian Sea. Scientists say that the biodiversity loss is perhaps the most serious impact of all.

But even as we face these and other dangers, we should focus on the opportunities involved, and here India has a tremendous opportunity to lead the world. You have proven with the information technology revolution that you can quickly get up-to-speed and up-to-scale and astonish the world. Introducing new levels of efficiency in the way we use energy is the number one solution to the climate crisis. New design, new use of information technology and metrics in order to guide ourselves toward the solutions is important. A rapid shift toward renewable energy includes not only wind energy and second and third-generation biofuels, the sequestration of carbon in soils with sustainable agriculture and sustainable forestry, but a particular focus on solar energy because India has the greatest asset in insulation of virtually any nation in the world. India already has a higher percentage of its energy from renewables than does the United States or China and has an ambitious plan. I would argue, however, that much more should be done by every nation and that the opportunity for India is greater than has yet been fully grasped.

In closing, I just want to make one more point. This is an economic issue, a geopolitical issue, a national security issue, and an environmental issue, but it is also a moral issue. It gives the greatest opportunity to reduce poverty and to fight off extreme diseases. It also gives the opportunity to safeguard the future for the next generation. I was speaking with some entrepreneurs here yesterday. I was struck that two of them told me the real reason why they were putting so much energy into the development of new, renewable options was because their children had talked to them about it and in both cases their children had joined their firms and were a part of this frenzy of optimism and development to bring renewable energy forward. I was so excited by that.

The time has come for a big leap forward. I remember as a young boy of thirteen hearing President John F. Kennedy announce the goal of putting a man on the moon and bringing him back safely within ten years. I remember that he said we would do it not because it was easy, but because it was hard. I remember how many people said at that time it was an unwise challenge. It was going to be impossible to do. Yet, eight years and two months later, Neil Armstrong and Buzz Aldrin set foot on the moon. The moment they did so, there was a great cheer from the engineers at mission control in NASA's headquarters at Houston, Texas. The average age of those systems engineers that day was twenty-six, which means their average age when they heard that challenge was eighteen.

Today's young people are counting on us to meet this challenge and to make bold steps forward. We can't let them down because not too many years from now, this next generation will make an assessment of the world in which they live. Depending on the circumstances in which they find themselves, they will look back at us and our time and ask one of these two questions.

If they see a world of rising sea levels and hundred of millions of climate refugees producing instability; the collapse of sustainable agriculture and governance in developing countries; tropical disease ravaging areas that have never known them; deeper droughts and bigger floods; disruption of infrastructure and chaos and a sense of hopelessness, if they live in such a world, they would be justified in looking back at us and asking: 'What were you thinking?'

'Didn't you hear the scientists?' 'Didn't you see the damages that were already occurring?'

But if they live in a world with a sense of renewal with millions of new jobs being created and efficiency in solar and wind and biofuels and sustainable agriculture; and new designs and better more efficient buildings; if they have hope in their hearts and they look at their children and feel that they will have better lives still, then I want them to look back at us and ask: 'How did you find the moral courage to rise up and solve a crisis that so many said was impossible to solve?'

Part of the answer will be that in India in the fall of 2010 in Delhi, leaders from across this great nation became a part of a mass moral movement to determine that political will is itself a renewable resource.

Moderator | **Rajdeep Sardesai**

Editor-in-Chief, CNN-IBN,
IBN7 and IBN-Lokmat

Rajdeep Sardesai: Before we open this to questions, let me just try and add a bit of spice to what you have already said. You have been accused in the past, and some of your critics might accuse you even after today's speech, of being an unnecessary alarmist and a scaremonger. You throw these figures at us and some of us are frightened. But others worry after the Himalayan glacier controversy as to how much of this is based on fact and how much of this is alarmist?

Al Gore: The IPCC (Intergovernmental Panel on Climate Change) made a mistake on the Himalayan glaciers. But what many people don't remember is the report had three sections. The most important and most focused section was the first one on the science. It had a long section on glaciers, including the Himalayan glaciers and it got it exactly right.

It was in one of the later sections where another author used the wrong figure and, yes, it has been seized upon and, yes, they have acknowledged the mistake and corrected it. But that should not be seen as an invalidation of the report. Ninety-eight per cent of all the climate scientists in the world agree with the conclusions of the IPCC. Your own National Academy of Sciences, the National Academy of Sciences in the United States, in Great Britain, in Germany, in Russia, in China and in every single developed country, all agree with these conclusions. Every major professional scientific organization agrees with these conclusions.

Now, you have a few deniers out there. They have been backed by billions of dollars per year largely provided by some, not all, carbon polluters to give them an enormous megaphone as part of a calculated strategy to create false doubts. I would point out also that over the forty years that I have worked on this issue, there has been a clear pattern. Each time an assessment has been made, the scientists will say, "Ok, here is what we see – best case, worst case, medium case." Then a few years pass and they go back and reassess. On every occasion, the actual developments have been at or above the worst case. I would love it if we were wrong about this, but we have to face reality as we find it. If it is an 'inconvenient truth' – pardon the phrase – it does not mean that we have the luxury of ignoring it.

Q: Why is there a gross reluctance on the part of the American establishment to acknowledge some of the international obligations like the Kyoto Protocol? Why is it that America is so inward-centred as far as its own prosperity is concerned regardless of the consequences it is going to have for the entire world?

Al Gore: As I mentioned, my country most of all has a moral obligation to provide leadership and to do more. As you can imagine it is a source of deep concern to me that the US Senate has failed to pass legislation. Our lower chamber, the US House of Representatives, did pass legislation, but the US Senate did not and there are many parts of the answer to your question and I will be brief in summarizing them.

There was a period after the scientific evidence was established to link lung cancer and lung diseases to the smoking of cigarettes, when the tobacco companies hired actors and dressed them up as doctors and put them on television to say there is nothing wrong with smoking cigarettes. There is no reliable evidence that it causes lung diseases. Yet, more Americans died every year from smoking cigarettes than the number that died during all of World War II.

Some of the same people who were instrumental in that campaign are now active in this campaign to intentionally create false doubts and to deceive people into thinking that the science is not sound. Internal memos were leaked and printed in the *New York Times* and elsewhere that laid bare their strategy. Their internal deliberations led them to the conclusion that if they can make people doubt the science, then they can delay any kind of policy action. Hundreds of millions of dollars in the US alone are being spent each year on this. On Capitol Hill, there are now six anti-climate lobbyists for every single member of the House and Senate.

Add to that the fact that undeniably the magnitude of the change necessary is very difficult to accept for any of us. I acknowledge that. But we really have no choice and if we make one simple change, we can use markets as our most powerful ally in accomplishing this transition. I referred to the change earlier – put a price on carbon, so that when we choose between solar, wind and renewables on the one hand, and coal and oil, on the other we get an accurate signal so that the economy can make adjustments in a million ways every day. Instead, we render it invisible to the economy and continue massive subsidies for the excessive use of dirty, polluting, vulnerable, expensive carbon-based fuels that have a limited future.

We like to think of ourselves as the two greatest democracies in the world. You hear the phrase all the time. I want to be candid with you about what has happened to American democracy. When both of our democracies were founded, the dominant medium of communication was the printing press and newspapers. It has certain characteristics – it is easy for individuals to enter the conversation; ideas can be used as a substitute for money and power and it fosters an emphasis on the rule of reason and makes it more likely that reasoned debate will lead people to make compromises and share conclusions.

In my country, starting a half century ago, television surpassed newspapers. In our political system, the dominant means of communication now is 30-second television advertisements. Eighty per cent of the money that is raised by politicians in both major parties is used to purchase these 30-second ads and the cost continues to go up. The average American now watches television five hours per day. As a direct result, the average politician now spends five hours per day on the telephone begging special interest groups for enough money to purchase more of these ads than the Opposition. They don't go to the committee hearings as much. They don't participate in debates on the floor of the Congress as much. They spend most of their time in cocktail parties, receptions, and fundraising meetings to try to amass enough money to buy these television ads. When the next votes come up, they are often thinking less about what the public will see as their reasoned conclusions and more about what the impact will be on the receptivity of the special interest group that they call on the telephone the next day.

Q: Mr Vice President, I am twenty-two years old and my concern is whether I will have a healthy world to live in the next forty years. Most climate negotiations fail because even though the leaders agree at the policy level, citizens fail to implement any of the climate change measures being taken. My question is, where and how will real change actually begin?

Al Gore: Your point is well taken. Almost all of us drive cars. I will fly back on British Airways tomorrow. Yet it is just another way of underscoring the importance of the one most important solution: put a price on carbon. The solution is not going to come from individuals who make green choices though it is important to do that, by the way. I offset carbon and I have a Gold LEED[1] certified home and 33 solar panels on my roof and drive a hybrid. Yet, it is much more important to change policies because the only way we are going to solve this is with new policies that integrate the significance of global warming pollution into the economic choices that we make on a routine basis. That will give us the opportunity to use markets to manage this transition much more quickly.

The other option is to wait until the oil supply crisis reaches a point where the manifestations of these disasters become so intolerable that all of a sudden there is a huge adjustment. The reason I bring this point up is that it is very significant because it means that we can create the inevitability of a horrific catastrophe before the visceral impacts are obvious to us.

As human beings we perceive danger in different ways. The kinds of dangers that we respond to automatically are the kinds that we are hardwired to respond to. The kinds that our ancestors

1 Leadership in Energy & Environmental Design (LEED) is a green building certification system.

survived – snakes, spiders, other human scaring weapons, these kinds of things trigger automatic responses. We also have the ability to recognize more serious dangers with our reasoning capacity. But it is not automatic and it does not produce a visceral response. It requires communication. It requires sharing conclusions and holding them in common and using the parts of our brains that allow us to steer toward long-term goals based on our deepest values. We have that capacity. We have to cultivate it and we have to fight back against those who try to disrupt that process with falsehoods and deceptions because of a very narrow self interest that is directly opposed to the general welfare and, most of all, opposed to the welfare of the next generation whose future depends upon us reaching this conclusion and finding the moral courage to act upon it.

Q: I come from Latin America where, as you know, we are doing some innovative things in the Amazon basin. I think you are best positioned here to talk about the Guyana-Norway context and share it with our Indian brothers and sisters.

Al Gore: Yes indeed, in Guyana, thanks to some of our friends from Norway, there is an ambitious project to keep trees in the ground and to prevent the destruction of this great forest ecosystem in the northeast of South America and in general. These kinds of projects have a very important role to play. One of the possible advances at Cancun would be the completion of a global agreement on avoided deforestation. Approximately 17 per cent of global warming pollution comes today from the destruction of forests. We lose about one football field worth of forest every second, much of it due to burning and illegal logging.

The good news is that many countries, Brazil being among the leaders, are taking steps to try to cut down on the loss of these forests. When the forests are burned, we are hurt in two ways. First, by the carbon which is released into the atmosphere. And second, the ability to reabsorb the carbon into tree growth is cut back. So, planting billions of trees and shifting to sustainable forestry techniques is extremely important.

In developing countries this means finding financial arrangements that make it possible to protect the forest and replace the subsistence income that would otherwise go to some who cut it down and burn it. It is not viable to burn it in these soils and turn it into subsistence agriculture because the soils are so thin that you only get a few crops before the land becomes barren and infertile. So, the project underway in Guyana is a good example among many in the world of how to do it right.

Q: Vice President Gore, you are also a private equity investor. Would you like to share with the audience, which alternative energy technologies you have invested in and are betting on for the future?

Al Gore: I think that efficiency is the most important among solutions. Wind energy has a very bright future. In the last three years, wind has been the biggest new source of electricity in the US. India has already added a lot of wind generating capacity and has plans to do more. Offshore wind is going to play a significant role. In the long run, solar energy is the most important of these renewable options and it comes in many forms from solar hot water heating to thermal solar for agricultural food processing and photovoltaic energy, which is the form that converts sunlight directly into an electrical current.

India has astonished the world in the field of computing and information technology. The reason why computer processing has moved forward so quickly is because of something called Moore's law. It's the law that says the number of transistors on a chip doubles every two years. That means that the cost comes down by 50 per cent every two years. That is not a law of nature. It is not a law of physics. It is a law of investing. The reason it works is that at the beginning of the semiconductor age, many of the first CEOs understood how big this market was going to grow. Today, there are one billion transistors for every man, woman and child on the planet – soon to grow to two billion and then beyond.

Photovoltaics offer an opportunity to have a very steep cost reduction curve. Now it is about 15 per cent a year. But if India and/or the US and other countries decided to make a major commitment to create markets for photovoltaic panels in the near term at scale, you would instantly find that the companies in Germany, Taiwan, India and elsewhere would start pouring vastly larger sums of R&D into dramatically accelerating the cost reduction curve in photovoltaics. Your current national plan is to have photovoltaic energy that has grid parity by 2022 and coal parity by 2030. You could cut that timeframe in half. You can have coal parity within ten years. If there was a much larger commitment to creating the markets at scale that would accelerate this R&D and bring the cost down.

Rajdeep Sardesai: There is a question that has been put to you from someone who has been watching you on television: do you have to be rich to be green? We are a consumptive society. A lot of Indians are just coming out of years of being denied material pleasures. And now Al Gore is telling us to control consumption.

Al Gore: I did not use any of those phrases. I think that at the state of the technology today, take the solar panels that I mentioned, I can put thiry-three solar panels on my house, but the expense involved makes that option simply unavailable to many. But if there were different policies, then you could see options where somebody else owns the panels and simply sells the electricity. There are companies that are willing to sell the milk and not the cow. So, you could facilitate the wider-spread adoption of these renewable energy technologies in ways that make them accessible to those with low incomes.

With the right policies, those at the bottom of the income ladder can benefit the most. If the right approach is taken, it will make it much more feasible to electrify villages that do not have electricity in India today. You could substitute solar lanterns for kerosene lanterns and so on. The idea that there is a direct conflict between economic development and protection of the environment and for solving the climate crisis is an old and obsolete idea. Actually, the most effective way to fight poverty and stimulate sustainable development is by moving more aggressively into this transition.

Key Issues that
Confront Us

■

Arun Jaitley

■

Brinda Karat

■

Moderator

Sagarika Ghose

Senior Editor, CNN-IBN

Arun Jaitley

Leader of the Opposition, Rajya Sabha

A lawyer and prominent member of the BJP, Arun Jaitley is known to back his arguments with clinching facts. The BJP leader is a great persuader, a strong critic of the government and a savvy media presence. Whether it is issues of security or development, Kashmir or complicated civil nuclear liability, he articulates the best alternative point of view. No wonder, the government has loved to do business with Jaitley ever since he became the leader of Opposition in the Rajya Sabha in 2009. His ideas have often found acceptance across the political divide and aided solutions to tricky legislative issues. As commerce minister in the NDA government, he earned admiration for standing for India's – and the developing world's – rights at the WTO.

THERE IS A NORMAL PATTERN WITH REGARDS TO CONFERENCES AND SUMMITS OF THIS KIND WHERE WE START APPLAUDING OURSELVES AND THEN LOOK AT the immediate future as to what our targets are going to be. It is a very logical approach. But I want to deviate slightly from that.

If I look back at sixty-three years, there are a huge number of areas that every Indian can be satisfied about. We have grown; we have economically grown. Our institutions have strengthened themselves. Parliamentary institutions, which were crumbling across the world during this period, have strengthened. India has shown a tremendous amount of resilience despite wars, despite insurgency and despite internal conflicts, to emerge out of each of these and the last twenty years, at least in terms of growth, have been fairly satisfying.

Whenever we are in government, and most political parties have been in government in the past structure at some stage or the other, we tend to fall into a trap to take credit for everything that is happening in the system. But there are a lot of things which are happening independent of the system. I have always been certain that at the pace we have been growing in the last ten years even if India didn't have a finance minister, we would probably have had a very reasonable rate of growth.

Instead of pondering over what is going to happen in the coming days of the session of Parliament or the next one or two years, I have been thinking about a question that was put to me recently by a delegate who had accompanied the US president on his India visit. He asked me: 'How do you see India twenty years from now?'

Regardless of which government is in power, and whether you have an 8 per cent or 9 per cent growth, there are a few things I can obviously see down the tunnel. We will grow. We will grow quite well. Our services sector will be the mainstay of our economy. Its growth will perhaps be even accelerated. Its impact will be seen not only in India but even outside. It is a sector which is quite capable of growing in spite of governments. It is hugely entrepreneur-driven. We missed the industrial revolution in the first instance but manufacturing is growing and, despite the problems within the political system, there are a few reforms necessary. We can accelerate that process too if we are able to implement these reforms. One advantage we will have is from the overpopulated rural sector. We need to bring out a lot of people into jobs in the other sectors. That is how economies all over the world have progressed. Logically, I also see poverty levels declining. Twenty years from now, it may perhaps be closer to a single digit.

But there are also going to be some problems. When you speak in terms of challenges that will confront us twenty years from now, we would have overcome a large number of them. Yet, even though we would have grown and rural infrastructure would

Will the quality of politics in India improve even two that we face, there has been some measure of satisfaction not in terms of the quality of our politics.

have picked up, urbanization will expand and the middle-class size will expand, there still will be a large part of India which will be living in poverty.

The other area I am particularly worried about where I don't see, even across the next two decades, any significant movement taking place is bang in the centre of India – in the tribal areas. Some infrastructural improvements may take place. But what do we do with improving the entire lot of the population there? There will still be inequalities. Unless we are radically able to improve the living lot of the people there, make substantial changes, define and redefine our approach, we will not be able to rid ourselves of this problem.

Growth levels in our agricultural sector, for all the data we may give, have been nominal. Our population is perhaps over the next twenty years going to increase faster than our agricultural growth rate. Let alone our dreams of being a surplus food economy, we may well move into a food-shortage era. That is going to be one area of concern which we may have to address.

The third significant area – and we have lived with it for over six decades – are the issues arising in and on account of the Kashmir problem. Over the past six decades we have committed blunders that every generation has paid for. The government of the day needs to realize that the roadmap we embarked upon was erroneous and needs to be substantially changed. We need to honestly ask ourselves would we, even then be able to solve that problem even over the next two decades? Or will we be telecasting the same kind of news that you see every evening at 9 o'clock even two decades down the road?

I do not want to sound pessimistic but there is another area of concern I have. I have been asking myself this question almost like a confession: Will the quality of politics in India improve even two decades from now? When you speak in terms of challenges

decades from now? When you speak in terms of challenges in the past two decades with our economic growth but

that we face, there has been some measure of satisfaction in the past two decades with our economic growth but not in terms of the quality of our politics.

Political parties which were formed post 1990, after the huge reforms and emergence of the New India, have been caste-centric. The support basis was redefined on that basis, defying even performance and anti-incumbency. Social sanction is given at times to even those found lacking in integrity. Many political parties are centred around families. You can cut across states and you will see this with all the new emerging parties. Families and dynasties are replacing the criteria of merit.

This is one challenge that may impinge on the kind of thought process we have and the kind of perspective we have to the earlier issues. I think a lot of the rest is going to happen on its own, because governments are going to be in power and governments are going to be growth-centric. But these really are the challenging areas.

Brinda Karat

Member CPI(M) Polit Bureau

CPI (M) leader Brinda Karat has many firsts to her credit. She became the first woman in 2005 to be elected to the Politburo, the party's crucial decision-making body. One of the most prominent voices on gender rights in the country, Karat has made a mark in Parliament through her consistent interventions on health-related issues. A full-time party worker since 1971, Karat was one of the leading voices who advocated reservation of one-third seats for women in the Lok Sabha and state assemblies. She has been fighting for the rights of tribal communities and Bhopal gas tragedy victims. Karat has also acted in *Amu*, a national award-winning film, which was based on anti-Sikh violence.

I WAS INTRIGUED BY THE THEME OF THE SUMMIT, WINNING IN TESTING TIMES. I TRIED TO RELATE THIS THEME TO THE PEOPLE WITH WHOM I WORK OR THE KIND OF WORK that I do. I am sure all of us in different ways do face testing times and we all want to win. If we look at India as a pyramid, then I think the test for those at the top of the pyramid and the testing times for those at the base of the pyramid – a base which is growing wider and broader – a major area of concern must be the gap between the two.

It is true that we have a robust growth rate. It is also true that in many areas, India has much to teach the world. But at the same time do we believe that our nation, our democracy and our systems can be at all sustainable? If the base of the nation is so eroded by inequalities, then the most basic and crucial challenge before the nation today is the gap between the base of the pyramid and the top of the pyramid. I believe that the trajectory of growth and the path of development or so-called development have led to this and to the inequalities between the rich and poor, between men and women. Even though women have crossed many barriers, we are still disproportionately represented at the base of that pyramid.

Sixty-three years after India's Independence, we still have the most resilient anti-democratic caste system. We still have the most abhorrent practices of untouchability. We still have, as the Sachar Committee has pointed out, discriminations on the basis of religious belief. Unless we can evolve a system in which these basic inequalities can be addressed, we can never really become the India that we believed in when we became independent.

Among the plethora of issues which are of concern is the security environment and the issue of terror – and when I talk about terror and terrorism, I really must emphasize that we cannot define terror by the religion that it claims to represent because as we have seen there is terror and terror and, therefore, this is another issue – that confronts us today.

The security environment and how we deal with it is one of the issues of deep concern, regardless of whether we have double standards or whether mobilizations on the basis of religion can equip India strongly enough as we do not need to be equipped to deal with that aspect of terror. If you ask me about the terror of hunger or the terror of malnutrition or the terror of seeing your child die because you do not have access to healthcare, these are some of the issues which are of deep concern.

In my worldview, many of the practices of rich India are really part of the problem rather than part of the solution. You will excuse me for saying that. You may also think that my politics is not something which would suit you. But I do believe as Indian citizens, wherever we are on that pyramid, we cannot go into the future unless we believe that the elimination of inequality has to be a core agenda for all political parties.

The other very important concern that I have, is whether, as Arun pointed out, we as Indians can really be proud about

> **We are seeing developing in India a most malignant nexus bureaucracy and a section of big business. This nexus is not destroy, democratic institutions which are of value**

our parliamentary democratic institutions. It is something that has been resilient and has been able to overcome many of the challenges that we have faced over the last sixty-three years of our independence. But today where do we stand on the issue of parliamentary democracy? What is happening to our institutions? What is happening to those instruments of governance which are so crucial to ensure justice to our citizens?

Here I would particularly like to refer to the recent scam which has outraged the whole nation, the 2G scam. The reason that I am raising this is because I do not want to point fingers at this or that individual. This is not the platform to do so. In any case, this goes far beyond one or another corrupt individual. What I would really like to raise before you is that in my view we are seeing developing in India a most malignant nexus of certain forces: a section of politicians, a section of the bureaucracy and a section of big business. This nexus is developing in such powerful ways that it can subvert, if not destroy, democratic institutions which are of value to us as Indians.

How is it possible, for example, that the very nature of our politics is being determined by big money? It is a fact. Recently I came across a report by an association called the News Election Watch. It looks at who wins elections and who can win elections today. It analyses candidates who stood for elections and ultimately won, to show that only 0.44 per cent of those with an asset base of less than ₹ 10 lakh could win the election. Among those with an asset base between ₹ one and five million, 6 per cent could win. The win-rate among those with an asset base of between ₹ 5 and ₹ 50 million was 19 per cent. And 33 per cent candidates with an asset base of over ₹ 50 million won.

When we talk of 33 per cent, we are talking about widening the democratic base by bringing in more women into politics, for instance. But here we have a figure that only those with big money could win elections. I do not think this is a small thing. What we find – and I am happy to say that the Left parties are an honourable exception – is a direct link between big money and politics. Being in Parliament I have found this to be true on so many occasions and I want to share this with you.

of certain forces: a section of politicians, a section of the developing in such powerful ways that it can subvert, if to us as Indians.

We know how tickets are sold for money. We know about how money is used to come into Parliament. But when we see Parliament itself becoming the floor for the blatant promotion of commercial interests by people who are directly involved in industry – I am not against industrialists fighting elections; it is a democratic right of every citizen to do so – a question arises: is India going to allow such a deep conflict of interest in the practice of our politics and the practice of our Parliament?

These are uncomfortable questions. But we need to put a stop to the functioning of this nexus which is manipulating government policy to the extent that public policy is converted or transformed into an instrument to promote private interest. This is not something that is in the interest of our nation. These developments and this nexus directly impacts the formation of public policy.

For example, many of us here believed that once liberated from License Raj, there would be a control on corruption. But what do the latest figures show us? Between 2004 and 2008, almost ₹ 5 lakh crore of India's money went out of the country in illegal flows and, perhaps, had a roundtrip back in the form of election donations. Corruption and the use of power of the commercial interest is something that is a matter of great concern. What we are seeing in Parliament today is a reflection of the working of that nexus.

We look at our resources going out illegally and then we hear that six crore tons of food grain is rotting in government godowns. And yet, we do not have the money to set up a universal public distribution system. People ask questions: why can't you bring that money back? Why can't that money be used for the welfare and the rights of the poor? Why do we continue to have absolutely dubious methods of estimating poverty which keep the poor out of the safety nets that we promise them?

These are some of the issues of concern to us. I believe when India became free, the generations before us who made so many sacrifices did bequeath to us a dream of a resilient and a resurgent India. We have a very bright future in the sense of a demographic dividend with young people who can really be the wealth of our nation. But I do hope they are not going to say that the generation before us, bequeathed to us not a dream, but a nightmare of ruined dreams.

Moderator | **Sagarika Ghose**

Senior Editor, CNN-IBN

Sagarika Ghose: We have been very privileged this morning because we have had the prime minister give us the Congress vision of India; the Nehruvian consensus of India. Then we had Arun Jaitley of the BJP give us the BJP vision of India, the Right vision of India, and Brinda Karat give us the Left vision of India. What comes across in these three visions of India is the commitment and passion for Indian democracy and the future of the Indian nation. My first question for Arun Jaitley: why are you not allowing Parliament to function? The prime minister made an appeal today to say in the current scenario, given the kind of allegations and accusations flying around, he wants to speak. He wants to discuss. But he cannot do that unless you allow Parliament to function.

Arun Jaitley: The prime minister has a good track record of these so-called statements of intent but a very disappointing track record when it comes to penalizing and identifying the corrupt. We have seen this happen repeatedly. Two facts which stand out: institutions which were created to check corruption are being subverted to create an infrastructure of cover up. You have a very dubious appointment in the Central Vigilance Commission. You have the CBI which has become a cover-up organization. The government expects the Opposition to debate it so that the issue can be talked out in Parliament, and then forgotten.

It is about time that people are identified, prosecuted and, if need be, sent to jail. The prime minister's track record does not inspire any kind of confidence. Please remember Parliament is meant for debate. But when debate is meant and intended to be used only for talking out an issue and then forgetting it, then parliamentary obstructions are also a part of legitimate parliamentary tactics. That is when the government has to bend and that is when the guilty will be taken to task.

Brinda Karat: Try, try, try again. We are against the disruption of Parliament and we do believe that Parliament is a very important forum. People expect us to use Parliament to raise their issues. Therefore, we do not want Parliament to be disrupted. But unfortunately, Parliament is being disrupted by the government because of its defence of the indefensible. We have had so many occasions to discuss precisely the 2G scam in Parliament. The issues which have been so clearly delineated in the CAG report were raised by my party over a year and a half ago. But we have not got any or response. We have repeatedly raised this issue on the floor of Parliament in the most democratic way possible. But we have reached a situation where the integrity of the system is being questioned and the government still does not want to react.

Why did the minister not resign earlier? Did the minister resign only because the government did not want the inconvenience of Parliament being disrupted? Similarly, the reason why we are raising the demand for a JPC is, as Arun has rightly said, precisely because of the subverting of official institutions to narrow parties and interest. These instruments are used so deftly by those in power. Therefore, I appeal to the prime minister to ensure the functioning of Parliament and to find a way to end the impasse so that the people of this country can be assured that a parliamentary committee will look into the issues which have shaken the entire nation.

Arun Jaitley: We debated this issue in the Rajya Sabha for three days starting 23 July. All the facts came out clearly. In October 2009 the matter was referred to the CBI. The minister has not even been interrogated till today – for over a year and a half. But for this parliamentary pressure he probably would not even have resigned.

Q: The rise of regional parties has perhaps strengthened the federal structure of Indian polity, but isn't it true that most national parties pamper regional parties even when they are corrupt because of the nature of coalition politics? What is the solution to this problem? Can the BJP and Congress assure each other that if the top leadership of DMK is found to be involved in the 2G scam, neither will ever enter into an alliance with it? They have had this experience with Mayawati. They have had this experience with the Shiv Sena.

Arun Jaitley: The evolution of the regional parties is a fact of hard reality in India. While there were a few in the earlier decades, in the last two or three decades they have picked up. Probably one of the reasons for this is that the inherent parliamentary strength of the Congress, which was the principal political party with an ability to get 300-400 seats in Parliament, has come down. So now you have two principal political parties supported by various smaller parties.

Regional parties also represent regional aspirations, particularly in states and areas where the national parties are weak. This gives a federal polity shape. We have learnt over the last two decades to live an era of coalition politics. Most governments have been coalition governments. But when you run coalition governments, every coalition partner has a responsibility both to India and to governance. It is this point which your question highlights. I can't disagree with a broad presumption that you are drawing that at times regional parties, when they are a part of the coalition, want a lion's share without sharing responsibility.

Therefore, it is important that regional parties increasingly become national players as members of national coalitions. This leads to an increased responsibility in their political functioning. Now, if you want to ask political parties for a promise on who they will or will not align with in the future, then I do not think any political party can today see down the tunnel as to what is going to happen. They say a week is too long in politics. The answer to your question is not to bind political parties at the national level not to align with anyone but for regional parties to accept their sense of national responsibility in matters of governance, in matters of policy and also in matters of ethical governance.

Brinda Karat: It is wrong to assume that national parties have a monopoly over integrity and probity. It is the failure of the so-called pan-Indian parties which have led to a system which is truly multi-party and not bipolar. As far as politics is concerned, I do not agree with you. I think it would be insulting regional parties and insulting the voters who vote for regional parties again and again. If you would say that all regional parties are corrupt and the two major national parties are not, then the facts speak for themselves.

Q: The political machinery was created to enable good governance, at least in theory. But in reality the political machinery is nothing but a struggle for power. Is the existence of problems like poverty, corruption and terror fundamental to the very survival of politics? Or is there a clear will in Parliament to put power politics aside and think of just the people and their needs?

Arun Jaitley: That is really too cynical a view of politics. We also share concerns about the quality of politics. We are conscious about the kind of improvement that is required in the quality of politics. We see that as a possible major challenge. There is a large part of India's politics that is concerned about all these major issues: poverty, inequality and national security.

A very large number of Indian politicians actually come from the grassroots. They have constituencies. They have rural roots. They have worked amongst the people. They know the pulse of the people. If you follow some of the more serious debates, you will find the kind of concerns they have. That is how legislations get amended in standing committees. Government policy comes up for strict scrutiny. Pressures come up on the state to alter and governments have to occasionally hold out assurances and a large number of those issues even defy party differences.

Therefore, while sharing your concern about the need to improve India's polity, we do have people with actual commitment to the grassroots.

Q: My question to Brindaji: why is it that every time this nation has sought to win in testing times the Communists have put a spanner on the wheel, whether it is opposing Gandhiji's Quit India movement or our prime minister's nuclear deal?

Brinda Karat: I would really like to say that there are interpretations of history which may not always be based on fact. Perhaps a small lesson in history would be quite appropriate here that it was a Communist in India's freedom movement who spent the greatest number of years in jail. It was the Communists in India's freedom movement who were the very first to raise a demand for India's independence. Therefore, I entirely reject the implications of your accusation that the Communists are not patriotic.

If there is a patriotic force in India, it is those who speak the truth. The truth is that we cannot, as a nation, go forward unless we take along with us the large mass of our people. As far as the nuclear deal is concerned, we are proud to say that what we had said at that point was that the deal was not in favour of India's people. This is a deal to promote the nuclear industry in the United States of America. We have now brought a bill and thanks to the support that we got from the BJP, we are at least preventing a Bhopal-type gas disaster from happening again. These were lessons which could not be learned by this government that wanted to give carte blanche to the nuclear industry in America to come in here and take no responsibility for any accident which may have occurred. Therefore, I beg to differ with you. I appreciate your democratic right to use this platform to say what you want about us. But I am sorry, I cannot accept a single one of your premises and with good logic I might add.

Q: Brindaji, why is it that the support base for Left parties is consistently decreasing?

Brinda Karat: There is a difference between a mass base of a party and the translation of that mass base into votes. Our translation of votes, particularly in today's India, is becoming increasingly difficult because of the various factors I mentioned.

Unravelling the Brain's Enigmas:

What's New and Why You Should Care

■

Prof. Pawan Sinha

■

Prof. Drazen Prelec

■

Prof. Jitendra Sharma

■

Dr Ravi Gopal Verma

■

Moderator

Prof. Obaid Siddiqi

Research Professor, National Centre for Biological Sciences

Prof. Pawan Sinha

Professor of Computational and Visual Neuroscience,
Department of Brain and Cognitive Sciences, MIT

Pawan Sinha is professor of computational and visual neuroscience, department of brain and cognitive sciences at MIT. Using a combination of experimental and computational modelling techniques, research in Sinha's laboratory focuses on understanding how the human brain learns to recognize objects through visual experience and how the visual world is encoded in memory. One of Sinha's recent initiatives is Project Prakash which focuses on the large population of blind children in India. He is a recipient of several awards including the James McDonnell Scholar Award and the John Merck Scholars Award for research on developmental disorders.

BRAIN SCIENCE IS WITHOUT A DOUBT ONE OF THE FRONTIER AREAS OF MODERN SCIENCE. IF WE UNDERSTAND THE BRAIN, WE CAN UNDERSTAND something very fundamental about the world and about ourselves. This is one of the grand challenges that science faces.

I want to focus on a project that I call Project Prakash. Project Prakash is introducing a new paradigm to science research. It has led to insights about brain plasticity and most importantly, in this context, India has been critically important for Project Prakash.

As scientists we work with the hope that our curiosity-driven research will eventually lead to some tangible societal benefits. That translation can take a few years. It might even take a few decades. But we hope that the translation will happen someday.

Yet we can also ask: can we be a little bolder? Can we make these two enterprises overlap in time so that in acting upon the advancement of basic knowledge we are also making an impact on society? That is what Project Prakash tries to do.

Project Prakash has its genesis in the confluence of a pressing humanitarian need and a grand scientific quest. The humanitarian need is that of providing treatment to curably blind children. India has the world's largest population of blind children. They number several hundred thousand and many of them suffer from treatable conditions: corneal opacities or congenital cataracts. But very few actually get treated.

This lack of treatment has dramatic consequences on the life prospects of the children.

Their life span is greatly shortened. Childhood mortality is through the roof. Less than half of blind children live to their fifth birthdays. Less than 10 per cent get any education and less than one per cent is employed as adults. So there is a clear humanitarian need.

Project Prakash has tried to address this need by launching an ambitious outreach programme where we go to villages and screen as many treatable blind children as we can. What these examinations allow us to do is identify children whose lives we can improve. Sometimes we'll find a child with cataract. We can provide surgical treatment, remove the cataract and implant an intraocular lens. Through such eye camps and outreach efforts we have so far screened over 20,000 children in the past five years and provided treatment to over 700 of them.

That is the humanitarian side of Project Prakash. Embedded in this humanitarian mission is a truly unique, unprecedented scientific opportunity for us as neuroscientists. Project Prakash gives us a window into how the brain begins to learn to see after the onset of sight. But before we can get to the 'how' question we have to ask the 'whether' question. Can a brain that has been deprived of vision for the first several years of life actually acquire visual function? There is immense literature on something called the critical period. Simply put, the assumption is that if you deprive the

Can a brain that has been deprived of vision for the first Findings from Project Prakash show that the brain of a few months after the onset of sight. We can state plasticity even late into life.

brain of visual information for the first two or three years of life, the brain loses its plasticity. It cannot make use of visual information subsequently. This idea has taken root in neuroscience. It's one of the major tenets of neuroscience. It figured prominently in the work of David Hubel and Torsten Wiesel, who got the Nobel Prize for their explorations of brain mechanisms of vision.

But the amazing thing is that even though we take this as gospel truth, most of the data on critical periods come from animals, from kittens, and monkeys. There are hardly any data from humans. This is where Project Prakash has the ability to make an impact. With Project Prakash we can actually look at whether the human brain is subject to a critical period. What we have found is that recovery is possible. There doesn't seem to be the strict critical period that people have reported with kittens and other animals. In case after case, after the onset of sight we see that children are able to acquire significant visual function across a variety of very complex visual tasks. We can even peer into the brain using non-invasive imaging modalities such as functional magnetic resonance imaging. We can look at whether the brain changes its functional organization after the onset of sight.

Is there direct evidence of brain plasticity? Findings from Project Prakash show that the brain undergoes remarkable reorganization within a matter of a few months after the onset of sight. We can state with great confidence that the brain maintains significant plasticity even late into life. These results have been picked up and are beginning to have an impact in the scientific world. There have been articles in *Nature* and even in *Time* magazine.

This kind of awareness building is having the right kind of clinical impact. Ophthalmologists who might have bought into

several years of life actually acquire visual function? undergoes remarkable reorganization within a matter with great confidence that the brain maintains significant

the idea of critical periods and so might have refused treatment to older children, now provide treatment irrespective of the age of the child on the basis of the results that we have found. From a scientific perspective these results lead to a reconsideration of the notion of critical periods.

Furthermore, once we know that the brain can learn even after several years of deprivation then a whole host of questions becomes open to us. We can ask how specific skills develop. In looking at how children develop specific visual skills after the onset of sight, we are able to make mechanistic inferences about what kinds of processes lead the brain to develop knowledge about the world through experience.

One of the lessons that come up repeatedly in our work is the importance of dynamic information: the movement of the world or the time varying information in the world. That seems to be the crux of how the brain learns. All the other complex abilities of the brain get developed on top of that. This general framework that we are developing based on results from Project Prakash allows us to have an impact in many different areas.

One benefit of Project Prakash is that it is actually helping us understand the course of normal visual development. Even though we are working with children who have been deprived of sight for the first several years, the lessons we are learning from that population allows us to understand how a normal baby begins to learn.

Another benefit is to understand how the normal developmental process can go awry in conditions like autism. A normal child, for instance, is very sensitive to faces beginning at, say, two or three weeks of age. A child on the autism spectrum tends not to show that normal development of face perception. Project Prakash, quite unexpectedly, is allowing us to understand what might be going wrong in the brain that causes this kind of impairment.

Project Prakash is helping us develop rehabilitation procedures for facilitating recovery from other kinds of insults to the brain – stroke, for instance. From a very pragmatic perspective, the lessons from Project Prakash are allowing us to develop robotic systems that can have fairly complex visual abilities.

To summarize, Project Prakash is one of those dream neuroscience projects that has begun to have an impact in multiple areas. It has given us insights regarding brain plasticity and its learning mechanisms. It has unexpectedly provided us testable hypotheses regarding conditions like autism. It has guided the design of artificial intelligence systems. It has had an impact in the educational trajectories of students who have been involved in this project. And, most importantly, it has had an impact in the alleviation of childhood blindness, to a modest extent admittedly, but an impact nevertheless.

One challenge that we face is the magnitude of the problem. Project Prakash has just begun to scratch the surface of a tremendous health issue that we face as a nation. But the amazing thing is that it's also giving us an opportunity to make advancements in science even as we address this health problem. The challenges are overwhelming. But we have a moral obligation to address those challenges both as scientists and as Indians. As Einstein said, 'Those who have the privilege to know have the duty to act.' Project Prakash, given the scientific data that has flowed out of it, puts an addendum to this famous saying: And in that action lie the seeds of new knowledge.

Prof. Drazen Prelec

DEC LGO Professor of Management, Management Science and Economics, MIT

Drazen Prelec has been a member of the MIT faculty since 1991 and currently holds the digital equipment corporation LGO chair in management and economics. He has appointments at the Sloan School, the department of economics and the department of brain and cognitive sciences. He is known for his research on behavioural departures from rational choice and for work on the neuroscience of economic and financial decisions. Topics of longstanding interest include the psychology of pricing, credit card misuse, impatience and financial well-being, risky choice, addictive consumption, self-control, and the economic impact of religious beliefs. His research has been recognized by several awards.

I THANK YOU FOR THE OPPORTUNITY TO TALK ABOUT A VERY NEW DISCIPLINE CALLED NEUROECONOMICS. NEUROECONOMICS IS THE STUDY OF WHAT HAPPENS in the brain of a person engaged in an economic decision. The economic decision could be a purchase decision by a consumer or an investment decision.

This is clearly an important subject. It's easy to forget that the world economy is sustained by millions and billions of economic decisions done voluntarily, in private and independently of each other. We assume that the economic wheels will turn. But it's also possible that they will stop, as they did few years ago in the financial sector. So we really need to understand what happens in the head of a single person when he or she makes such a decision.

Neuroeconomics has been fuelled by two independent trends. One has been a development in the discipline of economics itself: a recognition that the individual is not rational the way it has been traditionally assumed by economic theory. The other development has been the development in neuroscience and our increased ability to use technology to measure what is happening in the brain.

Before we turn to neuroscience, I want to tell you about a simple demonstration that was done by some colleagues at the University of Chicago showing an example of human non-rational valuation. The question before subjects in this experiment was: How much value would you place on a panda bear? What is the most you would be willing to pay to save a panda bear? Some of the subjects were shown an abstract representation in the form of a dot and others were shown an actual picture. Those who saw a dot placed a value of about $10. Those who saw a photograph placed the value of about $20.

This may not seem very surprising. If you see a picture, it will trigger some emotion. But in the second part of the experiment, another group of subjects was asked the question: How much they would pay for four panda bears? Again, some were shown four dots and others were shown photographs. Those who saw four dots placed a value of $20 relative to when they saw just one. But those who saw four photographs placed a value that was exactly the same as those who saw just one photograph.

So what is happening? It seems that valuation here is the result of either an emotional process or a more rational abstract process. Once you trigger the emotional process, the actual quantity doesn't matter anymore. It is a phenomena like this that caught the attention of economists and spurred investigation into the non-rational aspect of human decision making.

The instrument of choice in neuroscience for measuring what happens in the brain when it makes decisions is the fMRI machine. This is a large magnet. The person spends about an hour looking at a computer screen and has the opportunity to make decisions. The instrument measures changes in the magnetic field produced by oxygenated blood which flows into parts of the brain that have

Neuroeconomics is the study of what happens in the brain decision could be a purchase decision by a consumer or

been more strongly stimulated. This happens several seconds after stimulation. So you get a delayed indicator of brain activity.

The first study done at Caltech by Hilke Plassmann and her colleagues asked a simple question: do prices provide pleasure? Subjects drank wine in an fMRI machine and were told the prices of wine. They had to rate the wine prices which ranged from $5 to $90. The trick in the study was that the wines were labelled as $10 or $90 but were actually the same. Wines that were labelled $5 and $45 were also the same. The question was, how did this affect their rating and how does this affect the brain's response?

Well, the rating was much higher for the $90 wine, again not surprisingly. But the question of interest is: was this a deception or does the brain also enjoy those wines more? The brain record for the $10 wine showed that the fMRI signal on the medial prefrontal cortex, which is an indicator of value, showed markedly different responses to the $90 versus the $10 wines. Both were exactly the same wine, yet there was enhanced satisfaction or presumably enhanced satisfaction. So, there is some direct benefit from prices itself. This is something that cannot happen in economic theory, at least in simple economic theory, because people have preferences, but prices don't interact. They don't communicate with preferences and most microeconomics falls apart if you allow for this kind of interaction.

The second study looked at what happens in the brain when we shop. The background question of interest here was the standard economic conception: when you are deliberating whether to purchase an object or not, you are weighing two pleasures against each other. One would be the pleasure obtained from the object and the other would be the utility that you get from the next best alternative if you forego that purchase and bought something else. The other view which we believe is more correct is that a purchase

of a person engaged in an economic decision. The economic an investment decision.

decision is actually causing a more realistic moment where you are really struggling between the temptation to purchase something and some pain associated with spending money at that time. So it's really a struggle between pleasure and pain as opposed to between goods.

Subjects of this experiment were shown for four seconds each an X, then some chocolates or product, then the price and finally, the decision point: yes or no. This happened 30 times in succession. There was real money for some of those purchases. Typical products were somewhere in the $40-50 range. When we looked at the brain, we found the responses exactly the same when the products were shown. But when the subjects were shown the prices, there was evidence of some displeasure.

To conclude, neuroeconomics is a very speculative new discipline. It is, at this point, largely defined in our position to economic theory and is generating a set of findings. Our understanding of what these mean is limited by developments in neuroscience itself. It's not as if we have the complete neuroscience of decision making. We know relatively little about what is happening in the brain. The findings that we see today are interpretations that could change as neuroscience matures.

Prof. Jitendra Sharma

Assistant Neuroscientist, Radiology, Massachusetts General Hospital & Harvard Medical School

Jitendra Sharma is on the faculty of Martinos Center for Biomedical Imaging at Massachusetts General Hospital and holds joint appointments as an instructor in Radiology, Harvard Medical School and research scientist at the Picower Institute of Learning and Memory, MIT, Cambridge. The focus of his research is plasticity in brain circuits and dynamics of interaction between top-down (or internal states) and bottom up (or external) inputs that guide behaviour. He uses diverse approaches to investigate these issues that include high resolution functional MRI, multi-photon imaging using viral and genetically modified cell specific reporters and multi-electrode electrophysiology. His recent work includes looking at 'space-time interactions' in the brain.

I'M GOING TO TALK ABOUT SOME OF THE NEW TECHNOLOGIES THAT HAVE REVOLUTIONIZED THE FIELD OF NEUROSCIENCE IN THE LAST FIVE TO TEN YEARS. THESE EXCITING NEW developments are a part of the neuroscientist's new toolbox, which will allow us to peer into the brain like never before.

The brain is a large network of an estimated 100 billion specialized cells, called neurons, which make trillions of connections and are organized into discrete processing systems. For example, there is the visual system, auditory system, olfactory system and so on. Each of these areas or systems process sensory information and allow us to interact with the world. Some of the most important questions neuroscientists ask concern brain networks: how is the brain wired? How do single neurons connect to specific groups of neurons? And how does the brain wiring create function?

If we understand how the brain wires itself, we will be able to understand how the function develops in a normal brain as

If we understand how the brain wires itself, we will be brain as well as in a dysfunctional, diseased brain where

well as dysfunction that arise in a diseased brain where wiring goes wrong. There are many disorders where underlying causes may be related to faulty wiring in brain circuits. For example neurodevelopmental disorders, such as Autism, Down syndrome and Rett syndrome – where genetic abnormalities may cause faulty wiring during early development when the brain is wiring itself. In case of neuropsychiatric disorders like schizophrenia, depression, and anxiety, the underlying causes can be traced to miscommunication between brain circuits. Then there are neurodegenerative disorders like Parkinson's, Alzheimer's and dementia, where the brain networks degrade with time. So, if we understand how brain wiring occurs and how it is maintained then we will be able to gain insights into many of these diseases.

With the development of new tools that I am going to give a brief snapshot of, we now have the ability to visualize single neurons and networks of neurons in their native environment. For instance, while an animal is watching a visual stimulus on a video screen, we can watch its brain in action at a single cell resolution and understand how specific groups of neurons are involved in processing specific features inherent in the presented images. We can also visualize local and brain-wide networks of neurons: see what connects to what and how they share information. Finally, there is exciting new technology using which we can control specific groups of neurons 'on demand'. We can activate them or shut them down at millisecond precision to understand their roles in visual processing and behaviour.

At the heart of many of these new technologies are two ground breaking developments that have revolutionized neuroscience research. One is development of fluorescent proteins and molecular sensors, genetically engineered to tag different brain cells when the brain is developing from an embryo or in later stages using viruses targeted to enter into the cells. When activated, these

able to understand how the functions develop in a normal wiring goes wrong.

cells can be imaged at very high resolutions with different groups of neurons showing hues of distinct colours. Dr Jeff Lichtman and his group at Harvard University have engineered such a mouse, aptly named the 'Brainbow Mouse', in which one can actually see multicoloured neurons in an intact brain. The second transforming technology comes in the form of high resolution laser scanning microscopy that uses ultrafast lasers (of the order of femtoseconds or 10-15th of a second) to excite fluorescently tagged neurons to visualize and study their function. Once we know how to visualize neurons, we also want to know how the local circuits and distributed brain-wide connections are made which will allow us to understand how they share information. This new area of tracing the brain wiring, unsurprisingly called 'connectomics' is pioneered by a colleague of mine at MIT, Prof. Sebastian Seung in collaboration with Prof. Winfried Denk of Max Planck Institute in Heidelberg.

In the words of Sebastian, the ultimate goal of connectomics is to create a complete circuit diagram of the brain. For example, a connectome of a 1 mm cube of the retina of a rabbit, which Sebastian's group has just completed, shows that despite the complexity you can trace every element of this network down to a synapse. There is another technique that I'm particularly interested in, called diffusion spectrum imaging or diffusion tractography, pioneered by another colleague, Dr Van Wedeen at the Massachusetts General Hospital. This is a technique by which you can track the distribution of water molecules in 3D space by using high resolution magnetic resonance imaging. One can actually trace the brain-wide networks and colour-code them by their directionality and make a 3D image of the whole brain.

Several years back in Professor Mriganka Sur's Lab at MIT, my colleagues and I had rewired an animal brain to re-route the connections from the eye to grow into an area in the brain that processes sound. As a result, these animals grew up 'seeing through their hearing area'. The success of this experiment gave us a very unique opportunity to understand how adaptable the brain is and what role the environment plays in creating sensory function. This kind of plasticity is very different from what Prof. Pawan Sinha talked about, where reversing blindness even late in life allows the brain to regain at least a part of visual processing. Our experiments address basic question, such as 'what is visual about the visual cortex' or how specialized functions develop and how malleable they are? Continuing this work, I have always wanted to see how the networks in the entire brain have been affected by 'rewiring', done at the time of birth. The technique of diffusion spectrum imaging has allowed me to do just that.

The third tool that the neuroscience community is excited about enables us to control specific brain cells on demand. This is a new field called called 'optogenetics'. At the heart of this technique are 'opsins'. Opsins are light sensitive pigments, also found in our retina. These are proteins that convert light into electrical impulses, which is how the process of vision gets initiated.

About five to seven years back, Prof. Karl Deisseroth and his students Ed Boyeden and Feng Zhang (both are now at MIT) at Stanford University used naturally occurring 'opsins' to infect brain cells of a mouse. One of these opsins, called channelrhodopsin, when activated by a blue light can excite a cell, causing it to 'fire' or become electrically active. Similarly, another protein they later discovered is called halorhodopsin, which can be used to deactivate a neuron. So now we have an ability to shut down the cell or activate it using light pulses with very high precision. These proteins can be put inside a cell using viruses, but amazingly the cells remain fully functional. One can actually have a mouse running whenever a blue laser light is turned on or running in leftward circles because the right side of its brain or the right motor cortex is infected by blue light activated opsins.

I hope in this short presentation, I was able to convey some of the excitement pervading the field of neuroscience right now. As scientists, we feel that we're armed and ready, to uncover some of the greatest mysteries of the brain.

Dr Ravi Gopal Verma

Professor and Head, Department of Neurosurgery, M.S. Ramaiah Medical College, Bangalore

After completing his MS in general surgery, Ravi Gopal Verma, professor and head, department of neurosurgery, M.S. Ramaiah Medical College and Teaching Hospitals, Bangalore, went on to do his MCh in neurosurgery from the Sree Chitra Thirunal Institute for Medical Sciences and Technology, Trivandrum. His interest in the developing frontiers of neurosurgery led him to a fellowship in stereotactic and functional neurosurgery from the University of Western Ontario, Canada. He has since tried to make cutting-edge treatment available in India. At the M.S. Ramaiah Medical College and Teaching Hospitals, he set up a state-of-the-art functional neurosurgery unit, and is working on setting up a one of its kind neurosciences institute in the country.

MAN HAS ALWAYS HAD A DESIRE TO CREATE PROSTHESIS. THERE HAVE BEEN TRIALS OF CREATING A NEW HAND, A NEW LEG, ETC. BRAIN STIMULANTS in the form of drugs, food or exercise also have existed for some time in memory.

We have artificial limbs, artificial eyes and, even, artificial hearts. These have been found, described and are in research. But what about an artificial brain? The plan is probably to have one by 2035. I don't know how they are going to do it because if you look at the brain, it's a master system where everything is coded: your experience, your life and so on.

So, if you take a brain out and put it on someone else like a transplant, it will not be like putting a hand or a leg into a person. What do we do about this? Can we alternate? Can we change the way we deal with the brain? Can we modify or reorganize the brain to produce things that we want to do? That was probably the essence from which deep brain stimulation was spun.

What is the basic assumption? As Dr Sharma has already said, we think of the brain as an electrical and a chemical combined structure which processes information in terms of sequences of electrical impulses. That sequence produces a train of electrical activity that goes to a synapse. Once it goes to the synapse there is a neurotransmitter, which is the messenger which would combine few neurons together in an area to leave a message. That is the formulation of information. Finally, that information is sent to your hands and limbs for the particular work you're doing: lifting a cup of tea, for instance; that information tells you how to do it and makes your muscle work on those lines.

Coming to the abnormal situation, where do we have abnormality? It's at the synapse. When you have wrong information, you have abnormal function and that abnormal function is seen by us as the signs and symptoms of a disease. Now we all know that the brain is electrochemical. So if a message is fundamentally electrical then arguably the message can be altered electrically. That is common sense. That was the basis of the DBS (deep brain stimulation). With DBS you are able to treat Parkinson's disease, tremors, epilepsy, morbid obesity, and lot of psychiatric disorders like depression and obsessive compulsive neurosis. These are the areas in which DBS is showing results. The FDA has recently approved the effect on depression.

What is the procedure for DBS? We put in electrodes into the brain and we can do it in two different ways. One by generating impulses so as to mimic information or by disrupting activity so that there is diminished information.

I'll quickly go through the steps. We select a target on the brain, place electrodes within that target, and then we get to the target by fixating it on a frame that gives you X, Y and Z coordinates. When the frame is put on the head exactly in the middle of the brain you will know how these three coordinates will take you there. Once we

With DBS you are able to treat Parkinson's disease, tremors, like depression and obsessive compulsive neurosis. These

know where we are, we shift the patient to the operation theatre. He's awake. We talk to him and then as we put in this electrode within, we keep stimulating. How do we know we're in the right spot? We know because the electrical activity is recorded and also, we stimulate. So if there's a tremor and you're stimulated, the tremor stops. Once we know we're in the right place, we leave it there after we decide one channel.

To give you an example, we had the case of a thirty-three-year-old lady who came to us from a rural area in Andhra Pradesh and from a very low socioeconomic status. She noticed her first symptom at about the age of fourteen when she had developed involuntary vocalization by funny movements of the mouth accompanied by a flinging of the hand that kept progressing. She had no control of her system and from twenty-four years of age onwards it just started becoming so bothersome that she had to be bedridden.

When we investigated the patient we found that she had something called neuroacanthocytosis, which is a grave progressive degenerative disorder which has no medical treatment. Only when she slept was she without any activity. When we examined her, we had to sedate her slightly. Her husband hadn't slept peacefully for many years. She couldn't stand or go to the toilet. She had no privacy because two people had to hold her to get her to the toilet.

We decided that we would search the literature to find the treatment we could give her. We found an abstract that spoke about three similar cases, where there had been mild improvement in two. I told the husband, 'I don't think your wife is going to improve, but let's try it out.' He agreed. We did a surgery and placed an electrode. Six months later she was able to hold her hand. She was able to sit and lie down properly. Her movements were more under control. She was able to sit and drink water, which she hadn't done for the past ten years.

epilepsy, morbid obesity, and lot of psychiatric disorders are the areas in which DBS is showing results.

This is a story of winning in testing times. A patient for whom we thought everything was lost had DBS work for her. So individually it is winning in a testing time. Technology-wise, DBS has proved to be winning in testing times. In India where there are high-tech hospitals in urban areas and low availability of medical health in rural areas, we could do a surgery for patient for under US$ 15,000, whereas in USA the same surgery would have cost around US$ 60,000. I'm proud to be an Indian and working in India.

Moderator | **Dr Obaid Siddiqi**

Research Professor, National Centre for Biological Sciences

Q: My question is to Prof. Sinha. Can Project Prakash someday bring eyesight in adults also?

Prof. Pawan Sinha: That's a terrific question. In fact, that is exactly what we want to push on. In our work so far we have not found any upper limit to an age beyond which recovery does not seem possible. So it seems like the prospects are very good for even providing treatment to adults with congenital blindness.

Q: My question concerns what Prof. Jitendra Sharma spoke about neuropsychiatric disorders. Has there been any breakthrough on schizophrenia?

Prof. Jitendra Sharma: There is a lot of research going on in psychiatric disorders unfortunately many of them remain intractable. In particular, as Dr Verma has presented, research in DBS has shown a lot of potential in treating diseases like the one you have mentioned, obsessive compulsory disorders, depression and so on. A very depressed person suddenly starts smiling and even there are changes in one's mental state. So a lot of research is going on and current research should probably provide more answers in another two to three years.

Dr Obaid Siddiqi: Many of these questions would have to do with what discoveries are applicable and what are real and what are imaginary. This needs some discussion because there is a strong tendency, especially if these things come through newspapers and television, for people to believe that this is going to be done soon. But this is not the case. Therefore, a word of caution is necessary. We should simplify things, but not oversimplify as Einstein said. Schizophrenia is a very good example of this. It's been there for a long time and changes in treatment haven't really happened. So, one has to be cautious about what is real and what is imaginary.

Q: I'm curious to know about transplants of different organs. If there

is a brain transplant even if it happens in the 30s, what are the implications? If a terrorist's brain is transplanted will the recipient become a terrorist?

Prof. Pawan Sinha: Without a doubt if I transplant person A's brain in person B's body you really have person A. The brain is really the seat of all memories and one's personality. I can get a prosthetic arm, a prosthetic leg. I can even get an artificial heart. None of that makes me a different person. But if I get a different brain it will indeed completely change me. Not even the heart makes a difference. The heart is really just a pump.

Dr Ravi Gopal Verma: Your brain requires a new body. So your brain remains yours. The question probably needs more answers because you may not be able to transplant brains, but it has become possible to implant neurons and the stem cell growing. It will be possible, where the brain is damaged, to put neurons. I'm sure it will not be impossible for neurons to grow and spread and repair damage. But what these neurons will do will depend on something else.

Prof. Drazen Prelec: I just want to say that what Pawan has said is a belief and not a fact. But it's a belief that is shared by everyone working in neuroscience.

Q: My question is to Prof. Jitendra Sharma. Traditional Indian wisdom tells us that when the body sleeps, the mind awakes. What is the latest scientific research on this?

Prof. Jitendra Sharma: A colleague of ours at MIT has recorded evidence from multiple neurons in a mouse which was trained to go by a certain track in a maze. The mouse was then made to sleep while they recorded from its brain. What they found is that in its hippocampal area, the mouse actually replayed the whole experience when awake but in a much more compressed format. So it seems that we do 're-live' what we go through the course of the day, but in a shortened format. This is one of the latest things that have come out from the sleep research.

Q: I am interested in the ethical dimension of the research. What are the guidelines? You can get into fairly complex territory with this kind of research. How do scientists live with that?

Dr Obaid Siddiqi: How much animal experimentation is legitimate and how much is not? It is clear that a lot of what we understand about vision, for example, has been possible because of experiments on cats. But cats don't have colour vision so if you want to study colour vision and the psychology of colour vision, you have to go to primates. But primates don't do many things that we do. So if you want to do that, you have to go to humans.

There is a debate on what kind of experimentation is ethical and what is not ethical especially when it comes to humans. I would leave it at that because there are animal rights involved, and some people think that all animal experimentation can be dispensed with. So, there is no simple answer to your question. But it is well worth discussing.

Q: One of the biggest enigmas to human beings is the passion of dreams. How does medical science explain the phenomena of dreams from the human brain's point of view?

Prof. Pawan Sinha: Let me profess our ignorance in the field. Dreams are a fascinating aspect of our cognitive apparatus, our brain apparatus, but we don't really know why we dream. There are different hypotheses – maybe we are purging some of the memories that we don't really want to hold on to or maybe it's the converse. It's not really clear. As Prof. Sharma mentioned, there is work currently happening where it seems that rats exhibit replays of the kinds of activities that they would have shown while they were awake. They show replications of the same kind of activities while they were asleep. But it's anybody's guess as to what is the function of that replay.

What is known is that if you suppress dreams for a long period of time, it leads to cognitive impairment. So dreams are not useless. We need them, but we don't really understand how we need them or how they might make the brain a better functioning device.

Q: We often read that we're using only one or two per cent of our brain. Is there any research being done on this subject? How do we get the average human being to use more, to be more creative?

Prof. Pawan Sinha: It's certainly not the case that we only use one or two per cent of our brain. If that were the case, then evolution would have made our brains much smaller. All of our brain is actively used. Even when you do a very specific task, that task recruits large areas of the brain. So it's really a myth that we use only, say, 4 per cent or 10 per cent of our brain, and that if we used more we would be more intelligent. The brain is really very efficient in how it works.

Prof. Drazen Prelec: Let me add to this. For the visual system, there are thirty-eight areas in the brain that process visual information. What we see through our eyes is distributed into thirty-eight areas in the brain and is processed and integrated before we make sense of something. So the brain is actively engaged and doing a lot of processing.

Q: Instead of a total brain transplant, is there something like an electromechanical device where you have a problem with a particular connector which you bypass?

Prof. Jitendra Sharma: A new area of brain research concerning brain machine interface is fast developing. An area of the brain can be implanted with multiple electrodes to recording from hundreds of neurons. The data is processed and using sophisticated algorithms can be translated to control a machine or a robot. The same thing can be done vice-versa in the sense that a computer can be trained into doing some things and its connections can be brought back into the brain.

Q: The visual stimulus that we have is connected also to the memory we have. What role does memory have in neuroeconomics or when you're looking at pricing quotients of things?

Prof. Drazen Prelec: All reactions to price certainly depend on memory. For example, is there something special about the price number nine? There is some evidence that people react differentially to price nine. Let's say in the use of credit cards, if you show a visual display of the credit card logo then that creates an appetite for spending. That's clearly a cultural phenomena that has been created over repeated exposures to that particular stimulus. We're working with people who have experience and who have been culturally trained to respond to stimuli in particular ways.

Q: We're told that some of the greatest epics in ancient India history were conceived when the saints and the seers were asleep or in a trance. What is the latest scientific thinking on this?

Prof. Jitendra Sharma: Our understanding of sleep and the creativity which goes with the brain function when we're asleep is very minimal. Very few experimental studies have been done in this area. Sleep and the activity of the brain during sleep remains an enigma. Not much can be gleaned from some of the stories that we've read through scriptures, though they may contain some truths but are not verifiable as of now.

Q: Some time back there was a news item that said it's possible to take a backup of our memories. It sounded too good to be true.

Prof. Drazen Prelec: I think that's science fiction. It's not possible. It's simply not technologically feasible at the moment.

Q: How reliable are lie detector tests?

Prof. Pawan Sinha: This is something that we actually have some experience with. We do electroencephalography in our lab and lie detection is fairly crude. Even in the best of circumstances it's easy to fool the system. So whenever you hear about news reports that say that based on lie detector tests such and such person was convicted or released, one needs to take that with a great deal of caution because even the best technologies cannot reliably distinguish lies from truths just on the basis of brain scans.

'We have an unbalanced world economy. It requires more balance between what is consumed and what is produced. Over these next few years, India is going to be part of that solution. India has a major role to play not only in solving its own internal challenges of meeting the needs of its poor people but also in building a world economy.'

Lessons from the

Last Global Crisis

■

The Rt. Hon. Gordon Brown

■

Moderator

Vir Sanghvi

Advisory Editorial Director, Hindustan Times

The Rt. Hon. Gordon Brown

Prime Minister of United Kingdom, 2007-2010

Gordon Brown, the former British prime minister, became a Labour MP in the 1983 general election at the age of thirty-two. He was quickly promoted to the shadow cabinet as Trade and Industry spokesperson and in 1992 became Shadow Chancellor. He worked with John Smith, Neil Kinnock, Donald Dewar, Peter Mandelson and other leading figures in Opposition, but his greatest and most enduring political alliance was with Tony Blair. In 1997, Labour won a landslide victory and Brown became Chancellor of the Exchequer. During ten years at the Treasury, Brown masterminded many of Labour's proudest achievements including introducing the Minimum Wage and the Child Trust Fund. He moved into 10 Downing Street on 27 June 2007, and as prime minister made major changes to how Britain tackles health, education, defence, crime, energy, and foreign policy. He resigned as leader of his party on 10 May 2010.

WE'VE BEEN HEARING ABOUT THE PROGRESS THAT HINDUSTAN TIMES HAS MADE IN RECENT YEARS. I WAS ONCE A JOURNALIST AND A WRITER. THE MEDIA as you know stands for objectivity, impartiality, rationality – all the qualities you have to leave behind when you go into politics.

I have to congratulate the Hindustan Times. In a world of declining newspaper circulation, your circulation is growing and in a world where newspapers are challenged to deal with some of the big global issues, your newspaper reflects some of the great global debates that are taking place in every country of the world.

If you look at the history of the British Broadcasting Corporation in the early 1930s, we have come a long way from the time when the news would come on and the newsreader would say only a few words. I cannot imagine a circumstance in 2010 when any newspaper or radio station in the world could say just a few words. Of course, it was also a time when finance ministers presenting budgets, as in the case of Gladstone, would go to the dispatch box in the House of Commons and say, 'There is nothing to report.'

Can you imagine a situation today when any finance minister could hold his job if that was his annual report to the legislature of his country? I was a finance minister from 1997 onwards. I was a member of the G7 group of finance ministers, which is thankfully now involving India in the G20: I have always approved and supported India's membership of the G20 and also India's membership of the Security Council of the United Nations. At my first meeting of the G7 finance ministers in the wake of the Asian crisis, I arrived to find something very strange: there were only six ministers. The Italian finance minister had resigned between the invitation and the meeting. At the next meeting, which was six months later, I found that there were only four of the original seven. Such was the short tenure of finance ministers that the Russian finance minister had gone and so had the German finance minister. When Bob Rubin resigned as treasury-secretary of the United States of America, I had become, after only two years as finance minister, the most senior finance minister of the group, leading people to conclude that there are only two kinds of finance ministers: those who fail and those who get out just in time.

When I arrived at the Treasury as finance minister in 1997, there were three envelopes waiting for me. I was told to open them one at a time only if there was a crisis. When I came to the first crisis as chancellor, I opened the first envelope that my predecessor had left me. It contained the advice: 'Blame your predecessor'. Every finance minister and every government has been doing that for a long time. Then, things got a bit worse so I went to the second envelope and opened it and it said, 'Blame the statistics'. Then, when things got intolerably bad, I opened the third letter and it said, 'Start writing three envelopes to your successor'.

I am very grateful to you all for giving me a chance to speak about the global financial crisis. I want to say three very important things. First, I do not believe that the crisis is over but I believe there are a great number of things we can do to deal with it. Second, I believe that India has an essential and critical role to play not only in solving the problems around the world but in building the strong, sustainable growth we need for the future. I do not want you as a country to underestimate the critical role that you now play not just in the Asian economy but in the world economy. Certainly, I want to make the proposition that no one continent now can solve the challenges, whether it is climate change, economic growth, financial stability or security. These need an enhanced level of cooperation around the world.

My own love affair with India stretches back forty years. Close members of my family, like my uncle Jack who came on leave from Imperial College to the IIT and worked for four years as professor of electrical engineering there, would report home to us. As I grew up in the 1960s, he would give me books and documents about the march of India; about the ingenuity of Indian science; India's invention of mathematics; the great vision pursued by Nehru after the vision of Gandhi and all those who struggled so that this beautiful country and its people might be liberated from the yoke of Empire and the oppression of ages.

That inspiration which I got as a young child stayed with me as I entered adulthood. The struggle and example of Gandhi drove millions of us to support you and also support Nelson Mandela in his fight to free South Africa from the tyranny of racism. I understood from a very early age that the relationship of one of the world's oldest democracies to one of the world's largest had a huge part to play in the future of the world. That relationship thrives now on the modern cultural and business links we have forged. These are a shining example to the world of our shared faith in free institutions, free markets and free societies. Our understanding is that our two countries are not just intertwined but interdependent. For many years, Britain's public services, our professionals, our business and our culture and creative industries have been enormously enriched by the contribution of the Indian community.

I have visited India as prime minister in 2007, 2008, and 2009. I have tried to build the strongest possible relationships between our countries. I am very proud that Indian companies like Tata, for example, are now the largest employers of manufacturing workers in the United Kingdom. I am proud too that India is one of the biggest markets for British firms such as Vodafone and JCB. My constituents in Scotland are very proud to report that Indians are now the world's largest consumers of Scottish whiskey. You should be proud that sixty-three of the top Fortune 500 companies of the world have research and development centres in India. The figures from all sectors are staggering about the growth that you have achieved: 600 million mobile phone subscribers, Indian car ownership set to rise by 500 per cent over the next two years, a middle class that is rising in numbers from 1 per cent to 5 per cent and to what people expect to be 50 per cent in just thirty years.

It means that we in other parts of the world have got to engage in a fundamental reappraisal of what is happening to our world economy and what are the economic powerhouses of the world to be. Which other country, apart from you, has a twenty-year plan to create a thousand universities? Which other country has a high-tech company which is recruiting forty thousand new scientific workers a year but has a million young people applying for these jobs? Which other country is doing things at the speed and scale and scope that other countries dream of but with the diversity of culture, with the institutions of democracy and with a genuine heart that they wish to carry in the international community?

In the last few years, I believe we have lived through bigger changes economically than the first Industrial Revolution; bigger changes than we saw with the fall of the Berlin Wall; bigger changes than we saw with decolonization which happened over the course of the twentieth century. I want to summarize these changes and then look at their implications.

There has been an irreversible shift in power around the world. People look at what has happened to India, China and the rest of Asia. They look at what is happening to other countries in different parts of the world, including the Middle East. What we conclude is this: for two hundred years since the Industrial Revolution started in Europe, the majority of economic activity, trade, manufacturing, investments and consumption has taken place in Europe and America. For two hundred years, two continents with about 10 per cent of the world's population have monopolized growth, manufacturing, trade, investment, and consumption. By 2010, that had been completely reversed. It is changing fast from 1980, 1990, 2000 but, as a result of the financial crisis, it has changed irrevocably. Now only a minority of production, manufacturing, trade, exports are produced from these countries in Europe and America.

The truth, however, is that an imbalance has developed as a result in the world economy. While Europe and America produce a minority of the world's goods and are responsible for a minority of the world's exports, they are still responsible for a majority of the world's consumption. So we have imbalances between Europe and America and the rest of the world. That is what the next decade is going to have to sort out.

When I say that we are still in an economic crisis, it is that the imbalances are so big that until we get to a situation where India, China, and Asia are consuming far more of the world's goods and services, the world economy will remain unbalanced. Of course, this is a huge opportunity. This is my second point: the size of the Indian economy will double over the next ten years. More people will join the middle class. We have just seen how the technology of India is good enough to sell to the rest of the world. You are part of the solution – not only to your own problems of poverty but to the challenge of having sustainable growth in the world economy. At the moment, we have an unbalanced world economy. It requires more balance between what is consumed and what is produced. Over these next few years, India is going to be part of that solution. India has a major role to play not only in solving its own internal challenges of meeting the needs of its poor people but also in building a world economy where there is sustainable growth without crisis and without the boom and bust cycle that we saw in the world economy as a result of the financial crisis in the last few years.

The third point I want to make is that this will not happen successfully without international cooperation. You could look back to an old world where nations themselves did all the things that were necessary to achieve economic growth in their country. You can think even back to the 1930s where the way out of a world recession was for America to do certain things and for Britain and Europe and the rest of the world to take certain action. But we know now that you cannot have financial stability in the world just by the actions of one country. One country's actions will not be enough to secure financial stability for every country. You need coordinated action around the world.

I am sure Al Gore said that climate change cannot be solved by one country. You cannot deal with it if only one continent is in action. It needs the whole world. That is true of growth as well. If we do not have agreements on trade, then we shrink the world economy because individual countries and individual nations themselves cannot ensure that they are able to export when they want to do so, even if they are prepared to import more goods in the future. That is why it is important to have world trade agreements.

My view is that in the next year or two it is possible for us to create perhaps fifty million jobs around the world, take a hundred million more people out of poverty and achieve in the world economy probably 4 per cent additional growth. It is possible to do this if we coordinate our policies. That will require certain people to consume more. It will require certain countries to invest more. It will require a multi-year approach on how we deal with deficits in different countries, but recognition that deficit reduction must happen in a situation where we are encouraging growth, not destroying it.

The alternative, in my view, is a retreat into protectionism. What is happening in individual countries is that in the absence of a global vision about what we can achieve by cooperating together, countries are retreating into their own shells. The result is that they are pursuing protectionist policies whether on currencies, trade, preventing foreign purchases or generally restricting import of goods from other countries.

There are two options available to the world. We cannot stand where we are at the moment because we will retreat and slip into protectionism. But you can pursue the idea of a global growth pact built around the commitment to global financial stability. That would mean that the countries that are capable of growing will be given greater impetus to do so. India can make the reforms it needs – reforms in labour markets, products markets and capital markets – in a context where the world is growing rather than in a context where the world is sluggish and cannot generate sufficient growth to buy the exports that you are prepared to sell to the rest of the world.

You in India have a special responsibility to the poor of your country. I admire a government which in difficult economic circumstances around the world has created a right to work, a right to food and a right to education. I am particularly interested in how you can get more young children into school, college and university because India is a knowledge superpower and the talents you have will be even more enhanced by the ability to get millions of children into schools, college, and higher education.

Your ambitious plans for the future are a beacon of hope for the world that every child, no matter where they come from, no matter what their background should have the chance to bridge the gap between what they are and what they have in themselves to realize their full potential. The growth strategy I propose for the world allows India to make the investments that are necessary in the education system that you need which will mean that you will have broad-based prosperity in the future. You are leaders of the world in IT, leaders in many other knowledge industries, leaders in many of the services sectors of the world. But you can be leaders in a far wider range of sectors if you are able to educate and have a more trained and skilled working population for the future.

So, if at the moment I am presenting a picture of the world where there is still a crisis, because there are imbalances between different continents of the world that are not easily solved, I am also picturing a world that in the longer run by solving these imbalances can make for sustainable levels of growth that can considerably reduce unemployment in the West and reduce poverty in your country and in many other countries.

I used to be the chairman of the IMF's committee and we used to meet every six months in Washington. There were many anti-globalization demonstrations when we used to have these meetings. At one meeting, I remember seeing a demonstrator with a placard and a very simple slogan: 'Worldwide campaign against globalization'! You can see what the person meant but you can also see the contradiction. In France, they had another campaign when they were worried about the effects of globalization. They ran it in 2008 and it simply said: 'No to 2009'. That was the mood of the people about the difficulties with globalization.

I, however, see globalization as an opportunity. I have just come from Harvard University where I gave a speech on international development. It is now fifty years since John Kennedy was elected as president of the United States of America with the hope and optimism that he brought not just to our continent but to your continent as well. John Kennedy is remembered for his inaugural address that was an absolutely brilliant testimony to the responsibilities of politics and public service. Many of you would remember and have read the great words that he used about the torch passing to a new generation: 'Ask not what your country can do for you. Ask what you can do for your country,' and, 'Never negotiate from fear, never fear to negotiate'. Richard Nixon, by the way, was once asked which of his words he would like to give if he had won the presidency of 1960 and he said, 'The only words I want to get for my speech are "I hereby accept the office of president of the United States of America".'

I was also asked and I am privileged to be a part of a recording from different political leaders around the world of that great inaugural address. The words they asked me to record in Harvard are relevant to this gathering today because Kennedy also said in his inaugural address in 1960: 'United there is little that we cannot do in our host of cooperative ventures. Divided there is little we can do for we dare not meet a powerful challenge at odds and split asunder.'

'Together,' he said, 'we can struggle against the common enemies of man: tyranny, poverty, disease, and war itself.' I was very pleased to be able to also read these words: 'We can forge against these enemies a grand and global alliance, North and South, East and West, that can ensure a more fruitful life for all mankind.'

So, yes, we have an economic crisis to deal with. Yes, India has got a huge part to play in the solution of the economic challenges we face in the future. And, yes, we will do best as a world where we see prosperity as indivisible and see that the prosperity to be sustained has got to be shared. I think this is a message we can all take to the rest of the world.

Moderator | **Vir Sanghvi**

Advisory Editorial Director,
Hindustan Times

Vir Sanghvi: We are going to throw this open to the audience but I first have a few questions of my own. You said you are writing a book on the world economy. Can you give us some details? Is it a memoir?

Gordon Brown: It's a book about the financial crisis – my views on looking for the national solutions to global problems. Everybody is finding it difficult to find the solution to the problems that have been raised by the financial crisis. If we keep believing that we can solve these global problems by national solutions, we would probably fail. We have got to have more cooperative action across the globe.

I was not really interested in doing a memoir, maybe because I feel I'm young at the moment. To be honest, you can either look at history and politics in terms of the sort of intrigues of a few people at the top or you can look at history in a broader sense of understanding huge forces of work. Unless democracy can capture these forces and make them work for the betterment of people's lives, then all of us are sound and fury signifying nothing.

Vir Sanghvi: There have been many books written about the Labour government and the New Labour experiment. Many of them portrayed you as a sort of aggressive bruiser. You were also an endless source of trouble for Tony Blair. Did you never feel like responding?

Gordon Brown: I'm not really interested in the gossip. You have got to see history and the development of the world in a broader context. An over concentration on who said what at a particular point of time doesn't really tell us much about the future. I am interested in what is going to change our society over the next ten years, what I can do and what others can do to make that difference. That is what I want to write about.

Vir Sanghvi: I take it then that you haven't read the other books that I referred to.

Gordon Brown: I haven't actually read the other books.

Vir Sanghvi: Not even Tony Blair's?

Gordon Brown: I have been too busy writing myself and I haven't read it. Tony is a great guy and he did a wonderful job as a prime minister. I think he has been an accomplished person and spoken very eloquently. He is very engaged in the Middle East peace process which I applaud him for. It's a very important thing to have people who are prepared to devote their time to dealing with these great issues. I think Tony would prefer to talk to you about the Middle East peace process. Here I'm talking about the books and memoirs.

Vir Sanghvi: Alright, Just a few questions relating to your speech; you spoke about how we can get out of the global economic crisis. The question many people will ask is whether chancellors, finance ministers, and people like you did too little to avert the crisis. Did you not regulate enough?

Gordon Brown: I think we have got to be honest, yes. We assumed that the risks that banks were taking were diversified. In other words, there were different instruments. We did not know at that time how entangled the banks were with each other and how instead of diversifying risk, the risk had become very concentrated. We didn't know because the banks themselves weren't completely honest about the position. We didn't know because the system of regulation had been looking at individual companies and not at the connections between them and other companies. There was a general need for global regulation and not just national regulation. For ten years I have been saying, 'Look, we need to have some form of global supervisory body. We need to have an early warning system to see what's happening in different countries.' But we still had national regulators dealing with the global problems. That is where the mistake was made.

We have done quite a lot to change that but there's still a long way to go. Why I say there is still a crisis is because I can't be satisfied that the global financial system is wholly sound. I believe that some of the changes that we need to make are not being made. But equally, there is a crisis of growth because Europe and America are not in a position to grow at the levels they need to keep unemployment low and to keep prosperity up. There is a lack of global aggregate demand which can be filled by India, by China, by Asia but it is not being wholly filled at the moment. We are now in a transition stage to a point in which the consumption in Asia will rise substantially but it hasn't yet happened. Therefore we have economies that are lurching from crisis to crisis.

Vir Sanghvi: I don't think there are that many opponents of globalization in India but those who do oppose it have reservations and generally make the same point that in many ways globalization has been a bit of a con; that it is an attempt for American companies and others to access the Indian market. But when we want to get access in their markets, even on things like outsourcing, there is huge resistance.

Gordon Brown: That is why there has got to be appropriate debate because it's not honest for people to say they are proposing free trade or open trade when they are putting protectionist restrictions. One of the problems I got into in Britain was that I see this as a global story. It's very difficult to explain a global story to national audiences. National audiences will increasingly feel, as they face their own problems, that they are right to take protectionist attitudes. You can understand why Americans see imports coming into their country and saying, 'What about our jobs?' But you can also understand that America needs to get out of the crisis to double its exports. You are not likely to be able to double your exports in a situation where you are pursuing protectionist policies further restricting trade. We need this open debate and we need to respect that some developing countries need to have some ability to develop their manufacturing basis. But that can be a part of the trade discussion. The problem is that if we continue to just have national discussions about what is happening in our national arena and don't have discussions about how we can work together to solve these problems, then these problems will not even be addressed.

Vir Sanghvi: Right, let's throw this open to the audience.

Q: Why is Ireland in a denial mode and not willing to accept aid?

Gordon Brown: The problems in the European Union at the moment started with the difficulties that are faced by Greece, by Ireland and then by Portugal. These are relatively small countries but important countries in the European Union and each one has a different problem. Ireland's problem is that its banks were far bigger than the size of its economy. One of its banks was bigger than its whole economy. Ireland's problem is that its banks have accrued many bad debts. There are assets that they have to write off and the government has given a guarantee that it will stand behind the banks. Therefore, there were huge liabilities that are added now to the public sector deficit and then the public sector debt. The liabilities are such that Ireland's deficit is now 30 per cent of its national income and its debt is rising beyond a 100 to 150 per cent, what the final figure will be, I do not know.

So you have got a country where the private sector banks have failed but are very big banks in relation to the size of the Irish economy. They failed partly because they have bad debts and partly because the property market in Ireland collapsed. You have now a situation where the government, trying to resolve this problem, has taken on the liabilities of these banks and needs funding to do so. The issue is, what sort of arrangement can Ireland reach with the rest of the European Union and with the Euro areas because it is part of the Euro currency, not Sterling? The talks are about what sort of financial support might be given to Ireland.

Greece is a bit different because Greece was primarily a fiscal deficit. Nobody was paying sufficient taxes in Greece and the public services were running at a higher expenditure than their income. They have a deficit of 15 per cent but no way of paying it without major changes because they already have very high debt in the first place.

So, different countries have different problems but they raise the question of how Europe can grow in the next few years. One of the drivers for growth in Europe, and the inevitable response in Europe, is to contract. Of course that means that it's got a smaller share of the world economy. It means it's not able to import as much from the rest of the world and therefore the world economy shrinks. So I believe the solution to the problems in Europe is in the interest of India as well as in the interest of Europe.

Q: India just managed to create 54,000 jobs for the United States and we signed millions of dollars of deals with the United States. Looking at the fact that we have Dmitry Medvedev, Nicolas Sarkozy and the Chinese premier visiting the country very soon, what do you see as India's role in the next ten to twenty years especially with regard to the United Kingdom?

Gordon Brown: India could be the fastest growing economy of the next ten years. So let's start from India's economic position being one that is incredibly strong and growing. The reason I say this is that more people are joining in the workforce in India. More people will be getting qualifications and skills. More women will be starting to work. More people will be coming from the rural areas into the industrial economy. It is reckoned that there will be hundred million new industrial or potentially industrial and service workers in the Indian economy. This means that the growth that you are capable of achieving is perhaps higher than the 8.5 per cent you have had recently and perhaps over 10 per cent during the next decade.

India, as I said, will have an economy that, in my view, will double in size in the next seven or eight years, certainly by 2020. Therefore you will be a very powerful player in the world. The issue, however, is that while America and Europe's consumption represents 35 per cent of world economic activity, Chinese consumption is only 3 per cent and India's consumption is only 1 per cent. So you have a long way to go to raise the standards of living of people in India and to expand your middle class.

I saw that you are one of the big consumers as well as one of the big producers in the world. I see India in a position to lead a global debate alongside other countries that are willing to do so. I actually first advocated your membership of the Security Council fifteen years ago. So I am pleased that other countries are also supporting you. But I think your role in the G20 is absolutely critical as well because for the first time the G20 is the premier arena for economic cooperation. It's no longer the G7 or the G8 and it's no longer meetings between American and European leaders every six months. India is right at the centre of these discussions and has a very important role to play.

My view is that India should be pushing for a world growth strategy because you can make the reforms that are necessary. I know you have got many reforms you want to make to improve the way your labour markets and your capital markets work. But you can make these reforms that you want to make in a growth environment where the world is growing. It is in India's interest that the world economy is growing fast. So my advice is to play the fullest possible part that you can. World institutions do not underestimate your strength as a democracy and your strength as an industrial and economic power. They do not underestimate the strength of your leaders to make an influence on the rest of the world should you choose to do so. I see India playing a far more prominent role in world affairs over the next few years. I will be delighted that Europe and India have the strongest possible relationship in doing so.

Q: When you talk about the need for a fundamental appraisal, is it because Europe and America are losing their competitive edge and can no longer produce quality things at a competitive price? Your remedy that we should increase our consumption really means putting a premium on the inefficiency of America and Europe.

Gordon Brown: I don't believe so because my recommendations for Europe and America are that they have to invest substantially in better skills, better education, better infrastructure and in science and technology. The world economy moves forward as people invent new things, as new technology develops, as people are ready to apply these to new processes. What is different from fifty or thirty years ago is that we have global sourcing of goods. You can buy goods from any part of the world now in theory. In some cases, there are restrictions in practice. You have global flow of people. That can attract investment from any part of the world for projects that are underway.

In the next ten or twenty years, it's not a question of whether it might happen. It will happen. India, China, Asia will consume a great deal more. There will be a market for people in this country and in the rest of Asia wanting goods and services. They will want to buy the best goods, the best services, and the best quality, at the lowest prices. It's up to Europe and America to be competitive. But the opportunity for India is even greater because India has the chance by growth to eliminate the poverty that is distinctive to your national icon for many, many decades and also to have a rising middle-class people with skills and education get the best opportunities around the world. That is why this is not a zero-sum game. It's a win-win for every continent. The problem would be if each continent restricted and shrank back into itself. It is by cooperation and by working together to look at the broad picture for the future that we can find the solutions.

Q: When you are talking about reforms based in India like labour reforms and capital reforms, do you hope India's political leadership has the entrepreneurial courage to take this opportunity?

Gordon Brown: I am certain you have the entrepreneurial talent and leadership in this country. You should be very confident and optimistic about your future. I wrote a book on courage and one of the people I had actually wanted to write about, though did not do so was Gandhi – one of the great courageous figures of the twentieth century. He brought to people's attention the evils of colonialism. It is to his credit that he did so in a way that was non-violent. Courage is not the sort of military battlefield bravado which is only one form of courage. Courage also comes from strength of belief and strength of willpower. It's where you have a combination of strong humanitarian beliefs as we saw with Mandela and have seen with Aung Sang Suu Kyi. We have seen it with many leaders around the world including Gandhi.

When it comes to Indian enterprise and industry, there is a strong belief in what Indians can do and achieve and in the potential of industry and technology. Everybody sees the Indian economic progress as a result of courageous people making difficult decisions with strong willpower and a determination to do the best. I applaud this success of Indian companies and Indian entrepreneurs.

Q: Mr Brown, I have two questions. You quoted Kennedy in the 1960s who said if we stand together we can fight illiteracy, poverty, injustice but corruption was missing in that list. Corruption is now a big issue at least in my country. What would be your remedial solution to it? Second, what are your thoughts on outsourcing?

Gordon Brown: Let us be honest, corruption is a problem in every continent of the world. We can appeal to people to operate in lawful ways. But sometimes we have to force them to do so by pain of punishment and retribution. The best answer is to create a more transparent system of governing which includes openness and accountability. There is a huge initiative deal with resources, oil and other natural resources, which affects mainly Africa. It's called the Transparency Data that forces companies to reveal all payments they are making. That is, of course, a way to make sure that the searchlight of transparency, openness and accountability will shine on all dark corners where people are hiding things from us. So I think the answer is greater transparency.

President Obama's visit to India was a great visit for both America and India. I applaud what he said to the Indian Parliament: although past American opinion might have been seen to be too protectionist, he wanted to open up trade routes to India and wanted the relationship to be based on far more trading opportunities between the two countries. Increasingly, America realizes that if it is going to rebalance its economy, it has got to increase its exports. Its exports are relatively low in comparison with its imports. So America has got to be able to increase its exports but can only do so in circumstances when it supports open trade. It's hardly likely to increase its exports by 200 per cent if it is trying to restrict its imports by protectionist measures.

I feel the mood in America is going to change. While it is true that you have lots of protectionist legislation going to Congress in America, it is also true that there is recognition, at least among the leaders of America, that a stronger economy requires growth. They require 3 to 4 per cent growth a year to keep unemployment from rising and this growth depends on more trading with the rest of the world. My fear, to be honest, is whether we think we are doing it or not, lots of countries in the world are in danger of retreating into the policies of the 1930s. You see a problem you would identify as national debt or deficit when it is actually a problem of growth, or the lack of it, which is causing the deficit to rise. You are dealing with the symptoms not the cause.

That is what happened in the 1930s when people restricted their imagination to look only at their own country and did not see that there was a world problem. People looked at the symptoms of the problem and not at the causes. The result was that we had ten years of lost growth and all the social tensions that arose from that.

We must be far more far-sighted now. Any debate about growth and employment that affects Europe and America involves India and Asia too. You have a right to say what is in the interest of India for the future and see whether as a world we can come to an agreement about how consumption, production and trade would change over the next few years so we can create more jobs and create more prosperity. This is within our hands. We can create stronger growth and higher levels of employment in the world economy and help you and other countries that have large numbers of poorer people to reduce the numbers in poverty very quickly.

Vir Sanghvi: I'm going to ask the last question. You were part of the cabinet that voted to go into Iraq. If you knew then what we know now, would you have voted the same way?

Gordon Brown: I would not change my position. But there are three questions. The first question is: Was action against Saddam Hussein justified? Had he broken the rules of international community on such a regular basis that the international community had a right to take action against him? Yes, the French and the Germans and all those who did not eventually support [going into Iraq] believed that we had the right to do so.

Secondly, did we allow enough time to see whether there could be a peaceful solution? This is where the opinion is divided. To be quite honest, it is not the issue of principle, it is the issue of strategy and tactics of that time. I was a part of these discussions and it seemed at that time that there was no way forward in relation to the diplomatic process. But historians will be able to judge in the future when they see all the papers of each side that on the basis of evidence we had at that time, we did not believe that Saddam Hussein would have responded to diplomatic pressure. But there would be evidence on all sides that would come to bear and it is a question that historians and others will look at.

The third question: there was definite failure on our part and all of us, and that is the reconstruction of the war. There was no proper preparation for what was eventually not simply a population wanting a change of government but a population that needed to be persuaded that this was not an American invasion but an attempt at a national reconstruction. It took some years before that policy was pursued. Now people have got to answer for why the pre-planning of that was so bad. But in the end, I think that is what gave the American intervention such a bad name.

Vir Sanghvi: If you had known that the Americans had no plan for reconstruction, would you have voted to go in?

Gordon Brown: The issue then is, if you had made up your mind that this was a historical necessity, you would have helped to make the preparations. So, I think it is the other way around. I think everybody should have been more vigilant in ensuring that preparations for reconstruction were made. It took some time for the strategy to change. From effectively dismantling every institution of Iraq where you worked with the existing institutions of Iraq so that there was a national interest in reconstruction and not simply a foreign or external interest in reconstruction. So I would come to the conclusion that that does not change your answer to one, and two but those people who made these decisions about the reconstruction have got answer why it took so long for that reconstruction policy to actually become the right one and not the wrong one.

Vir Sanghvi: The obvious follow-up from that: do you believe that your government's willingness – you were not the prime minister but you

were a part of the government – to go in and do pretty much what the Americans suggested hurt the Labour Party?

Gordon Brown: I was prime minister when we came out of Iraq. But when I became prime minister, we made a decision that the work that we could do in Iraq had came to an end. So we left Iraq before the Americans, as you know. We left having succeeded in very specific objectives we had set ourselves. I saw that we had to deal with the problems of Iraq in a different way. We had to help Iraq re-establish its economy and create jobs for the people because at that time they had no sense that they had a stake in the future. We had to build up the police in Iraq and help the army become self-sustaining as an armed force.

Our troops were able to leave Iraq as they did with a stronger local police force, stronger local army and a commitment that was being followed through with lots of foreign investors for economic development. In Basra elections were being held with hundreds of candidates. There was a local government base where terrorists and insurgents were being challenged by local people believing in the democratic process.

Vir Sanghvi: That is great but you have not answered the question: Do you think the Labour Party lost because you were seen as being in George Bush's pocket?

Gordon Brown: You have got to do the right things. As I say, the issue about whether more time was needed is still a big burning question. That is where most of the criticism lies. Yes, reconstruction should have been done a lot better and I think people should be honest to say that the Iraqi people lost out because we did not have jobs for them. We did not have plans for rebuilding their industry. We did not have plans for creating opportunities for young people or building schools that had been damaged quickly enough. We have got to answer that question.

But I think you have got to do the right thing and however it seems historically, in relation to America or in relation to the Western world, as a nation you have got to do the right thing. This was not done for America's interest. This was done because it was a national decision that we made.

Vir Sanghvi: So 'yes' to there was a case for going in and a 'maybe' to whether it was the right time to go in at that stage?

Gordon Brown: No, our judgement was the right thing. I agree that historians will look at this and look at the question of whether Saddam Hussein planned to make further concessions if he had been given more time. Was it possible to replace Saddam Hussein by other leaders?

Vir Sanghvi: And if you had known that there were no WMDs?

Gordon Brown: And if you knew what the position was there. But I do say the reason for taking on Iraq in the first place was not that they had weapons but that they had persistently refused to honour their obligations to the international community. I do say as we go through the twenty-first century, we will find that unless there is international law and unless people are prepared to abide by international law, the world will be a chaotic place. I believe that if someone promises to uphold the international law and then defies international community with impunity, then the world is a less safe place.

Vir Sanghvi: So would you vote the same way again and if it hurt the Labour Party, will that be the cost of doing the right thing?

Gordon Brown: Sometimes when people talk about politics, they assume that everything is done purely for self-interest or electoral manipulation. That is not true. I think you can stand up and be counted for what you believe in. When I talk about courage and the courage that Gandhi showed, I'm talking about someone who had the strength of belief to be committed to a cause, irrespective of the electoral or temporary advantage; someone who had the willpower to see it through. These to me are the people who are public servants who are to be admired.

The Rise and Rise of China:

What it means for India

▪

Dr Kenneth Lieberthal

▪

Prof. Yasheng Huang

▪

Prof. Richard Rigby

▪

Moderator

Raghav Bahl

Founder-Editor, Network18

Dr Kenneth Lieberthal

Senior Fellow, Foreign Policy Studies, The Brookings Institution

Kenneth Lieberthal is senior fellow in the foreign policy and in the global economy and development programmes and director of the John L. Thornton China Center at the Brookings Institution. He is professor emeritus of political science and of business administration at the University of Michigan. Lieberthal served as special assistant to the President for National Security Affairs and senior director for Asia on the National Security Council from August 1998 through October 2000. He has written and edited sixteen books and monographs and authored about seventy periodical articles and chapters in books. He has consulted widely on Chinese and Asian affairs and serves or has served as a consultant for, among others, the US departments of state, defense and commerce, and the World Bank.

IT'S REALLY A PLEASURE TO BE HERE TODAY TO TALK ABOUT WHETHER INDIA SHOULD WORRY ABOUT THE RISE AND RISE OF CHINA. FIRST OF ALL, LET ME MAKE A FEW comments about the continuing rise of China.

China's GDP growth, obviously, has been spectacular but future growth faces serious challenges. China will rapidly move from a demographic surplus to a demographic deficit in terms of the age structure of its population and this is going to happen within a couple of years. Secondly, social strains in China are high and environmental problems loom extremely large. The capacity of the system to become a much more innovative economy, to make the kinds of adjustments that you just heard about is in some question. There is a lot of effort being made but there are a lot of impediments, given the way the system functions.

The other side of the ledger is that there are just huge drivers of ongoing growth in China. To me the major ones are the scope and scale of urbanization, which requires tremendous infrastructure investment. That pace is actually quickening and is already at a historically unprecedented level. The demands of a rising middle class in China – a middle class that is fairly broadly-based and very consumer-oriented – and the simple analytical capacity of the system to mobilize resources to accomplish its top goals (and one of its top goals is clearly rapid economic growth) mean that on balance you are looking at a five to ten year perspective, trying as its overall GDP growth is likely to remain very impressive.

Based on behaviour today, a much larger Chinese economic presence is likely to produce ongoing efforts to leverage its economic muscle in order to encourage political outcomes that it favours internationally. The increases in the size of the Chinese economy, especially given its large manufacturing base, also means that the greenhouse gas emissions from China are going to continue to go up at an extremely rapid rate, probably accounting for about 30 to 40 per cent of the global increases in greenhouse gas emissions between now and 2050. This is despite their major clean energy initiatives.

There will be significant increases in Chinese overseas direct investment, both to obtain needed energy and other natural resources and also to buy into manufacturing and service sector opportunities. We are going to see major development of China's conventional force projection capabilities and significant increases in China's activities in both regional and global international organizations. In short, India is going to have to cope with a China that is a major player regionally and, increasingly, globally for some years to come.

China's foreign policy is going to be focussed on acquiring necessary resources for its economic development – it is a resource scarce society – domestically and in protecting its territorial integrity, which is to say it is going to be focused primarily on fairly narrow Chinese interests, rather than on the kinds of obligations that you normally associate with a truly global player. Domestically, China will be focussed on maintaining basic social and political stability and preserving its one party system of governance.

China is and will remain a serious challenge for India in the in an all around way, generally to India's disadvantage.

What are the implications for India of this kind of quick overview profile? Let me divide this into shorter implications and longer term implications and just give you a framework for each. In the short run, I see three major implications or sets of implications, two of which are favourable, one of which is a challenge. On the favourable side, China's rise is actually producing increased diplomatic room for India. All major countries now and most countries throughout Asia view India's success as a necessary component of a dynamic equilibrium that restrains the negative sides of China's rise. If you look at India's list of guests recently, you will find the leaders of all of the major countries of the world coming to visit. This is not totally divorced from what is happening with China. Secondly, India is also attractive because of its commitment to democratic values and human rights as Prime Minister Manmohan Singh has stressed eloquently.

In short, China's rise is in a variety of ways increasing India's diplomatic opportunities.

The second broad area of opportunity is economic. China's market is attractive. It is large and growing very rapidly. Sixty billion US dollars of India's total four hundred billion dollars in foreign trade is with China and that is likely to grow substantially. Of course, India will have to be tough on issues like market access to realize full benefits of this, but India is fairly capable of pursuing this. China is also a source of capital and of capability that can be used in helpful ways for India's infrastructure development, if the Indian government acts to shape this in a way that is most effective for India's goals.

Finally, my own sense is that China's development is itself a spur to India's rapid economic development. China has shown that you can grow at 10 per cent a year for a long period of time. It has shown the leverage you could get from major infrastructural development, the leverage you get from improving the quality of

neighbourhood. China is very likely to stick with Pakistan

education. All of these things are helpful as India increases its aspirations and moves ahead very rapidly.

The area where China's rise is most problematic is in the security arena. China is and will remain a serious challenge for India in the neighbourhood. China is very likely to stick with Pakistan in an all around way, generally to India's disadvantage. China will also seek expanded ties in Afghanistan, especially as NATO forces draw down there and possibly also in Iran. China will continue to build its military forces in order to protect its increasing dependence on sourcing energy and other materials from the Middle East and from East Africa.

In the long term, the scales tip a little more in the negative direction for India as China rises. I would note four major issues. First China's ongoing rise will continue to push up prices for energy, food, and raw materials in the international arena and that is going to affect India's cost structure. Second, China's rise is going to make climate change far worse. Probably the biggest single impact of China on the global arena in the coming decades is in the area of climate and none of the news there to my mind is good. India is going to be subject to the downside repercussions of that as much as any place.

Third, China will remain a counter point to India's core values and, therefore, potentially to the power of the Indian model in the international system. Finally, there are uncertainties about how successful China will be in its global role, especially in multilateral, regional and global organizations in the future. If it is highly successful, that will pose its own set of issues for India as it tries to come up to China. So, in all four of these ways, China ends up being more of a challenge than an opportunity for India. Yet, it is an existential challenge; one that needs to be engaged. You cannot deny it or shun it. You have to figure out how to leverage it so that you do best in the face of that reality out there.

Raghav Bahl: You talked about how after 2008, we are beginning to see more assertive foreign policy movements from China, while China's entire twenty-five year economic reform history before that was predicated on peaceful rise. What kind of negative impact will this new Chinese foreign policy have on their economic growth rate?

Dr Kenneth Lieberthal: The short answer is that if they keep behaving in this clumsy fashion as they have in the last year and a half, it is going to affect not so much their short-term economic prospects – those have their own drivers – but will create an increasing perception of a threat in countries around their periphery. That is what is drawing in the United States more heavily than we otherwise might be drawing in. That is really counterproductive from their own interest point of view. We will have to see if they sit back, reassess, and readjust.

Prof. Yasheng Huang

Professor of International Management, MIT Sloan School of Management

Yasheng Huang is professor of political economy and international management and holds the international programme professorship in Chinese economy and business at Sloan School of Management, Massachusetts Institute of Technology. He also holds a special-term professorship at School of Management, Fudan University and an honorary professorship at Hunan University. In addition to academic journal articles, Professor Huang has published *Inflation and Investment Controls in China* (1996), *FDI in China* (1998), *Selling China* (2003, Chinese edition, 2005), *Financial Reform in China* (2005, co-edited with Tony Saich and Edward Steinfeld), and *Capitalism with Chinese Characteristics* (2008, Chinese edition, 2010), a detailed narrative account of the history of economic reforms in China, which was selected by the *Economist* magazine as one of the best books published in 2008.

AS A CHINESE ACADEMIC I HAVE LONG BELIEVED IN THE INDIAN GROWTH STORY. IN 2003, I CO-AUTHORED AN ARTICLE WITH MY INDIAN COLLEAGUE AT HARVARD University, Tarun Khanna with the title 'Can India Overtake China?' It's easy to sing the praise of the Indian motto when that motto is producing growth at 7 to 8 per cent. In 2002-03, India was growing at the 4 to 5 per cent range. One of the reasons why we arrived at that conclusion is because we looked at the data from the corporate sector at a microeconomic level the returns on capital in India and found that even when India was growing at 4 to 5 per cent and China was growing at 8 to 9 per cent, at the microeconomic level, the returns on capital in India consistently outperformed return on capital in China.

Prime Minister Singh said today 'we must be doing something right'. It's a memorable phrase coming from the head of a state.

China has a lot of issues – economic policy issues, political the country as growing very fast is not a wrong one.

On the other hand, I agree with Ken that the Chinese growth story is one of a long duration for reasons that are not terribly difficult to understand.

If you look at the countries or economies that succeeded after World War II in catching up and overtaking the developed countries – meaning their per capita GDP reaching or surpassing the per capita GDP of developed countries – each single one of them is located in East Asia, starting with Japan, South Korea, Taiwan, Hong Kong, and Singapore – if you think about the country as culturally East Asian because its majority is Chinese.

With two substantial exceptions in East Asia, North Korea and China, there is something about the region that makes for economic growth. Maybe it's the rise, maybe it's the food or maybe it's something else that positions that region for high growth.

China has a lot of issues – economic policy issues, political practices and things like that – but the long run story of the country as growing very fast is not a wrong one. Let me talk more about China-India comparison rather than just China itself. It is really a sort of Mumbai consensus vis-à-vis Beijing consensus way of thinking about these two countries. But before I do that, let me give you some characteristics of the two countries.

The phrases Mumbai consensus and Beijing consensus were apparently coined by Larry Summers when he visited Mumbai recently. Mumbai consensus refers to liberalization Indian style, at a gradual and deliberate pace. Beijing consensus is the view that China has grown because of the strong government interventions; huge, massive, most of the state-directed investments and infrastructures, smart policies by bureaucrats and much more. So, these are two very different conceptions about how an economy can grow.

Before I get to the specifics of Mumbai and Beijing consensus let me give you the characteristics of the following country and so you can think about what that country is. This is a country where the GDP growth exceeded 10 per cent for a long time. Agriculture employment fell by one-third, there was massive FDI, a high level of income inequality by which we measure income inequality by the Gini-coefficient: the higher you are in Gini-coefficient, the more unequal you are. This country has a Gini-coefficient of 0.45, which is a very high level of income inequality. State-owned enterprises play a very important role in this economy; 75 per cent of the top hundred firms' assets belong to the state sector. There is no political competition. It's a one-party system, so obviously this is not India. The Wall Street Journal had an editorial in praise of this country by arguing that this country has something to teach the United States about economic management and economic growth. When I gave these characteristics to a Chinese audience, I asked them to guess which country I was talking about. They said China: state interventions, no political competition, lot of FDI, GDP growth

practices and things like that – but the long run story of

extremely fast, and urbanization at a very fast rate. But actually the country I was talking about is Brazil.

Specifically, from 1964 to 1974 Brazil experienced extremely rapid growth of GDP. In fact, the word 'miracle' was for the first time applied to describe the economic performance of Brazil. Before that, the word miracle usually was associated with a religious phenomenon, rather than with an economic phenomenon. But the problem is that the Brazilian miracle didn't last.

In the 1970s their economy crashed. In the 1980s they lost ten years of growth and in the 1990s they struggled and recovered. Since 2002-2003 the country has moved on to a sustainable growth trajectory. Brazil started out in 1950 much richer in terms of per capita GDP as compared with Taiwan and South Korea. Now, its per capita GDP is about one fourth of Taiwan and South Korea.

Let me conclude by saying there are many differences between China and Brazil. But in terms of massive state investments, massive infrastructure spending in Brazil there are a lot of similarities as well. But if this is not supported by private sector growth, by entrepreneurial dynamism, that motto, as the Brazil story would tell us, is not sustainable.

So on that score I am more optimistic about India, even though recognizing that in India there are a lot of problems – policy and political paralysis and so on. The good thing about this country is the dynamism of the private sector and NGOs and its democratic practices. This is a page that China can take from India.

Prof. Richard Rigby

Executive Director, The ANU China Institute, Australian National University

Richard Rigby, executive director of the Australian National University (ANU), China Institute, graduated with first class honours in History at the ANU in 1970, and went on to do his PhD under Professor Wang Gungwu in the then department of Far Eastern History (now the Department of Pacific and Asian History). Rigby joined Australia's department of foreign affairs in 1975, where he worked until the end of 2001. Postings included Tokyo, Beijing (twice), Shanghai (consul-general 1994-98), London, and Israel (ambassador, 2000-01). He then joined the Office of National Assessments as assistant director-general, responsible for north and South Asia, where he worked until taking up his current position with the ANU China Institute in April 2008. While engaged in government work, Rigby continued to pursue academic interests. His personal interests in Chinese studies are literary and historical.

THE MOST OBVIOUS IMPLICATION OF THE RISE AND RISE OF CHINA FOR INDIA IS THAT THE WORLD INTO WHICH INDIA ITSELF IS RISING IS GOING TO BE ONE IN WHICH China is going to be a far more powerful and influential player than it has been for a long time. Of course this poses challenges – and note I do say challenges, not threats – to India as it does to all of us.

I am very well aware of the problems that you have: on the border, including China's tougher approach to Arunachal Pradesh, the Kashmir issue, China's support for Pakistan, the Dalai Lama-Tibet issue, Chinese involvement with other South Asian states and so on. Moreover, we have emerging problems concerning the great river systems rising on the Tibetan Plateau. I don't underrate any of these questions at all. The government of India has the absolute

I have always been struck by the degree to which India if ever, it will catch up. China, of course, doesn't think country, it is with the United States.

duty to secure the security of the state and its citizens which is something I fully understand and acknowledge.

If we look at China's strategic intentions, I would list the following as most important. One, maintain regime survival, with all that this means including securing continued economic growth, access to resources and so on. This is fundamental. It is domestic issues that keep the leadership awake at night, not how to take over the world.

China certainly wishes to be the preeminent power in the Asia-Pacific region and, over time, become an increasingly important global player and leader. They want to prevent Taiwan independence, leading over time to re-unification. They want to develop a Blue Water navy to operate in the Pacific and Indian oceans as well as neighbouring seas.

Clearly all of these pose some problems for India. But in all of this, in Chinese eyes, it is not India that is the principal potential revival; it is the United States. The United States is the potential strategic adversary and, given that, China's programmes are actually consistent with these objectives.

I have spent a lot of my ad-hoc life looking at and thinking about China and living there for some twelve years. But I have also come to India over the last decade and am very well aware of the degree to which China looms large on India's horizon. Indeed it should. But I do wonder at times whether the national security perspective doesn't tend to overwhelm the other aspects of the relationship. This isn't to criticize the Indian military or military related-think tanks with which I have spent a good deal of time. That is their job. For many years after 1962 there wasn't much more to the relationship other than the national security side of it.

My sense is that, even today, the broader discussion about China and India is not always as balanced as it could be. Another way of putting this would be to say that the people who look at the economy and the remarkable growth of economic links between the two countries, the people who look at Chinese history, culture, and language, the people who look at the Chinese political system, the people involved in the educational exchanges, the people involved in NGO contact and so on and so forth, perhaps need to be talking to each other in a more systematic and structured way than it is possible in this case.

measures itself against China and the concern over when, this way about India. If China compares itself to any other

The rise of China is a very complex phenomenon and there are no easy answers on how best to deal with it. In fact at the national security level the answer is possibly the most simple: prepare for what might happen if things go wrong and through adequate preparation help ensure that things don't go wrong.

But looking at the question more broadly, when we think about the rise of China, it seems to be that while it is important to estimate what China's overall per capita GDP will be in such and such year, how many aircraft carriers it will have, how many missiles will it have pointing at Taiwan and elsewhere, the total volume of trade investment and so on, we also need to try to form some opinion of what sort of a China it will be in 2020, 2030, 2050. We can probably assume that China in 2020 won't be very different from what it is now. But the further we look to the future, the less sure we can be about the answer.

I would argue that this makes China very different from India. The lack of surety as to what sort of a country China will become against the high likelihood that the nature of the Indian state is unlikely to change radically, however much more wealthy or influential India becomes, is a strong point in India's favour. It gives grounds for uncertainty about China's future. But I should add that the manifold questions about what sort of a China are being asked very vigorously within China itself. One thing that people often don't realize is that despite the best efforts of the authorities to maintain a surface appearance of ideological unity, China in fact is a place where just about everything is debated – and often debated very vigorously particularly within the organs of state and party.

I have always been struck by the degree to which India measures itself against China and the concern over when, if ever, it will catch up. China, of course, doesn't think this way about India. If China compares itself to any other country, it is with the United States; not that it wants to be exactly like the United States but the United States is the exemplar to which it looks and not the model. It is the country with the indicators against which it is to prove itself. Perhaps it should be thinking more about India and as the evidence of India's full-fledged emergence, as noted recently by President Obama, becomes more apparent to all, I am pretty sure it will.

I believe that the competition between the two countries – I am excluding strategic competition – should actually be good for both. For most of the time since independence, India has not really had a worthy competitor against which it matches itself. None of the other regional states have come up to the mark. But since opening reform in China, followed a decade later by India's own moves in the same direction, India finally has a worthy rival and competitor in Asia's other great ancient state and culture. It is perhaps no coincidence that both countries are now on the way to reassuming the prominent roles that they have played for most of human history.

China's remarkable growth obviously has a lot to offer to India both positively and negatively. India has a great deal to offer to China too; I would argue possibly more and more in the future, particularly in the areas of the values of democracy and an open media. Regardless of who in the long term wins the race, the rabbit or the hare, the dragon or the elephant – choose your own metaphorical menagerie – what really matters is that both countries are on their growth trajectory which should be good for them and for the world.

Both countries are facing a very challenging decade. I won't list the ways they are being challenged but if both countries get through the next decade in reasonable form, it is going to indeed be a very different world.

In his recent masterful work *When a Billion Chinese Jump,* Jonathan Watts writes of the environment and how the world community needs to shift away from nationalist competition to consume towards internationalist cooperation to conserve. That is right but I think it should be applied more widely. Just think out of the box for a few seconds.

Outside the box, just imagine what a radical improvement of India's relations with Pakistan would mean for India's concerns over the nature of the relationship between China and Pakistan.

What about China actually inviting India to invest in a port and a pipeline in India to solve China's Malacca Strait dilemma? What about the principal reasons why China feels the need to have its navy in the Indian Ocean or at least have India-China naval cooperation safeguarding SLOC? Now, let's get back into the box.

In reality, it is clear the relationship is going to be one of competition and cooperation with continuing security challenges and occasional crises that will need to be managed within a broader framework. Greater trust and understanding is needed. There is a pressing need for serious investment of money, personnel and time in India through the creation of serious world-class institutions devoted to the study of China institutions that will inform government, media and the wider population and be responsive to their needs.

It won't come easily and it won't come quickly. We've been going through this process in Australia. India and China need to know each other better and this is a really serious issue. In this regard the media also have a very important role to play and I thank the Hindustan Times for organizing this discussion.

Moderator | **Raghav Bahl**

Founder-Editor, Network18

Raghav Bahl: I just want to get in two questions, one economic and one political and then we will open this to the audience. First, the economic question: we have seen that a lot of the Chinese bounce-backs since 2008 have happened on enormous amounts of debt. China's debt went up by one trillion dollars in six months in 2009. The entire banking system of India has lent only half a trillion dollars, so in six months they created two times India's banking system. The question is China suffered a big erosion of assets in the late 1990s. How much of a threat is that now that they would have a big bad debt problem?

Prof. Yasheng Huang: Both China and India seem to have fared relatively well in terms of GDP growth but they have done this through dramatically different mechanisms. In India it is mostly because of a combination of two things. If you look at the composition of Indian growth, it is mainly from domestic consumption, so it is really fairly balanced. You could argue that investment should go a little bit higher and so on.

Before the financial crisis, China was very much dependent on export wealth. I would argue that this has nothing to do with difference in terms of savings rate; the private saving rate in the two countries is about the same. But they got themselves into that situation, so the only way to bounce back was to undertake a massive investment programme on top of the investment programme they already undertook between 1998 and 2008.

Raghav Bahl: They wrote off roughly 20 per cent of their bank assets in 2000. So if you write off 20 per cent, that is a trillion dollars wiped off the economy.

Prof. Yasheng Huang: China was able to grow out of that write-off between 1998 and 2008 because of the strong export demand from the United States. We know how that happened. My question is that the geopolitical situation is going to be a little bit different from the one that we faced between 1998 and 2008 and whether or not you can grow out of it.

Dr Kenneth Lieberthal: China's growth dependence from 1998 to 2008 was mostly on exports and investment. When the 2009 trade crisis hit, they had to shift in the direction of more domestic investment. They emerged with an uncertain level of bad debt on the books in the banking system but they emerged with the lowest level of government debt of any reasonably developed economy in the world. They have a history of taking bad debt from the banking system and have the government absorb that debt and relieve the banks of it. They have the capacity to do that again. So I think they may have a banking problem in the future but by no means one that they cannot manage because they have kept government debt to relatively lower levels compared with all the other major players in the world.

Raghav Bahl: While government debt in China is low at 30 per cent of GDP or thereabouts, the fact is they have a lot of off-balance-sheet government debt. The fact is most local provinces have been underwriting loans. If you club the two, there are some estimates which say that it could be 120 per cent of GDP, which is a big problem.

Dr Kenneth Lieberthal: Most countries have off balance debt.

Raghav Bahl: Yes, but India declares its off balance sheet debt. Now, my political question has to do with the prospect of political change in China in 2012. People like President Hu, and Prime Minister Wen Jia Bao are known to be people who have come up from the bottom and people with more democratic inclinations than some of the other Chinese leaders. By contrast, very little is known about the man who is coming in now. He is traditionally thought of to be a 'princeling', someone who would like to go back to the old model. What is your assessment of political change in China in 2012?

Dr Kenneth Lieberthal: At the highest levels of the Chinese system, there will be 70 per cent turnover in 2012. They have never had such as large turnover before. This is in the standing committee of the politburo, the politburo itself and the military commission. So this is really an extraordinary level of change. On the one hand, you are moving from people who went bottom up to people who have been near the top by family ties for a long time. But you are also moving from the generation that got its start during the Cultural Revolution to a generation that has been much more exposed to the international system, especially to the West in their careers. Frankly, we don't know what the implications are.

But it is always fun to look at China from the United States. In the United States you have a president who has come in on the promise of change. In China, if you are going to aim for the top leadership, you spend four years or so before that making sure you do nothing but praise current policy and indicate that you will simply continue it. So you really have no idea what these people will do when they become the top dogs in the system. We will just have to see.

Prof. Richard Rigby: Although we don't know a great deal about Xi Jinping, we know some things about him. He is somebody who seems to have a pretty good grasp of the way the world works. He is certainly not somebody who would take things back. Western political leaders seem by and large to be pretty impressed by him. They see him as somebody who is a flexible thinker. Obviously, we are not talking about major change, particularly not major change in the first one or two years of the new leadership. But the suggestion that things might go back to some earlier pattern are not appropriate. We should have grounds for being cautiously optimistic.

The vast array of problems in China is sooner or later going to demand some really radical action. Most Chinese people, including leaders of whom you speak, know that. They know that they can't keep on going exactly as they have been going. But there is a question of when is the right time to move; who has the overall courage and the ability to push everybody with him? That is the question which is still unanswered.

Q: China is today the largest single foreign investor in Latin America. We know of the race between India and China for raw material. Where do you see Latin America feature on the India-China rivalry?

Prof. Yasheng Huang: China is more engaged in Latin America because it needs it. Chinese energy per GDP ratio is much higher than the energy per GDP ratio in India. So is the energy and intensity of Chinese economic growth. So, they need Latin America, they need Africa.

Q: My question is for Richard Rigby. You mentioned that the debate in India is not quite balanced and there is a bias towards the security side of it. But there is a larger question and that is China's engagement with Pakistan. The Chinese have very cleverly used Pakistan to keep India anchored in this region.

Prof. Richard Rigby: A quick word about Pakistan. Yes, I understand that aspect of the Indian argument and I think that is true. But there is another reason why China does what it does with Pakistan, which is because if it does not do it, it feels that Pakistan will belong completely to the United States. So there is a strong US element involved in that as well: it does not wish to gift Pakistan to the US completely.

I completely understand from the point of view of India and defence planners why you want to keep a very close eye on what the Chinese are doing in the Indian Ocean. But let's not forget that the String of Pearls concept was dreamt up by a young person writing a study contracted by the US Defence department. It was a young American back in 2004 who drew some lines and dots. If you look at what has really happened, there is no real suggestion that these are going to become Chinese naval bases or that they would be actually particularly suitable for the navy. Anybody who really knows about the conditions in Chittagong, Hambantota etc., knows this.

Dr Kenneth Lieberthal: Fundamentally, I agree with what Richard Rigby just said. I would just add two points. One, that it is very tempting for quite understandable reasons to see everything China does as being strategic and aimed at one objective. The reality is that China's biggest concern in this part of the world is protecting its energy supply lines from the Middle East. So a lot of what it is doing militarily in terms of moving toward the Blue Water navy is aimed at protecting supply lines rather than aimed at containing India. The reality is that from Beijing India is not inconsequential, but it not the only thing out there.

Q: How far will the Chinese leadership, regardless of what change happens in the top, be able to contain the democratic aspirations of its people especially with regard to the recent standoff they had with Google, for instance? Do we see that in the context of their leadership aspiration to control the national information highways or is it going to insulate the population from what is happening around the world?

Prof. Yasheng Huang: Everybody wants to know the answer. But the answer has to be short. It's an excellent question, but I would argue that the democratic aspirations are more broadly based just among the Western educated Chinese. It's coming up now from people who lost their land. It's coming from the urban citizens who suffer because of the pollution. If you look at Taiwan and South Korea in the 1980s when those societies began to move toward democracy, the first movement was in the environmental arena. The reasons were simple because everything else – education, health, traffic – can have private solutions. You can send your children overseas. You can send your children to better hospitals.

But air, no matter how powerful you are, you have to breathe the same air. So there is more alignment in terms of issues regarding pollution and environment. There is more NGO activity in the environmental arena compared with other arenas. Let me just quickly add one point and this is Indian's strength: technology. Technology is changing Chinese politics. You mentioned Google, but I think the interpretation of what happened is a little bit more complicated than the one you laid out. The fact is before Google left, 70 per cent of the search engines were the result of the Chinese internet companies. Even though the Chinese, because of the great firewall, cannot get information about India, the things that they're interested in is actually not news from America or news from Hong Kong but really peer to peer communication: Twitter, blogs, these have been very effective in terms of voicing democratic aspirations. And the government is beginning to listen to that voice now, which is a very good development.

Raghav Bahl: Will they become democratic or not, in the political sense?

Dr Kenneth Lieberthal: First, China is becoming an enormously more information-rich society than it has been in the past. The feeling of people who travel abroad and who access the international arena is that China is doing extremely well.

Second, when you look at public opinion polls in China by foreign firms – these are not rigged polls – what you find is overwhelming levels of support for the direction in which the country is moving: 90 plus per cent is the kind of per cent that no other country in the world gets.

Third, you find deep dissatisfaction with local conditions: environment, corruption, land deals and so forth. There are high levels of local dissatisfaction and high support for the overall direction of the country. What the government is now doing is trying to respond by improving the quality of governance, not democracy, but improving the quality of governance itself. The question to my mind, therefore, is how effective can it be in moving to higher quality governance, given the structure of the system. But we don't have the time to get into that answer.

Prof. Richard Rigby: Why haven't the large and continually growing Chinese middle class already started demanding political democracy? I think there are two very quick answers to that. One is that for most of them life has been getting better all the time and they think that there is still further room for life to continue to get better. They know that this is being brought about as a result of the policies by this party. Yes, the party brought about all the disasters and crimes of earlier periods, but it also brought about what's happened over the last twenty to thirty years.

The second point is that while there has been virtually no progress in terms of political democracy and, here again, I'm talking principally about the well-off urban Chinese, their ability to control their own lives, their personal freedoms have grown incrementally. The things that you can do now as an urban Chinese, as long as you can afford it, are almost unbelievable for anybody who knew what China was like twenty years ago. This certainly slows down a great deal the pressure for a fundamental change of system. Add to that the concern over what might result from unknown change.

Raghav Bahl: So I think there seems to be great consensus here on the panel that China will not move to political democracy in the way that we understand that concept in this country. Of course underlying all three assessments is the fact that China will continue to grow at about 8 per cent because as long as there is economic prosperity, people may not want to build pressure for political reform. The joker in the pack is if China's growth rate drops to 4 or 5 per cent. Will that then unleash so much dissatisfaction that people would want to change the regime?

Q: With the growth of China as a financial and economic super power, will we see a more responsible and committed China towards global economic growth?

Prof. Yasheng Huang: Between 2008 and the end of 2009 there was some rhetoric and behaviour coming out of China that understandably provoked anxiety on the part of Americans, Indians and neighbouring countries. But I see this as a transitory thing. This year, for example, I have sensed that by going to conferences and talking to people that sense has changed. Beginning of the year the country experienced labour strikes, suicides, and some really nasty things. Inflation is 4 per cent and with inflation rising, Chinese attention is going to be increasingly focused on domestic challenges and trying to manage more peaceful relationship with its neighbouring countries.

Raghav Bahl: Is there evidence of that? The Chinese actually seem to be becoming far more aggressive in their foreign policies stance. The whole readouts thing happened just weeks ago over the fishing boat standoff with Japan. Then there was the whole South China Siege.

Dr Kenneth Lieberthal: Yasheng is right that what we're seeing over the last year and a half or so is out of character. The Chinese leadership tends to be very pragmatic. So they have made mistakes, but they have been very good at reviewing their mistakes and learning from them and adjusting policies. What's new is that since the global financial crises, China's relative position in the world has risen to the point where for the first time it feels it can take the initiative in international affairs, not simply be reactive.

The early evidence as to how they will behave as a major power frankly has not been very good. We have seen a much more arrogant and muscular kind of policy almost across the board. The question in my mind is: given that they don't really want a rise in the perception of China as a threatening power, are they now going to review those results and adjust accordingly? I think it's more likely than not that they will. But it is not clear. If they don't, we have a serious problem on our hands. Otherwise if this is what China will be like when China has the initiative, then we all have to do a fair amount of adjusting. But it is too early to tell.

Prof. Richard Rigby: I completely agree. There have been some signs of revision. Quite recently there was a series in Chinese media about how they're accepting that they have got an image problem in Southeast Asia. This would have been unheard of – their agreeing to some suggestions and not pushing quite as hard on certain questions relative to India. When you talk about things that have happened the last ten to fourteen days the jury is still out. Are we seeing what China is going to be like or is it a phase they're going through and will they pull back?

Q: If the motivation of the Chinese is to wean away Pakistan from USA why would it go to North Korea to pass on nuclear secrets? There was no possibility of USA sharing its nuclear secrets with Pakistan. My second question: how do you compare agricultural production of China with that of India? And if China also has surplus food production in the agriculture sector, why is its rural population bent on moving to urban areas even though it is banned by law?

Prof. Richard Rigby: I said that China's engagement of Pakistan was one of two principal elements. I was simply adding that the desire to ensure that Pakistan didn't move completely in the US direction is also now their element. I don't think there's any evidence to suggest that the Chinese influence the North Koreans in doing what they did with Pakistan. Ken might know a bit better. I've done fair bit of work in that area though I haven't seen that myself.

Dr Kenneth Lieberthal: It is no longer correct that farmers cannot go to the cities. In fact I mentioned that urbanization in China is taking place on an unprecedented scale and scope and that transfer of rural to urban dwellers in China annually is 15 million people a year. That is one of the major drivers of development in China. China itself is now on balance an agricultural importer. It both exports and imports with the balance on imports, partly because rural land keeps disappearing at the rate of about one per cent per year and partly because Chinese people are eating a lot better and demanding a lot more. I'm not sure how all that compares with India, but that is the Chinese profile.

Q: How do you perceive the role of China in Myanmar and in Tibet? Second, I don't think you covered the issue of the Chinese currency. In your perception do you feel that the government is artificially keeping it low, and if so, why?

Prof. Richard Rigby: The Chinese are very pragmatic in the way they seek to pursue their interests. In Myanmar they are interested in results. They are interested in access to the sea. Of course they like to have as many good relationships with governments in their periphery as they can possibly have. But they don't give two hoots about whether they're nice governments or nasty governments and that is a problem for people who care about good governance and some of the other standards that we have.

On the other hand, the Burmese are by no means completely in the hands of the Chinese and I would actually think it would be better for India to continue being involved in Burma.

Tibet is the most problematic. I wish that the human rights of the Tibetan people were better preserved and protected as I do the rights of all people living throughout the People's Republic of China. But I don't think China is ever going to let go and it doesn't really matter whether it's a Communist government in Beijing or not.

Dr Kenneth Lieberthal: China recognizes it is supporting a very unpopular government in Myanmar. The Chinese themselves and Myanmar are running into a lot of problems. But they don't feel they have much choice and they will continue to do what they're doing.

On the currency issue, China acts very forcefully to hold down the value of its currency and that has less impact on the US-China economic relationship than it does on most developing countries around the world, including India. That is somewhat misplaced from a US perspective, but from the global perspective and especially from an emerging market perspective it is a very serious problem. Within China there are a lot of people who understand that China's current currency policy is not serving them well. But this is a government that now has to play to a lot of different domestic interests and among those interests are exporters. Exports are enormous job generators and the Chinese are worried about stability and what happens if those exporters who work on thin margins and labour-intensive industries suddenly are no longer viable. That is what is really slowing them down. I believe they have realized the downside of their current policy. But they're just being too cautious to move away from it in any serious fashion.

Prof. Yasheng Huang: I agree with Ken on why China is keeping the currency value low. But it's not irrational actually. Let me lay out what the context is. The context is that the household consumption with GDP started around 45 per cent in the early 1990s. Now it's down to about 35 per cent, India 65 per cent, US 70-75 per cent. China has one of the lowest service sectors in GDP ratio. India is powered by its service sector. China's service sector to GDP is about 35 per cent. In India or any other developing countries, the service sector is the most labour-intensive sectors. IT is one thing but we're also talking about selling vegetables and eggs on the street. It is common knowledge that the export sector is the job generator. But that happened in the context of other policies suppressing other sources of job growth and employment growth.

I think China will move away and is beginning to move away from this irrational policy of suppressing service sector growth. This is really one reason why a lot of Indians when they go to China, Shanghai and Beijing come back impressed because Beijing and Shanghai look extremely clean. They are not chaotic, they are very well regulated. But many Indian visitors have no idea that the cleanliness of Shanghai and Beijing is being achieved at the expense of service sector growth which puts all the burden of job creation on the exports sector. This is how it has come about and it will require some structural reforms to liberalize the service sector growth and then China will move away.

Raghav Bahl: Whenever we talk of the Chinese currency being kept at the value it is there is a lot of discussion on impact on exports but not that much discussion on the value of the foreign exchange results that China holds because those come down dramatically in value. If 20 per cent of the currency revaluation happens, they lose almost half a trillion dollars.

Prof. Yasheng Huang: The issue is this is not a narrow financial consideration. The bigger issue is jobs. There was an earlier question about restricting the Chinese movement. Those restrictions just don't work anymore. There are 430 million rural migrant workers and not all of them work in the export sector, but many of them do. From a political point of view these are the last people that you want to upset. I would argue that, yes the Chinese look a little bit strange from the outside. But from the inside it is both politically and economically rational to do what they have been doing. But the trick is to move away from that system as fast as possible.

Dr Kenneth Lieberthal: I agree, but let me say I also agree with your point. China holds an extraordinary percentage of its foreign exchange in US dollars. It is caught in the dollar trap. It holds so many US dollars that it cannot exit from the dollar rapidly at a level significant enough to make a difference and so you notice China's currency has been devaluing with regard to almost every other currency in the world except the US dollar. Their problem is that they over-invested in the US dollar and they now have very little flexibility available to them. That certainly produces some caution vis-à-vis the exchange rate with the dollar.

ADITYA BIRLA GROUP

Presenting Partner

A US $29 billion corporation, the Aditya Birla Group is in the League of Fortune 500. It is anchored by an extraordinary force of over 1,30,600 employees, belonging to 40 different nationalities. The Group has been adjudged among the top six great places for leaders to work in the Asia Pacific Region (The Hewitt Associates, The RBL Group and Fortune Magazine Study 2009). Over 60 per cent of its revenues flow from its overseas operations.

The Group operates in 27 countries – Australia, Bahrain, Bangladesh, Brazil, Canada, China, Egypt, France, Germany, Hungary, India, Indonesia, Italy, Korea, Laos, Luxembourg, Malaysia, Myanmar, Philippines, Singapore, Sri Lanka, Switzerland, Thailand, UAE, UK, USA and Vietnam.

GLOBALLY THE ADITYA BIRLA GROUP IS:

- A metals powerhouse, among the world's most cost-efficient aluminium and copper producers. Hindalco-Novelis is the largest aluminium rolling company. It is one of the 3 biggest producers of primary aluminium in Asia, with the largest single location copper smelter.
- No.1 in viscose staple fibre.
- The 4th largest producer of carbon black.
- The 4th largest producer of insulators.
- The 5th largest producer of acrylic fibre.
- The 9th largest cement producer globally.
- Among the best energy efficient fertilizer plants.

IN INDIA:

- A top fashion (branded apparel) and lifestyle player.
- The 2nd largest player in viscose filament yarn.
- The 2nd largest in the Chlor-alkali sector.
- Among the top 3 mobile telephony companies.
- A leading player in Life Insurance and Asset Management.
- Among the top 3 super-market chains in the Retail business.
- Among the top 10 BPO companies.

Rock solid in fundamentals, the Aditya Birla Group nurtures a culture where success does not come in the way of the need to keep learning afresh, to keep experimenting.

BEYOND BUSINESS – THE ADITYA BIRLA GROUP:

- Works in 2,500 villages.
- Reaches out to 7 mn people annually through the Aditya Birla Centre for Community Initiative and Rural Development, an initiative spearheaded by Mrs. Rajashree Birla.
- Focuses on: health-care, education, sustainable livelihood, infrastructure and espousing social reform.
- Runs 42 schools providing quality education to 45,000 children. Of these, over 18,000 children receive free education.
- Its 18 hospitals tend to more than a million villagers.
- In line with its commitment to sustainable development, has partnered the Columbia University in establishing the Columbia Global Centre's Earth Institute in Mumbai.

- To embed CSR as a way of life in organizations, has set up the FICCI – Aditya Birla CSR Centre for Excellence, in Delhi.
- Transcending the conventional barriers of business because we believe it is our duty, facilitate inclusive growth.

BPTP

Associate Sponsor

BPTP Limited is a real estate development company with operations primarily in various parts of the NCR, including Gurgaon, Faridabad, NOIDA and Greater NOIDA. We are involved in residential and commercial real estate development projects ranging from integrated townships, plotted development, group housing consisting of high rise and low rise apartments and villas to other commercial properties including district and convenience commercial and retail centres, IT and cyber parks and IT SEZs.

BPTP Limited is the largest real estate development company in the Gurgaon- Faridabad-NOIDA market in terms of the number of apartments launched and sold, and the third largest real estate development company in terms of the sq ft launched and sold, in each case during the period from January 2005 to July 2009 (source: Prop Equity).

BPTP Limited is one of the few companies in India that have investments from major global investors both in our Company and in certain of our Subsidiaries. CPI invested ₹ 3,225 million in our Company in August 2007. HVIHL, an affiliate of J.P. Morgan Chase Banks, invested ₹ 2,150 million in our Company in July 2008. CPI India invested an aggregate amount of ₹ 3,990 million in three of our associate companies and one of our Subsidiary's owning SEZ projects in Faridabad, NOIDA and Greater NOIDA in April 2008. We also own 51% in our Subsidiary, Vital Construction Private Limited, which has developed 'BPTP 'i' Park', an IT park located on NH-8 in Gurgaon, and the remaining 49% shareholding interest in this Subsidiary is owned by Merrill Lynch International.

Our promoter and founder, Mr. Kabul Chawla, has vast experience in real estate development industry and been associated with the real estate development business since 1995. Prior to the commencement of construction of our Ongoing Projects, Mr. Chawla has, through joint ventures, developed two IT and cyber parks in Gurgaon and NOIDA covering an aggregate of approximately 0.99 million sq ft of Saleable Area and two shopping malls in Delhi covering an aggregate of approximately 0.27 million sq ft of Saleable Area. Mr. Chawla has been primarily responsible for the direction and growth of our business and has been instrumental in identifying our current development projects, including identifying Faridabad as a destination and our signature integrated township project, BPTP Parklands.

IFCI LTD.

Associate Sponsor

IFCI Ltd, the first Development Finance Institution of the country, was set up in 1948 to provide impetus to industrial development through medium and longterm finance. In over 60 years of its existence, IFCI has evaluated more than 4800 projects, with a well-diversified sector portfolio and extended cumulative financial assistance of over INR 400 billion.

IFCI, along with undertaking techno-economic and financial viability studies for projects and extending financial assistance, is today an organization providing a host of specialized services in the areas of Corporate Advisory, Project Development, Project Appraisal, Risk Analysis, Credit Syndication, Placement of Debt and Equity, Corporate Restructuring, Infrastructure and Legal Advisory.

Through specialized subsidiaries and associate organizations, IFCI has emerged as a major player providing comprehensive financial solutions ranging from Merchant Banking, Insurance Broking, Venture Capital, Depository Services, Factoring Services, Asset Reconstruction & Securitization to Education and Infrastructure

IFCI has come to be rated amongst the world's top 500 global financial brands. A lean and dynamic management team comprising of highly motivated and seasoned industry professionals with values rooted in excellence, integrity and innovation, make it uniquely poised to emerge as a major player in corporate finance.

SUJANA GROUP

Associate Sponsor

Sujana's place amongst the emerging organizations, with a significant footprint in each of its diversified success, is based on sound facts - A turnover of INR 5,573 crores (USD 1.23 billion), and an emphatic presence in verticals like Steel, Power & Telecom Infra, Light Engineering Components ,Home Appliances, Energy which accounts for the Group being one of the largest business conglomerates in South India.

Sujana has single-handedly transformed steel from a commodity into a service, introducing innovations such as Smart Steel, Sujana Plus and Sujana TMT, delivering ROI to customers.

Power & Telecom Infra is another core area where Sujana offers holistic solutions in Telecom infrastructure leveraging its design and engineering capabilities. Customers have the dual benefit of Sujana's EPC's capabilities and a 'single window' solution throughout the project life right from conceptualization to commissioning.

Sujana's Light Engineering portfolio has set benchmarks in precision and quality while its product innovations in Home Applications has resulted in the creation of brands that are today household names across consumer durables.

Continually seeking new growth opportunities Sujana has made recent forays into the Energy segment to tap potentials in Concentrated Solar Thermal & Photo Voltaic Power Generation, LED lighting applications, EPC and Energy Management Consulting. Manufacturing expertise, technology edge, in-house R&D makes Sujana's solar solutions total and relevant to India's needs, costeffectively.

An ever increasing presence across India supported by a worldwide presence with offices at Singapore, Hong Kong, UAE, Mauritius, Kenya, Zambia, Malawi, and the USA, Sujana is rightly positioned to evolve into a vibrant, dynamic, global entity.

OIL & NATURAL GAS CORPORATION LIMITED

Associate Sponsor

Oil and Gas division was formed in 1955 out of GSI and was subsequently converted into Oil and Natural Gas Directorate and finally into Oil and Natural Gas Commission on 14th August 1956. In 1994, it became a Corporation, and in 1997 was given status of 'Navratna' by Government of India. ONGC was recognized as a "Flagship" Oil PSU in the year 2000.

ONGC is one of the largest E&P companies in the world in terms of reserves and production, with hydrocarbon reserves exceeding 1 bn tonnes of Oil and Gas and produces more than 1 mn Barrels of Oil Equivalent (MMBOE) per day contributing around 80% of domestic production. It also contributes over 3.5 mn tonnes per annum of Value-Added-Products including LPG, C2-C3, Naphtha, HSD, SKO and ATF.

ONGC has created and sustained unprecedented wealth in its business, a trillion Indian Rupees, for its owners, a billion citizens of India.ONGC has established 6.4 bn tonnes of in-place hydrocarbon reserves with 339 discoveries of oil and gas. Out of these in-place hydrocarbons on domestic acreages, ultimate reserves are 2.3 bn tonnes of oil plus oil equivalent gas (O+OEG). In fact, six out of seven producing basins in India have been discovered by ONGC, from where ONGC and all others produce oil and gas. It has cumulatively produced 753 mn metric tonnes (MMT) of Crude, 442 bn Cubic Meters (BCM) of Natural Gas and 54.2 mn tonnes of Value Added Products (VAP) from 136 domestic onshore production fields and 7 domestic offshore fields.

ONGC as an integrated Oil & Gas Corporate has in-house capability in all aspects of the business i.e., Acquisition, Processing & Interpretation (API) of Seismic data, drilling, work-over and well stimulation operations, engineering & construction, production, fractionation, refining, transportation, applied R&D, training and marketing.

The Company operates with 32 seismic crews, manages 225 onshore production installations, 131 offshore well platforms, 160 drilling and work-over rigs, owns and operates more than 15,000 kms. of pipeline in India, including 3200 kms. of sub-sea pipelines. With its Tatipaka mini-refinery and acquired MRPL refinery, it has almost one tenth of India's refining capacity. ONGC has also started taking interest in downstream sectors through investments in LNG.

Petrochemicals, Power and Infrastructure sectors. ONGC, the 369th ranking Fortune Global 500 Company (2007) has also been ranked as Numero Uno E&P Company in Asia and the third largest E&P Company in the world in Platts Energy Business Technology Survey 2007- based on Assets, Revenues, Profits, EPS and Return on invested capital. ONGC is 21st among the top 50 publicly traded global Oil & Gas companies (PFC Energy ranking, January' 2007).

GLOBAL GROUP

Associate Sponsor

Global Group is India's leading business group focused on Network Services and Shared Telecom Infrastructure.

Global Holding Corporation Pvt. Ltd. is the holding company of "Global Group" that has 7 companies, two of which are listed on Indian Stock Exchanges. The Group owns more than 32,500 towers, cross revenues of US$ 1.5 Billion, Balance sheet size of over US$ 4 Billion, and more than 35,000 professionals (FY 2011E). The Group has operations across 46 countries, employs people of 22 nationalities and supports 18 social causes.

For over 2 decades Global Group has been partnering with leading telecom operators and OEMs offering its expertise in wireless communications. From 2G Networks to 3G, from WiMAX to IPTV, Global group provides complete lifecycle solutions around Network Services. The services include Network Planning and Design, Network Deployment, Network Operations and Maintenance, Infrastructure Management, Energy Management and Professional services.

Global Group Enterprises have received more than 35 accolades and awards for excellence in Business, CSR and Corporate Governance. The group's flagship company GTL features in the in the S&P's ESG India Index, is the recipient of "Outstanding Achievement" trophy from IMC RBNQA, "Certificate for strong Commitment" from CII-ITC for Sustainable Development and "Greentech Environment Excellence" Award. GTL Infra has won "Best Independent Infrastructure Provider" from Tele.Net, "Innovative Infrastructure Company of the year" by CNBC TV18 and "Top Independent Infrastructure Provider of India" by V&D. Global Towers has been awarded the "Best in class Innovation in Manufacturing Award" at International India Innovation summit, 2010. The Group offers excellent working conditions and provides social benefits like free Medical Care and Insurance for the employees' families.

By 2013, the Group plans to Erect, Engineer and Manage 100,000 Cell Sites across 150 Networks. These Networks are expected to connect more than 100 million subscribers in 50 countries across the world.

PARKER - THE LUXOR GROUP

Summit Partner

Founded in 1888, PARKER has been an inspiration to people around the globe. A brand dedicated to passion for perfection, and driven by bold innovation, Parker's philosophy is to put consumers and craftsmanship first and this is what makes Parker the most recognized fine writing pen brand in the world.

Launched in India in 1996 by Luxor Writing Instruments Ltd., a pioneer in the writing instruments market in India, PARKER offers an exclusive range of luxurious writing instruments, legends in their own right, and lifestyle statements relevant to every generation.

Parker has made a mark on the nation so much so that it has been awarded 'The Most Trusted Brand' for five years in a row. Available all across the country, Parker has served professionals impeccably with writing solutions that are a perfect combination of elegance, reliability, durability and timeless style. The very reason why Parker has been writing thousands of success stories over the years.

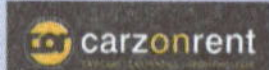

CARZONRENT

Summit Partner

"Carzonrent" & "EasyCabs" have been established today as the most used and preferred Indian brands for car rental, limousine service, operating lease and radio cabs services.

Deep domain expertise, on schedule delivery & cost effectiveness, excellent staff training on systems and procedures and ensuring exceptional delivery standards has helped Carzonrent stand out as a clear leader in the Car rental Market with the largest market share, a fact also confirmed in the recent Euromonitor International Report about the Car rental Industry in India. In addition, other accolades which Carzonrent has been bestowed upon owing to its customer focused approach are: -

- "Best Car rental Company in India"
  Financial Express Business Travel Awards India in 2004
- "Best Car Rental Company in India"
  Galileo Express Travel World Award 2008
- "Excellence in Customer Experience"
  Bird Express Travel World Award 2009
- Best CTO award under the process excellence category
  Dun & Bradstreet Awards 2009
- Best CTO award under the logistics & transport category
  Dun & Bradstreet Awards 2009

The company is committed to provide the best in class services and customized 360° ground mobility solutions. Since "Personal Ground Transportation" is its "Core business", the company chose the letters 'COR' to represent the brand and company – Carzonrent.

Reiterating on its commitment, 'COR' represents a zeal to keep on improvising operational and service innovations to serve better. "Carzonrent", now operates a fleet of over 6000 cars providing Car Rental, Limousine service , Operating Lease and Radio Cabs services to over 20000 travelers on a daily basis.

hindustantimes.com

HINDUSTANTIMES.COM

Media Partner

HindustanTimes.com, with over 5 mn unique visitors and 100 mn page views per month, is one of the largest news portals in the country. Ranked amongst top 10 global news sites by Forbes, the site is today one of the most popular destinations for news and information content seekers on the web.

In keeping with the objective of continuous improvements to enrich the user experience, HindustanTimes.com brings to its loyal and discerning audience exclusive, high-calibre content along with in-depth reportage that allows its surfers to follow a story in depth.

The site also provides sections written by popular columnists, along with indepth web exclusives on politics, business, new economy, entertainment, fashion and lifestyle apart from interactive features like celebrity chats, business tools, discussion forums, blogs, newsletters, alerts and rich multimedia.

THE NATIONAL HIGHWAYS AUTHORITY OF INDIA

Summit Partner

The National Highways Authority of India (NHAI) was constituted by an Act of Parliament, namely the National Highways Authority of India Act, 1988. It is responsible for development, maintenance and Management of National Highways vested or entrusted to it by the Central Government and for matters connected or incidental thereto. The authority became operational in February, 1995.

The National Highways Authority of India (NHAI) is mandated to implement National Highways Development Project (NHDP) which is India's largest ever Highways Project in a phased manner. The national Highways have a total length of 70,548 km to serve as the arterial network of the Country. Although national highways constitute only about 2 per cent of the road network, it carries 40 per cent of the total road traffic. Rapid expansion of passenger and freight traffic makes it imperative to improve the road network in the country. Accordingly, Government of India has regularly launched major initiatives to upgrade and strengthen National Highways through various phases of National Highways Development Project (NHDP).

POWERGRID

Summit Partner

Power Grid Corporation of India Limited (POWERGRID) is the Central Transmission Utility (CTU) of the country and one of the largest and bestmanaged transmission utilities in the world. POWERGRID owns and operates more than 95% of India's interstate and inter-regional electric power transmission system.

In that capacity, as at September 30, 2010, POWERGRID owned and operated 79,556 circuit kilometers of electrical transmission lines and 132 electrical substations. In Fiscal 2010, POWERGRID transmitted approximately 363.72 billion units of electricity, representing approximately 47% of all the power generated in India. The company has been able to consistently maintain the availability of this gigantic transmission network at over 99%.

According to Booz & Company's comparative benchmarking across global transmission companies, POWERGRID was rated as one of the best in terms of system availability in Fiscal 2010. POWERGRID was conferred the status of "Navratna" by the Government of India (GoI) in May 2008 and the Company has received the highest annual performance rating of "Excellent" from the GoI in each year since Fiscal 1994.

CHIVAS

Summit Partner

Created by the merger of Pernod and Ricard (1975), the group has undergone sustained development, based on both growth and acquisitions. The purchase of part of Seagram (2001), the acquisitions of Allied Domecq (2005) and recently of Vin & Sprit (2008) have made Pernod Ricard the world's co-leader in wines and spirits with consolidated sales of € 7,203 million in 2008/09.

Pernod Ricard holds one of the most prestigious brand portfolios in the sector: Absolut Premium Vodka, Ricard Pastis, Ballantine's, Chivas Regal and The Glenlivet Scotch whiskies, Jameson Irish Whiskey, Martell cognac, Havana Club rum, Beefeater gin, Kahlúa and Malibu liqueurs, Mumm and Perrier-Jouët champagnes, as well Jacob's Creek and Montana wines.

The Company demonstrates strong presence in India with leading brands like Royal Stag, Blenders Pride and Imperial Blue whiskies; and iconic international brands like Chivas Regal, Absolut, The Glenlivet, Jameson, Martel, and Havana Club. Pernod Ricard India has ventured in to the wine segment and launched its Nine Hills wine brands, being well recognised for their quality and having received several awards.

Pernod Ricard is strongly committed to a sustainable development policy and encourages responsible consumption.

PETRONET LNG LIMITED

Summit Partner

Petronet LNG Limited, a Joint Venture company, promoted by ONGC, IOCL, BPCL and GAIL India was formed in the year 1998 to set up LNG Terminals in the country. The company established South East Asia's first LNG Receiving and Regasification Terminal of 5 MMTPA capacity at Dahej, Gujarat in April 2004 and expanded its capacity to 10 MMTPA in 2009-10.

Presently, PLL Dahej Terminal is operating at a capacity of 10 MMTPA (40 MMSCMD), out of which, 7.5 MMTPA is being sourced through Long Term Contract with RasGas (Qatar) and additional LNG is being sourced through contracts. PLL's Dahej terminal is meeting approximately 20% of India's total gas requirement.

Petronet has taken another initiative by starting construction of the Kochi Terminal of 2.5 MMTPA (10 MMSCMD), expandable to 5 MMTPA, which is scheduled for mechanical completion in April 2012. PLL has already tied up 1.44 MMTPA LNG on long term basis from Exxon Mobil's Gorgon Project (Australia) for supply to the Kochi terminal. With the commissioning of Kochi LNG Terminal, the natural gas market share of the company in the country is expected to go up to about 25%.

AIRPORTS AUTHORITY OF INDIA

Summit Partner

Airports Authority of India (AAI) is a leader in building airport infrastructure through the country. AAI came into being on 1.4.1995. AAI manages 115 airports including 23 Civil Enclaves. In addition, AAI also provides CNS-ATM facilities at 11 other airports. About 2.8 million nautical square mile area of the national airspace has been assigned to AAI for provision of Air Traffic Services.

Airports Authority of India has undertaken plans to upgrade infrastructure at airports across the country. In terms of Capital Expenditure Outlay, AAI has increased it from ₹ 3534 cr . in the Xth Five Year Plan to ₹ 12,964 cr. in the XIth Plan. The annual expenditure of ₹ 2742 crore during 2009-10 is estimated to go up to ₹ 3600 cr. in 2010-11.

Development at four major airports has been undertaken under a SPV, i.e. Delhi & Mumbai airports through a Joint Venture route and Bangalore & Hyderabad Airports as Greenfield airports, involving a planned expenditure of more than ₹ 30,000 cr.

Modernisation of Kolkatta and Chennai airports has been undertaken by AAI at an estimated cost of ₹ 4340 cr. (Rs. 2325 cr. for Kolkata & ₹ 2015 cr. For Chennai). These projects are likely to be completed by the year 2011.

NORTH DELHI POWER LIMITED

Summit Partner

North Delhi Power Limited (NDPL) is a joint venture between Tata Power and the Government of NCT of Delhi with the majority stake being held by Tata Power. NDPL distributes electricity in North and North West parts of Delhi and serves a populace of 50 lakh. It started operations on July 1, 2002 post the unbundling of erstwhile Delhi Vidyut Board. With a registered consumer base of 12 lakh and a peak load of around 1315 MW, the company's operations span across an area of 510 sq kms.

NDPL has been the frontrunner in implementing power distribution reforms in the capital city and is acknowledged for its consumer friendly practices. Since privatisation, the Aggregate Technical & Commercial (AT&C) losses in NDPL areas have shown a record decline. Today they stand at 14.47% (as on March 31, 2010) which is an unprecedented reduction of around 74% from an opening loss level of 53% in July 2002.

NDPL is the first power distribution utility from India to have received the prestigious Edison Award 2008 (international category) and again in 2009 for Policy Advocacy. Some of the other key recognitions include Palladium Balanced Scorecard Hall of Fame Award- 2008; SAP Ace Award 2008; UPN, USA Metering Award; Asian Power Award 2009 (3rd consecutive years) and the Asian Power Most Inspirational CEO of the Year 2008 Award.

CITY UNION BANK

CITY UNION BANK LTD

Summit Partner

City Union Bank, one of the oldest private sector banks of the country was incorporated in 1904 at Kumbakonam Town, in the delta district of Thanjavur, Tamil Nadu, with a mission of providing quality banking services to the public.

Today, City Union Bank stands as one of the most trusted bank in the private sector with more than 225 branches across India. All the branches come under the CBS system engineered by TCS, offering effective and efficient services through multiple delivery channels, significantly contributing to the growth of the individual and the nation.

During the FY 2009-10, City Union Bank has crossed the milestone of ₹ 17,000 Cr in total business with all-round growth in various parameters above the industry benchmarks. Its portfolio of services offers several saving account, fixed deposit, loan, NRI and SME Services, each tailor-made to cater the specific needs of customers of all generations and of all walks of life. Recognitions

- Awarded No.1 in Customer Satisfaction by IBA in 2008.
- Ranked No.1 private sector bank by "Chartered Financial Analyst"
- Awarded the "Sir Visweswarayya Award 2010"

HINDUSTAN

Media Partner

Hindustan is HT Media Group's premier Hindi newspaper with a daily reach of 10 million that makes it the 3rd largest read daily in India. Hindustan has consistently been the fastest growing newspaper in India, a result of its unwavering commitment to high standards of journalistic integrity and reader connect. The newspaper is in a process of constant self-renewal and continues to make a mark through its impactful journalism.

This year has also seen a transformation in the status of the newspaper. Hindustan Media Ventures Limited, an HT Media Group company and thepublisher of Hindustan daily, went public through a successful IPO in July 2010.

Hindustan continues to consolidate its dominant position in Bihar and Jharkhand, both states that have come to be recognised for their economic transformation. Its market expansion in Uttar Pradesh has moved it to a position of strength, challenging the traditional leaders.

Hindustan continues to make rapid strides in its quest for becoming the most read daily in India.

MINT

Media Partner

Mint, India's second largest national business daily is published by HT Media Ltd and has an exclusive content partnership with *The Wall Street Journal*. Since its launch in 2007, *Mint* has consistently delivered on its promise of bringing 'Clarity in Business News' - a need that has been clearly and repeatedly articulated by business news readers across the country.

Mint is today the preferred business daily of top decision-makers across the country, 80% of whom do not read any other business paper. Available in Delhi, Mumbai, Bangalore, Chennai, Kolkata, Ahmedabad, Chandigarh and Pune. Mint gives clear, relevant and insightful news & analysis on key business developments in India and abroad.

Mint's clear and distinct content and ability to efficiently serve readers across multiple formats such as print, web, mobile and events has also found strong support from leading advertisers both in India and abroad.

FEVER 104 FM

Media Partner

It was in 2007 that two media powerhouses, HT Media and Virgin, joined hands to launch Fever 104 FM. With the technical collaboration with Virgin and the media strengths of the Hindustan Times group, it was only a matter of time before Fever 104 FM took the FM industry by storm.

Launched in the 4 major cities of Delhi, Mumbai, Bangalore and Kolkata, with a positioning based on strong consumer insight, Fever 104 FM has grown from strength to strength and has achieved leadership position in most markets.

With innovation as a core value, Fever 104 FM has constantly redefined the standards in the radio industry – whether the IPL partnerships, the Fever Music Mahotsav, or more recently the Fever Radio Ramayan. Today, Fever 104 FM is considered a young, vibrant and one of the most aspirational radio brands. It has grown from strength to strength, and is today poised to become the No.1 FM brand in the key metros. With strong talent, youthful and innovative programming, and undoubtedly the best music, Fever 104 Fm is considered a thought-leader in the radio space.

CNN-IBN

Media Partner

CNN-IBN is India's No.1 English News channel and has been the world's window to India and India's window to the world. The channel is one of the most respected and trusted sources for news and information in the country today. CNN-IBN has been the 'thought leader' and has pioneered several path breaking initiatives that include CNN-IBN Indian of the Year, Real Heroes, Citizen Journalist Awards, the bi-annual poll State of the Nation, Citizens for Earth, etc

Since its inception in December 2005, the channel has been reaching out to an average of 45 million households every day, dedicated to becoming an engine of new journalism by treating news as sacred and giving the viewer a voice. Over the past five years, CNN-IBN has developed into one of the most respected and dynamic media brands in the country today. The channel's distinctive philosophy '9i's of journalism' ensures that its news is Insightful, Investigative, Informed, Independent, Impactful, Interactive, Inclusive, Immediate and Innovative.

IBN7

Media Partner

India's Channel of Impact - IBN7 is a Hindi News Channel with a single motive and promise to present the news in a "no nonsense manner" and deliver truth in context to the discerning viewer.

Guided by the same principles which made CNN-IBN a cult brand, IBN7 with its committed journalistic force that embodies and believes in the spirit of 'Khabar, Har Keemat Par' has the highest share of impact across all TV channels.

Within 4 years of its inception, IBN7 has emerged as the thought leader in the cluttered Hindi news space with initiatives like IBN7 Diamond States Awards, IBN7 Super Idols, the Citizen Journalist Awards, the bi-annual poll State of the Nation, etc.

CNBC-TV18

Media Partner

The undisputed leader in business news and information in India, CNBC-TV18, is trusted by business leaders for its insight, analysis and real-time market coverage. With one of the largest and most comprehensive television content libraries in India, CNBC-TV18 has been the platform for thought leaders across India, giving India's decision makers unparalleled news, analysis and perspective.

Not only has the channel revolutionized business programming in India, helping viewers to understand and profit from the markets and from their businesses, it has also built loyal communities, by interacting with people of all ages through non-markets programming, special on-ground events and a series of awards that have set the standards for industry benchmarks.